Beyond the Welfare State?

The New Political Economy of Welfare

Second Edition

Christopher Pierson

Polity Press

First edition published 1991
This edition published 1998 by Polity Press
in association with Blackwell Publishers Ltd.

Editorial office:
Polity Press
65 Bridge Street
Cambridge CB2 1UR, UK

Marketing and production:
Blackwell Publishers Ltd
108 Cowley Road
Oxford OX4 1JF, UK

ISBN 0-7456-1902-9
ISBN 0-7456-1903-7 (pbk)

A catalogue record for this book is available from the British Library.

Typeset in 10 on 12 pt Times New Roman
by Ace Filmsetting Ltd, Frome, Somerset
Printed in Great Britain by T.J. International, Padstow, Cornwall

This book is printed on acid-free paper.

Contents

Acknowledgements

Much has happened to the welfare state since the first edition of this book was published in 1991. This second edition has been fully revised to take account of these changes. I continue to be indebted to those who helped to make the original writing of this book possible: Virginia Bovell, Peter Flora, Anthony Giddens, David Held, John Keane, Desmond King, Meridee Pierson; participants at the British Sociological Association Annual Conference, the American Sociological Association Annual Conference, and at seminars in the Departments of Politics and Sociology at the Universities of Edinburgh and Stirling. Research for the first edition was supported by the Carnegie Trust for the Universities of Scotland and the University of Stirling. In preparing the second edition, I was fortunate enough to spend a period as a visiting research Fellow at the Australian National University in Canberra and my work there and in New Zealand was supported by the British Academy and the Carnegie Trust for the Universities of Scotland as well as the ANU itself. I have learned a great deal from staff and students at the Public Policy Program in Canberra and at the University of Nottingham. I am especially grateful to Professor Francis Castles for sharing his expertise about the Australian system of social protection (and much else).

Thanks are due to all the editorial staff at Polity Press, to April and Laura for their technical support and to Meridee, Ailsa and Lewis (who is also new to the second edition!).

The book remains dedicated to my mother, Margaret, and to the memory of my father, John. He really wanted me to be a Professor of Physics at Manchester but would certainly have settled for one of these ambitions being realized.

Christopher Pierson
Nottingham

The author and publisher would also like to thank the following for permission to reproduce material in the book:

HarperCollins Publishers Ltd for table 4.8 from R. E. Goodin & J. E. Le Grand: *Not only the Poor: The Middle Classes and the Welfare State* (Unwin Hyman, 1987); and figure 2.1 from C. Offe: *Contradictions of the Welfare State* (Hutchinson, 1984).

International Social Security Association for table 5.1 from N. Ploug: 'The Welfare State in Liquidation?' in *International Social Security Review* 2 (1995).

Organisation for Economic Co-operation and Development, Paris, for figure 4.3 from *Social Expenditure 1960–1990*, © OECD 1985; and for figure 4.2 and table 4.5 from *The Future of Social Protection*, © OECD 1988.

Prentice Hall for table 4.7 from M. Godfrey: *The Economic Approach to Social Policy* (Harvester Wheatsheaf, 1986).

Sage Publications, Inc. for table 6.1 from J. Alber: 'Continuities and Changes in the Idea of the Welfare State' in *Politics and Society* 16:4, p. 452, copyright © 1988.

Solo Syndication Limited for the Evening Standard for cartoon by David Low from the *Evening Standard*, 1950.

Transaction Publishers for figure 4.1 from A. Flora and A. J. Heidenheimer: *The Development of Welfare States in Europe and America* (1981), copyright © 1981; all rights reserved.

Introduction

Transforming welfare is now at the top of almost every politician's agenda. The welfare state, which was once a defining cause for social democrats and, by turns, a source of despair and indifference for those on the right, is now the object of almost universal demands for urgent and profound change. The stakes have been raised, as welfare reform has been transformed into the key strategy for 'reviving the economy' and 'mending the social fabric', but faith in traditional solutions is in seemingly terminal decline. We are told that, in anything like its traditional form, the welfare state cannot survive. But, as yet, the workable alternatives are quite unclear. Indeed, we are now confronted with a perplexing diversity of possible futures, all of which somebody promises will resolve our current difficulties. What explains this change in the terms of the welfare state debate and where is it headed? How do we pick our way through the abundance of competing explanations? Most importantly, are we really moving, as some suppose, to circumstances that are 'beyond the welfare state'? These are the questions addressed in this book. We shall find that the answers are more complex (and the process of reform more difficult) than many contemporary commentators suggest. We shall find, too, that to understand the newer trajectories of reform we need to know rather more about how we got to be where we are and, indeed, to understand rather more clearly just how and for whom existing welfare states work.

Welfare States: The Changing Object of Debate

For a lengthy period after the Second World War, the dominant academic view was that the emergence of the welfare states could be seen either as the completion of the centuries-long movement towards full and equal citizenship or else as the price exacted by the organized labour movement for a cessation of open hostilities with capital. For some, the institutionalization of the welfare state represented a decisive victory for the political arm of the labour movement, a vindication of the 'positive-sum' reformism of social democracy. For others, it was the technologically, rather than politically determined 'side-effect' of industrial and economic progress, the final act in the process of 'civilizing' the brute forces of industrialization. Again, while for some it consummated the transformation of capitalism into a distinctively new form of social and political organization (which might or might not be called socialism), for others it represented the further and benevolent development of capitalism. For the latter, the welfare state constituted a form in which the excesses of nineteenth century *laissez-faire* capitalism had been curbed and a more rational, equitable, sociable (and thus secure) basis for the private ownership of the economy put in its place. As we shall see, such views were never universally shared, still less unequivocally welcomed. Some on the left insisted that the rise of the welfare state sapped the transformative energies of the working class while subsidizing the reproduction costs of capital. At the same time, critics to the right maintained that the welfare state undermined the fundamental premises of the liberal society that had been created by the great revolutionary movements of the seventeenth and eighteenth centuries. But despite these dissenting opinions, enough of a common view prevailed in the post-war years of Western economic growth and welfare state expansion for us to speak of a widespread (though often unarticulated) professional consensus upon the broad lines of welfare state development.

Just as certainly, we may speak of the last twenty-five years having seen an extremely widespread challenge to this orthodoxy. This dissent has been heard from most points of the political compass. In the heyday of 'post-war consensus', outright hostility to the welfare state settlement was widely characterized as a maverick disposition of the political extremes of both left and right. But this was to alter under the pressure of the economic reverses and social upheavals of the late 1960s and early 1970s, and the political changes these brought in their wake. In this period, the belief that the welfare state was 'in crisis', indeed, that many of the social, economic and political ills of the modern era were directly attributable to the continuing growth of the welfare state, established itself with astonishing rapidity as something like a new orthodoxy. Elements of both the New Left and the New Right found common ground in identifying the incompatibility of a working market economy with the state provision of welfare. At the same time, criticism of the particular consequences of the welfare state for women and for ethnic minorities, long a suppressed undercurrent in social policy, gained a new prominence with the general resurgence in feminist and anti-racist writing and thinking from the early 1970s onwards. Still more recently, the impact of the Green movement, with its characteristic concern for the harmful consequences of unsustainable economic growth and bureaucratized public services, has represented a further challenge to the benign assumptions of the defenders of the social democratic welfare state.

Paralleling this increased political interest and controversy has been a change in the academic study of the welfare state. However wrongly, the welfare state was for long seen as the worthy, if rather dull, province of a group of concerned specialists, mostly in the fields of social policy and social administration, working on a particular and practical agenda of (diminishing) poverty and (expanding) welfare provision. By contrast, in the last twenty years, the welfare state has increasingly been colonized by students of political theory and the 'new political economy' who have drastically broadened the domain of welfare state studies, seeking, under this rubric, to construct broad explanations of the general nature of the social, economic and political arrangements of advanced capitalism. In the most recent period, with the demise of the Soviet Union and the seemingly uncheckable advance of a fully globalized capitalism, the 'problem' of the welfare state has (once again) been presented as amenable to a technical fix – only this time the 'fixers' are more likely to be economic specialists from the World Bank than the 'traditional' welfare professionals of the post-war period.

From both these political and academic sources has come, in recent years, increasing support for the claim that the advanced capitalist societies are undergoing a process of transformation which is carrying them towards social and political arrangements which are, in some sense, *beyond the welfare state*. Most prominent among these claims are the following:

Proposition 1
In the long term, the welfare state is incompatible with a healthy market-based economy. Only the exceptionally favourable circumstances for economic growth of the post-war period allowed simultaneously for an expansion of the economy *and* the welfare state. Under changed international economic conditions this means, for the political right, that economic growth can only be restored by severely lessening the drain of the welfare state upon the productive economy. For the left, it has implied that the welfare aspirations embodied in the idea of a welfare state can only be met by instituting new forms of economic organization and ownership.

Proposition 2
The development of the welfare state was an integral part of the evolu-

tion of modern capitalist societies. However, the period of its remarkable growth was also historically unique. The welfare state has now 'grown to its limits'. Wholesale dismantling is neither necessary nor likely, but any further (costly) growth will begin to undermine the basis of its popular support.

Proposition 3
Changes in the international political economy, above all the processes of *globalization*, have undermined the circumstances for the promotion of national welfare states. The powers of national governments, national labour movements and nationally based capital – between whom agreements about national welfare states were typically constructed – have been undermined by the greater internationalization and deregulation of the modern world economy. The Keynesian Welfare State is incompatible with this new international political economy.

Proposition 4
The post-war welfare state represented a 'historic compromise' between the powers/interests of capital and organized labour. That 'compromise' has now broken down (in some accounts because of the comprehensive defeat of the labour interest). While at one time welfare state policies served both capital and labour, it is now becoming increasingly unattractive to both and will be able to mobilize decreasing support within both camps. At the same time, these interests have been reorganized in ways which make any future return to corporatism improbable.

Proposition 5
The development of welfare state provision (especially in public health and public education) has itself generated social changes which undermine the continuing necessity for state welfare provision and attenuate the basis of continuing support for public provision. In particular, the development of the welfare state has transformed the *class* structure of advanced capitalism in such a way as to undermine the *class* basis for its own continuation. Most significantly, these changes undermine that alliance between middle and working classes (or, alternatively, that commonality of working class experience) upon which the welfare state was built. This furnishes for an ever growing section of the population an incentive to *defect* from (the support of) public welfare provision.

Proposition 6
The welfare state represented an appropriate institutional means for delivering certain welfare services at a given level of social and economic development. Continued economic growth has rendered these forms of welfare provision increasingly inappropriate. Most notably, the expan-

sion of consumer choice/affluence within Western industrialized economies engenders increasing dissatisfaction with state-administered welfare
and a greater defection of consumers to market-provided welfare services.

Proposition 7
While the welfare state political project should be understood as historically progressive, further progress cannot be effected through the continued promotion of conventional welfare state policies. This is because the
welfare state is tied to a productivist/economic growth strategy which is
not (any longer) consonant with the meeting of real human needs and the
securing of genuine social welfare.

It is with these claims about development 'beyond the welfare state' that
this book is principally concerned. It is not, however, a study in futurol-
ogy. Future 'tendencies' in the welfare states must depend upon their
historical evolution and those powers and structures that they currently
embody. This is reflected in the structure of the book. The first three
chapters deal with the major theoretical approaches to the welfare state
out of which prognoses for its future development arise. More specifically, they are concerned with the relationship between the welfare state,
social democracy and the structure of advanced capitalism. To assist the
reader through this minefield of competing explanations, I include at the
end of each section a brief thesis summarizing the main claims that have
been outlined. Chapter 4 reviews major trends in the international development of welfare states down to the early 1970s.
   For most commentators, the conditions for moving 'beyond the welfare state' have only ripened or become manifest over the past twenty-five
years. This is the period that has been dominated by the spectre of a
'crisis in the welfare state'. Correspondingly, the fifth chapter gives detailed consideration to varying explanations of this crisis and measures
these against the actual experience of developed welfare states since the
early 1970s. The final chapter returns explicitly to our propositions about
developments 'beyond the welfare state' and makes an assessment of
these in the light of the evidence considered in the rest of the study. While
we shall see that the casual elision of social democracy and the welfare
state is historically and theoretically misplaced, especial attention is directed throughout the book to the changing relationship between the
welfare state and social democracy.

1
Capitalism, Social Democracy and the Welfare State I
Industrialism, Modernization and Social Democracy

The purpose of these first three chapters is to establish how the (contested and changing) relationship between capitalism, social democracy and the welfare state has been understood. It would perhaps be as well to begin by clarifying how these terms will be employed within this study. *Capitalism* refers to an economic (and social) system based upon the production and exchange of privately owned commodities. *Advanced capitalism* refers to this economic (and social) system as it has evolved within the most developed societies of North America, Western Europe, Japan and Australasia. Both systems are seen to be more or less dependent upon markets, but neither is premised upon pure 'free' markets in either labour and/or commodities. *Social democracy* refers to those political movements, ideologies and practices which are founded upon the reformist promotion of the interests of organized labour within a developed capitalist economy. It tends to afford definitive status to the development of representative democratic institutions within capitalist societies as the means of gradually reforming these societies in the direction of greater fairness and equality, largely through the promotion of welfare state strategies.

Use of the expression *welfare* has always been inexact. At its simplest, *welfare* may describe 'well-being' or 'the material and social preconditions for well-being' (*Shorter Oxford English Dictionary*; Weale, 1983, p. 23). As such, it may be distinguished from three common subclassifications: (1) *social welfare*, which broadly refers to the collective (and sometimes sociable) provision or receipt of welfare, (2) *economic welfare*, which usually describes those forms of welfare secured through the market or the formal economy and (3) *state welfare*, which refers to social welfare provision through the agency of the state. A good deal of confusion has arisen from the tendency of commentators to argue as if one of these subclassifications was exhaustive of *all* forms of welfare or as if they were interchangeable (as, for example, in the supposition that state welfare is the same as social welfare). These definitional issues have been extensively discussed elsewhere (see Titmuss, 1963; Madison, 1980, pp. 46–68; Weale, 1983, pp. 1–21; Jones, 1985, pp. 13–14; Rose, 1981; on classical definitions of economic welfare, see Pigou, 1912, 1929). Here, comment can be confined to two points. First, in this study the primary focus of attention is upon *state*-provided forms of welfare and their interconnection with the structure of the formal economy. Secondly, and given this emphasis, it should be stressed that the ways in which welfare is delivered *outside* of the state or the formal economy, through the church, through voluntary organizations and, above all, through the family, is just as important.

In a narrow sense, the *welfare state* may refer to state measures for the provision of key welfare services (often confined to health, education, housing, income maintenance and personal social services). Increasingly broadly, the welfare state is also taken to define (1) a particular form of state, (2) a distinctive form of polity or (3) a specific type of society. In this study, the *welfare state under capitalism* is generally understood in this third sense as defining a society in which the state intervenes within the processes of economic reproduction and distribution to reallocate life chances between individuals and/or classes.

Capitalism against the Welfare State: Classical Political Economy

In this book, attention is focused upon the nature of the relationship between capitalism, the welfare state and social democracy. In considering the competing ways in which this relationship has been understood, perhaps the most primitive line of division is between those who perceive the welfare state to be *incompatible* with the principles and practices of (any form of) capitalism and those who understand the welfare state as a possible or even as a *necessary* component of any developed capitalist economy. Both forms of explanation can be seen to focus upon (differing) aspects of capitalism as a market-based form of economic organization. For both, social democracy may be either an indispensable third term or else largely irrelevant.

The conviction that state responsibility for social welfare is incompatible with the efficient working of a capitalist economy can be persuasively retraced to capitalism's greatest advocate – Adam Smith. In common with many later commentators, Smith understood welfare, or the means to welfare, rather narrowly, as being secured primarily through the production and exchange of goods and services within the formal economy.

Since, he argued, the general welfare of society is but the sum of the welfare of the individuals within it, social welfare would be best secured by maximizing the sum of individual welfares. Such maximization could best be achieved by allowing individuals, within an overall legal framework of tort and contract, to pursue their own economic interests without external restraint. The form for such economic maximization was a freely competitive market economy in which production was directed solely by the laws of supply and demand and in which all sought to maximize their welfare within the market-place by selling dear and buying cheap such marketable resources or 'commodities' (including labour) as lay within their command. The great beauty of the market economy – its 'cunning of reason' – was that though every man entered into market transactions solely to serve his own selfish (and generally short-term) ends, in so doing he was 'led by an invisible hand to promote an end which was not part of his intention', that is the maximization of general social welfare or the common good (Smith, 1895, p. 345). If not quite the product of either God or Nature, markets nonetheless maximized the liberty of the individual and effectively directed people's (natural) self-interest and greed towards the optimization of general social welfare.

Smith, like the more thoughtful of his latter-day followers, was not an uncritical admirer of the market. He noted, for example, the pernicious effect that the minute division of labour might have upon the labouring poor. Nor did he discount the importance of a state exercising centralized political authority. However, the proper exercise of such state power was limited to: (1) the defence of the realm against external assault, (2) the guarantee of the rule of law and (3) the maintenance of 'certain public works and certain public institutions' which the market could not competently provide. Even were the latter to include some sort of state responsibility for the relief of destitution, it is clear that the state could not have a *duty* to provide (nor its citizens a corresponding *right* to claim), generalized social welfare.

Just why such a welfare-securing state was incompatible with a capitalist market economy is made clear in the work of other classical political economists, notably by Nassau Senior and Thomas Malthus (Senior, 1865; Malthus, 1890; see also Bowley, 1967, pp. 282–334; Rimlinger, 1974, pp. 38–47). Within a capitalist economy, the 'free' owners of labour power – as Marx ironically noted, 'free' in the twin sense of being legally at liberty to sell their labour power to an employer and being 'free' of any other means of supporting themselves – *must* be obliged to sell this labour power *at the prevailing market price* in order to support themselves and their families (Marx, 1973a, pp. 270–1). Without this compulsion to work – the requirement to undergo the disutility of labour in order to enjoy the utility of welfare – an efficient (and welfare-maximizing) market economy could no longer function. If welfare were to be granted, still more were it to be guaranteed, independent of the willingness (and/or capacity) to work, there would remain no incentive for workers to sell their labour power. Workers could then dissipate themselves (as Malthus feared) in idle living (and breeding) at the expense of the productive members of society, and the economy would in turn be undermined to the eventual ruination of the whole society. Thus, it was the very uncertainty of the wage-earner's continued welfare that was the mainspring of capitalist economic growth.

Capitalism against the Welfare State: Marx

Marx was perhaps the most sophisticated (and admiring) critic of this classical political economy. In turning to his account of the relationship between capitalism and welfare, we find broad agreement about the structure and dynamics of the capitalist economy and about its incompatibility with state-secured welfare. As the status of his definitive study of *Capital* as 'a critique of political economy' suggests, Marx's intention was to take the work of the classical political economists and to press what he saw as their authentic premises to radically new conclusions (Marx, 1973a). The radical divergence between Marx and classical political economy lies not in his view of the relationship between capitalism and the welfare-securing state, but in his account of the (ever more acute) inability of capitalist economic organization to secure 'genuine' individual and social welfare.

At the heart of Marx's critique of capitalism were three basic claims drawn from classical political economy: first, that capitalism is an economic system based upon the production and exchange of privately owned commodities within an unconstrained market; secondly, that the value of any commodity is an expression of the amount of human labour power expended upon its production. Upon these premises, Marx develops an account of capitalism as a necessarily exploitative and class-based system, one in which unpaid labour is extracted from the sellers of labour power by the owners of capital under the form of a 'free and equal exchange' in the marketplace. Such market exchanges do not, however, optimize individual (and thus social) welfare. Rather, the radically unequal exchange (the extraction of surplus value) that is masked by a formally 'free and equal' market in commodities means that capitalist economic organization only secures the welfare of the capitalists (as individuals and as a numerically declining class) while prescribing *dis*welfare for the great majority of the exploited working class.

The third element that Marx derives from classical political economy is the claim that capitalism is a dynamic system in which the competitive search for profit, and responses to the long-term tendency for the rate of profit to fall, lead to the intensification of exploitation and the heightening of class conflict. It is also a system chronically prone to periodic crises (of overproduction). While such crises do not straightforwardly occasion the economic collapse of capitalism, they do determine a cyclical intensification of the contradictions that are to lead to its eventual demise. As a part of this process, capitalism in its historically 'declining' phase comes to be ever less efficient and less equitable in delivering individual and collective social welfare.

This radical inequality of welfare outcomes is endemic to capitalism and, for Marx, not open to remedy or amelioration by an interventionist state. As we shall see later, views on the welfare state in twentieth-century Marxism are complex and sometimes contradictory. However, the most essential points of Marx's own understanding of the state, and of its capacity to secure general social welfare, may be summarized as follows:

1   While some insist that Marx's central works of political economy constitute not an economic but a *materialist* critique of capitalism, the core of Marx's historical materialism depicts the political in general, and the state in particular, as derived from essentially economic relationships.

2   That economic relationship which the state and politics expresses is one of systematic class-based exploitation. In every age, the state mobilizes *exclusively* the interests of the ruling class. This is true of the capitalist state, as it will be of the proletarian state under a transitional socialist order. Only under communism, with the final elimination of class oppression, will the state 'wither away'.

3   The state cannot serve two masters (or classes), nor can the transformation from one type of state to another be peaceful and/or gradual (other than under very exceptional circumstances). The bitter historical experience of the workers' movement has been that the existing state has to be 'smashed' and replaced with new and distinctively proletarian state institutions. (Marx, 1973b, pp. 71, 125; Pierson, 1986, pp. 7–30)

4   This relationship is not changed by the winning of popular parliamentary democracy. Certainly, Marx held democracy to be a progressive principle but he rejected the claim that the winning of parliamentary democracy so transformed the existing order that it became possible to effect transition through the institutions of the existing state. (Marx, 1973b, pp. 190, 238)

In summary, the state under capitalism might intervene in the reproduction of social relations; however, it could not (1) intervene in such a way as to undermine the logic of the capitalist market economy or (2) act against the long-term interests of the capitalist class. Whatever institutional form the state under capitalism might take, (and even under the governance of social democratic forces), it remained in essence a *capitalist* state. For Marx, securing the *real* welfare of the broad working population and articulating their *real* needs were simply incompatible with the structure of a capitalist economy.

It is possible then to find in the work of classical political economy and its fiercest opponent a broadly shared view of the incompatibility between capitalist economic organization and the state provision of welfare. The distribution of utilities under capitalism is taken to reflect not 'needs', however these are understood, but market capacity. It was not so much this analysis of the nature of the capitalist economy that divided socialists from capitalism's defenders. Rather it was the socialists' argument that responsiveness to markets rather than 'needs' made capitalism unacceptable and required that it be replaced by a form of social organization of production (whether communal, co-operative or state-directed) in which the distribution of welfare reflected 'real need' rather than 'market capacity'. Down to the early twentieth century and the prospect of the welfare state as an alternative socialist strategy, this was a view embraced not just by revolutionary Marxists but also by most other (and more circumspect) species of socialism. The defenders of liberal capitalism responded to this criticism by insisting that, while not perfect, markets were the most effective way of promoting general and improving levels of welfare. If the anonymous and impersonal 'coercion' of the market were to be removed and society's material needs still to be met, this would require *more* oppressive and directive forms of coercion by the state (Kristol, 1978).

Capitalism and the Welfare State: Symbiosis and Support

There were those writing in the eighteenth and nineteenth centuries who believed that capitalist economic organization was compatible with securing collective provision for the welfare of the working class (Owen, 1927; Paine, 1958, pp. 246ff). However, down to the last third of the nineteenth century there was widespread agreement among both capitalism's defenders and its detractors that state welfare was incompatible with the dynamics of a capitalist economy. The twentieth century saw opinion much more evenly divided. Indeed, in certain phases, there was a broadly based consensus, again shared on both left and right, that the state provision of welfare is fully compatible with, or even indispensable to, a developed capitalist economy. This mutual compatibility of capitalism and state welfare is not always welcomed, and some see the welfare state as a way of reinforcing the inequitable welfare outcomes dictated by the market economy. But, whether for good or ill, in the period after the Second World War, the logic of *symbiosis* between the welfare state and capitalism came to define the prevailing orthodoxy.

The context for this changed approach to the relationship between capitalism and the welfare state was the emergence or maturing of a series of deep-seated economic, social and political changes in the structure of the developing capitalist societies towards the end of the nineteenth century. For those who perceive a symbiotic relationship between capitalism and public welfare, the emergence of the welfare state can be understood in terms of those societal changes which arose out of the great historical transformation from essentially agrarian, localized and traditional to definitively industrialized, (inter)national and modern societies that occurred between the eighteenth and twentieth centuries. More specifically, these transformations could be traced to the interaction between industrial revolution (expanding from its origins in eighteenth century Britain), and political revolution (most spectacular in America and France in the eighteenth century, but just as importantly in the widespread extension of democracy in the late nineteenth and early twentieth centuries).

Summarily, the most important of these societal developments were:

1 **The impact of industrialization.** The coming of large-scale industrial production led to:
   - a long-term decline in agricultural employment and the rural population;
   - extensive urbanization, the growth of large cities and of typically urban 'ways of life';
   - the creation of a landless (manual) urban working class, concentrated in particular economic sectors and based in distinctive urban neighbourhoods.

   Its *further* development led to:
   - the requirement for a (partially) skilled, literate and reliable workforce;
   - the recognition of 'unemployment' as a condition in which workers were *involuntarily* unable to find paid work;
   - the growth of white-collar employment and the middle classes;
   - the creation of societies of historically unprecedented wealth (however inequitably this wealth might be distributed), and of sustained and long-term economic growth.

2 **Population growth and the changing social composition of the population.** Everywhere industrialization was accompanied by a rapid growth of population. It was also associated with other demographic changes:
   - changing patterns of family and community life;

- a growing division between working and non-working populations and between 'home' and 'work';
- decreasing infant mortality and increased life expectancy (at least in the long run);
- the emergence of publicly-sanctioned non-participation in the labour force (through retirement in old age, sickness, disability, childrearing, involvement in full-time education).

3 **The growth of nation states.** The locus of industrialization consisted increasingly of nations and states. In some cases, state formation and nation building were directly associated with the management and co-ordination of industrial development (as, for example, in Germany and Italy). The growth of industrialized nation states was itself widely associated with:

- internal pacification;
- the centralization of governmental powers;
- the development of a 'professional' civil service;
- growing state competence through new techniques of surveillance and advanced communications.

For most (though certainly not for all) significant commentators, one further element should be added to these basic characteristics of industrialization:

4 **The growth of political democracy/the rise of political citizenship:**
- the expansion of legal citizenship;
- the extension of the franchise;
- the development of social democratic parties;
- the increased salience of 'the social question'/ the political 'problem' of the working class.

For the great majority of more recent commentators, these constitute the necessary, but not sufficient, bases for an explanation of the development of the welfare state. There is some disagreement about which of these constitute the more important causes. For example, some commentators dismiss the independent impact of *political* forces in shaping the welfare state, while others regard political mobilization as indispensable. There is also violent disagreement about those other variables whose interaction with industrial development can persuasively account for the emergence of the welfare state. But it is widely maintained that without these basic processes of industrialization (the growth of industrial production, economic growth, urbanization, demographic change, state development) it would be impossible to imagine the modern welfare state.

Industrialism and the Welfare State

For some, the principal mobilizing force behind the growth of the welfare state was a *moral* one, based upon public or elite reactions against the excessive hardships inflicted by early industrialization. In such accounts, particular stress is laid upon the growth of humanitarian and charitable sentiment among the governing and middle classes, the growth of knowledge of social and medical conditions affecting the industrial population and a growing awareness of the nature and importance of public health provision. Thus, Penelope Hall, in a standard British text of the 1950s (and beyond), insists that the basis of the welfare state rests in 'the obligation a person feels to help another in distress, which derives from the recognition that they are in some sense members one of another' (Hall, 1952, p. 4). In a more historical mode, Derek Fraser writes of 'the public conscience . . . shocked into action' and Malcolm Bruce of the welfare state as 'the result of a fit of conscience' (Fraser, 1973, p. 23; Bruce, 1968, p. 294).

However much this 'moral' approach may continue to reflect popular justifications of the welfare state, its intellectual authority has been rapidly eroded over the past twenty-five years. Perhaps more lastingly influential have been those who depict the coming of the welfare state as a product of '*the logic of industrialism*'. From the perspective of (Anglo-Saxon) functionalist sociology in the post-war period, the rise of the interventionist state and the curtailment of the 'excesses' of liberal capitalism could be seen as a response to the new 'needs' generated by the development of industrial societies. Upon such an explanation, the origins of the welfare state were seen to lie in secular changes associated with the broad processes of industrialization and, particularly, the breakdown of traditional forms of social provision and family life. These changes included economic growth and the associated growth in population (especially of an aged population), the developed division of labour, the creation of a landless working class, the rise of cyclical unemployment, changing patterns of family and community life and industry's increasing need of a reliable, healthy and literate workforce.

The most authoritative advocate of this industrialism thesis has been Harold Wilensky, whose early work concluded that 'over the long pull, economic level is the root cause of welfare-state development'. Its effects are expressed 'chiefly through demographic changes . . . and the momentum of the programs themselves once established'. The effects of 'political elite perceptions, mass pressures, and welfare bureaucracies' may hasten its coming, but the welfare state is essentially a product of the 'needs' of an industrialized society. While Wilensky allows some weight at the margins to the influence of 'democratic corporatism', in essence, political ideology and political systems are largely irrelevant in explaining a technologically determined development which occurs more or less independently of the will of either political elites or mass publics (Wilensky, 1975, p. 47; Wilensky, 1976, pp. 21–3).

This thesis on the welfare state, which achieved its greatest prominence in the 1950s and 1960s, belonged within a much broader explanation of the evolution of industrial societies. This broader account enjoined that conventional political divisions between capitalist and socialist (or communist) societies were increasingly irrelevant. What characterized societies in the developed world (capitalist or communist) was that they were *industrial* societies, the nature of whose social and economic arrangements were given by the technological logic of industrial production and economic growth. Thus, Wilensky argued:

> economic growth and its demographic and bureaucratic outcomes are the root cause of the general emergence of the welfare state ... such heavy brittle categories as 'socialist' versus 'capitalist' economies, 'collectivistic' versus 'individualistic' ideologies, or even 'democratic' versus 'totalitarian' political systems ... are almost useless in explaining the origins and general development of the welfare state. (Wilensky, 1975, p. xiii)

Accordingly, such theorists maintained both that the welfare state was an indispensable part of this structure of the industrial societies and that 'the primacy of economic level and its demographic and bureaucratic correlates is support for a convergence thesis: economic growth makes countries with contrasting cultural and political traditions more alike in their [welfare state] strategy' (Wilensky, 1975, p. 27).

Thesis 1

The welfare state is a product of the *needs* generated by the development of industrial societies

---

Commentary: The Industrialism Thesis

As the orthodoxy of the 1950s and 1960s, the industrialism thesis – with its central claim that the welfare state was a product of both the new *needs* and the new *resources* generated by the process of industrialization – has received considerable attention. A series of empirical surveys (most influentially those of Cutright and Wilensky) suggested 'the primacy of economic level and its demographic and bureaucratic correlates' (Cutright,

1965, p. 537) in determining welfare state development. In a survey of 76 nation states outside Africa, Cutright found that 'the degree of social security coverage is most powerfully correlated with its level of economic development' (Cutright, 1965, p. 537). Wilensky's later survey among a range of 22 developed and underdeveloped nation states maintained that economic level, when combined with the dependent effects of the proportion of aged in the population and the age of the social security system, explained more than 85 per cent of the international variance in social security effort. Accordingly, 'there is not much variance left to explain' by other causes (Wilensky, 1975, pp. 22–5, 48–9).

However, this view has been frequently challenged. In a survey of 17 developed Western capitalist democracies, Stephens argues that Wilensky's 'finding that public spending is heavily influenced by the demographic and bureaucratic outcomes of economic growth does not hold' (Stephens, 1979, p. 101). Similarly, O'Connor finds very limited evidence of convergence in the OECD countries, and then only upon a very particular definition of 'welfare effort' and for a very limited period (O'Connor, 1988). In a survey of the long-term experience of four Western European states, Hage, Hanneman and Gargan find that 'previous research has overestimated the importance of GNP in welfare state development'. While 'social need is an important determinant of the growth in welfare expenditures . . . the availability of resources has no relationship to the growth in welfare expenditures' (Hage, Hanneman and Gargan, 1989, pp. 104–8). Indeed, in certain contexts, Hage, Hanneman and Gargan and David Cameron find that the growth of welfare expenditure is in fact *counter-cyclical*, that is it is negatively related to economic growth. (On France and Britain, respectively, see Hage, Hanneman and Gargan, 1989, p. 107; Cameron, 1978, p. 1245).

More recently, Manfred Schmidt has adapted the 'industrialist' thesis developed by Dethev Zollner to assess social policy development in a range of 39 'rich and poor countries'. Zollner's original thesis was that the share of social spending as a percentage of GDP (as a surrogate of welfare state development) could be correlated with 'the non-agricultural dependent labour force–population ratio' (as an index of industrialization). Amending the thesis so as also to include previous levels of affluence and of social expenditure, Schmidt finds that, in its amended form, Zollner's industrialism thesis will explain about 75 per cent of total variation in social spending effort among his 39 nation sample. The fit between the amended Zollner thesis and the empirical data is thus 'remarkably good'. However, for a small sub-sample of nine nations (both 'underspenders' and 'overspenders'), the fit was 'remarkably bad'. In the case of these 'social policy-surplus' and 'deficit' nations, Schmidt insists that an explicitly *political* explanation is required (Schmidt, 1989).

Schmidt's assessment may in fact direct us towards a more general conclusion about the utility of the industrialism thesis. Undoubtedly, the experience of industrialization and economic growth has had a profound impact upon the development of welfare states. Even among those who challenge the relationship of economic development to welfare state growth, there is widespread recognition of changing social need as a spur to social policy innovation. However, following Uusitalo, it is clear that the significance of economic development in explaining *variation* in social policy between nations depends very substantially upon the size and diversity of the sample under review. It may also depend upon the precise ways in which crucial variables, such as 'welfare effort', are specified (O'Connor and Brym, 1988). In samples which draw upon a wide range of very differently developed nations (as when, for example, contrasting the first and third worlds), economic development emerges as a very powerful indicator of welfare state growth. However, among similarly developed nations (for example, in studies confined to OECD countries), much less can be explained by variation in level of economic development (Uusitalo, 1984). Correspondingly, we can argue that the industrialism thesis (stripped of its teleological functionalist element) demonstrates that economic and industrial development has been a necessary background condition for the development of welfare states. However, given this premise, especially within the developed capitalist states, the *particular form* that the welfare state takes may be crucial, and it is here that the space remains for other forms of explanation.

This is an insight which was developed with particular effect by Goran Therborn. Concentrating upon the logic of market economies rather than the logic of industrialism, Therborn insists that the dominance of capitalist markets, far from eliminating the necessity of state institutions, generates new and pressing demands for (welfare) state intervention. He draws attention to what he calls 'the modern *universality* of welfare states', as the form which *all* developed and industrial societies (and not only capitalist ones) must necessarily take. For Therborn, such universality necessarily arises from a uniform feature of all such societies, namely '*the failure of markets in securing human reproduction*'. Echoing the classical analysis of Karl Polanyi on the coming of a market society, he insists that 'markets require states'. He identifies a 'double historical process, in which the modern welfare state emerged, a process of market expansion and a countermovement of protection against the market' (Therborn, 1987, p. 240). As feminist writers have done most to establish, the market has never provided competently for the reproduction of human labour power. For this it has always had to rely upon either private provision (through the family) or public provision (through the state's education and health services). Welfare states, then, are the necessary corollary of the rise of the market economy.

This account of the welfare state as provider of those conditions of

Table 1.1   Two types of welfare state

'Proletarian' welfare state	*'Bourgeois' welfare state*
1 Welfare state arrangements to assert workers' right to a livelihood	Welfare state arrangements adjusted to needs of capital accumulation, incentives to work, and so on
2 Right to work, right to safety at work, leisure and so on	Primarily geared to provision of skilled, able, loyal and fit workforce
3 Statutory public social insurance, public income maintenance, worker-controlled; (state-controlled a second-best option)	Limited (discretionary) system, administered by employers: (state-controlled a second-best option)
4 A wide coverage and uniform/ universal provision on a class (rather than 'social citizenship') basis	No uniform/universal provision; provision on a 'needs' basis
5 Redistributive financing	Financed on (actuarially sound) insurance principles

Source: Therborn, 1986, pp. 155–6.

human reproduction not secured by the market is developed through a further distinction between *public* goods and *private* goods.[1] Therborn argues that state provision for simple human reproduction and some provision for expanded reproduction constitutes a public good in virtually all developed countries. Some other public goods – beyond the simple reproduction of the species – are widely acknowledged (for example, in the area of natalist or health policies). Others have become more or less deeply institutionalized as 'national norms' or 'social citizenship rights'. However, the state provision of private (rivally consumed) goods is seen to constitute a much more fiercely contested area of welfare state policy. The provision of private goods, whether progressive or regressive, is, by definition, redistributive. It is here, over the redistribution of resources through taxation, pensions, social security transfers and so on, that the fiercest disputes occur.

In essence, Therborn's view is that a minimum of state provision of welfare (broadly that which can be understood as constituting public goods) is a necessity dictated by the structure of societies dependent on

---

[1] *Public goods* are 'non-rivally consumed' goods or goods from which the exclusion by non-paying consumers is impractical. *Private goods* are those which, even if provided by the state, are rivally consumed.

markets and is not vulnerable to political retrenchment. Only the form and extent of the welfare state, rather than its very existence, is a political issue in market-dependent societies, and this form will be largely determined by the balance of social forces in conflict. This may be illustrated through Therborn's own 'ideal types' of the welfare state as these might reflect the conflicting interests of owners and workers (see table 1.1).

A strong, interventionist welfare state is seen to be closer to the working class model and better able to resist pressure for retrenchment. By contrast, a market-oriented, weak welfare state is closer to the bourgeois model. However, the conflict engaged in is over the *form* or *extent* of the welfare state, not over the welfare state set against some other state form.

In this way, Therborn characterizes the welfare state as 'irreversible' or as a 'functional necessity'. It is an indispensable means of overcoming the limitations of market provision under any social formation. However, its actual form may represent the interests of either capital or organized labour. The balance of interests represented will be determined by the effective strengths of these (and other) opposing political forces. Therborn's account thus shares with the original industrialism thesis the claim that the welfare state is a product of the *needs* generated by the development of market-based societies. But he also maintains that the actual level of welfare state provision will be an expression of the strength of social democratic forces.

The industrialism thesis, in either its original or this amended form, remains of considerable importance. It is clear that massive changes in the social and industrial character of capitalist societies in the nineteenth century did transform the context for state action, and the view that the dominance of capitalist markets, far from eliminating the necessity of state intervention, generates new and pressing demands for state involvement carries considerable conviction. Nonetheless, such accounts are very significantly weakened by the misplaced assumption that the identification of changing 'needs' in itself *explains* the development of new institutions to meet such needs. In the case of Therborn's work, it is not clear that the identification of potential public goods makes their (indefinitely continued) provision unproblematic. Public choice theory makes it clear that there is no guarantee that a public good will be produced even if it is in the interests of every member of society to have such a good provided (Offe, 1987, p. 516; Olson, 1965). Furthermore, many of Therborn's proposed public goods, resting on 'national norms' or 'social citizenship rights', look extremely vulnerable to political retrenchment or 'redefinition'. Too often, the 'logic of industrialism' has been seen as a sufficient *explanation* of the rise of welfare state institutions, without identifying the political and historical actors/forces which were to make such changes happen.

Modernization and the Welfare State

The modernization approach may be represented, simply if rather approximately, as a *politicized version of the industrialism thesis*. It too is concerned with what distinguishes modern from traditional societies and sees the welfare state as a part of that complex which defines modern society. It too is shaped by a progressive–evolutionary logic, a historical transition towards more complex and developed societies which is seen to be carrying all traditional societies towards some variant of the modern form. But it can be distinguished from the industrialism thesis by the (differing) ways in which it complements the logic of industrialism with the dynamics of democratization. Thus modern societies are to be defined as much by the processes of institutional change that they have undergone under the rubric of political democratization as by the technological changes that have followed upon industrialization.

The modern world (including the welfare state) is seen to be the product of two revolutionary changes: not just the 'industrial revolution' but also the political revolution that transformed national publics from subjects to citizens. The latter process – most explicit in the revolutionary experience of France and America – saw its more prosaic but equally important fulfilment in the widespread universalization of the franchise around the turn of the twentieth century. In the words of Flora and Heidenheimer, the welfare state is 'a general phenomenon of modernization . . . a product of the increasing differentiation and the growing size of societies on the one hand and of processes of social and political mobilization on the other'. Thus, 'the historical constellation in which the European welfare state emerged' was one of 'growing mass democracies and expanding capitalist economies within a system of sovereign nation states' (Flora and Heidenheimer, 1981, pp. 8, 23, 22).

Theorists of modernization have not fought shy of identifying capitalism (as opposed to industrialism) as an important and independent component in the shaping of (at least Western) modern societies. They also confer considerable importance upon political mobilization and especially the mobilization of the emergent working class as an important component in the rise of the welfare state, particularly in the period before 1945.[2] However, at least in the modernization writing of the 1950s and 1960s, such political mobilization was depicted less as the implementation of the class aspirations of the organized working class than as the natural correlate of full citizenship (Lipset, 1969; Flora and Heidenheimer,

---

[2] Typically, Flora and Heidenheimer insist that 'up to 1914, and to a large extent through the inter-war period, the social forces most relevant to welfare state development were those of the working class' (Flora and Heidenheimer, 1981, p. 28).

1981). Certainly, the expansion of the franchise around the turn of the twentieth century did bring the working class more fully into political life. But perhaps more importantly for the modernization theorists, it tended in the longer term to de-emphasize class politics through (1) the social concessions made to the working class public (partly through social welfare) and (2) the shared status which everyone now enjoyed as full citizens of the nation state. Thus, the securing of the early welfare state was seen both to constitute a success for working class politics but also to lessen the requirement for further class-based political action. Indeed, it was suggested that in a reformed polity, the equality of political citizenship might predominate over the economic inequalities that arose within the capitalist market place. Thus Reinhard Bendix wrote 'it may appear . . . that the growth of citizenship and the nation-state is a more significant dimension of modernization than the distributive inequalities underlying the formation of social classes', while 'the growth of the welfare state . . . provides a pattern of accommodation between competing social groups' (Bendix, 1970, p. 313).

Upon this account, the coming of the welfare state is one aspect of a more widespread process of modernization. It is associated historically with the extension of political citizenship and especially the rapid expansion of suffrage (and the consequent development of mass political parties) of the turn of the twentieth century. It is seen as a response to working class political pressure (or, at least, the anticipation of such pressure), but also through its very institutionalization of social reform as a means of defusing the demand for further class-based and/or more revolutionary political action.

Table 1.2 Type of rights

	Civil rights	*Political rights*	*Social rights*
Characteristic period	18th century	19th century	20th century
Defining principle	individual freedom	political freedom	social welfare
Typical measures	habeas corpus freedom of speech, thought and faith; freedom to enter into legal contracts	right to vote, parliamentary reform, payment for MPs	free education, pensions, health care (the welfare state)
	————————▶ Cumulative ————————▶		

Source: Marshall (1963) pp. 70–4.

Perhaps the clearest statement of this position is to be found in the work of T. H. Marshall. Addressing the specifically British experience, Marshall characterizes the process of modernization over the past three hundred years as one of the general expansion of citizenship. It is a history of the expansion of the rights of the citizen and a growth in the numbers of those entitled to citizen status.

Marshall identifies three species of rights – civil, political and social – each with its own 'typical' historical epoch, which have been cumulatively secured over the last three hundred years (see table 1.2). The macro-history of the period since 1688 in Britain is seen as one of progress from the securing of a body of civil rights – the rights of the freely contracting individual, sometimes identified with the structure of a capitalist market economy – which, in turn, made possible the expansion of political rights – principally, the expansion of voting rights – which meant in its turn the enfranchisement of the working class and the rise of mass social democratic parties. The winning of civil rights (in the eighteenth century) and of political rights (in the nineteenth century) made possible the securing in the twentieth century of an epoch of social rights. Such rights, which Marshall describes as embracing 'the whole range from the right to a modicum of economic welfare and security to the right to share to the full in the social heritage and to live the life of a civilized being according to the standards prevailing in the society' (Marshall, 1963, p. 74), are frequently identified with a broadly based definition of the welfare state. Upon such an account, the coming of the welfare state is indeed a historical process, but one which is part of a broader progressive history of expanding citizenship. The coming of the welfare state in the early twentieth century is thus the product of the exercise of the expanded political citizenship of the late nineteenth century, broadly under social democratic auspices (Marshall, 1963).[3]

Thesis 2

The welfare state is a product of successful political mobilization to attain full citizenship, in the context of industrialization.

---

[3] In fact, Marshall's was not a straightforwardly evolutionary view. He repeatedly stressed the potential clash between citizenship equality and class/economic inequality (Marshall, 1963). For a critical commentary, see Barbalet (1988).

Traditional Social Democracy and the Welfare State

Very similar assumptions underlie much traditional social democratic thinking on the development of the welfare state. Here again there is an emphasis upon the process of modernization (associated with the rise of an industrial civilization), and once more an acknowledgement of the importance of the capitalist organization of the economy. Also repeated is the belief that political changes effected under the rubric of extended citizenship (and under the pressure of working class political mobilization) may, in fact, have *undermined* the conditions for further class-based political mobilization.

The distinctiveness of the traditional social democratic position may be established around three key points. First, while social democrats recognize that the birth of capitalism had severe and oppressive consequences for the formative working class, they insist that its further development has not, as Marxist critics have insisted, seen an inexorable worsening of the relative position of the working class. The situation of the urban-industrial working class (often through their own mobilization and agitation first in trades unions and then in social democratic political parties) has improved, not worsened. Thus, capitalism has proven capable of reform. The excesses of liberal capitalism have been checked by an increasingly interventionist 'social state' which has counteracted the inequitable outcomes of liberal capitalism through legislative interference.

Secondly, the class structure of capitalism, again in defiance of Marxist expectations, has not been increasingly polarized but has, in practice, grown to be ever more diffuse and differentiated. Significantly, the development of capitalism has been accompanied by the secular growth of the middle class. In the twentieth century, the growing division between the legal ownership of capital and its effective control (the 'managerial revolution') is seen to have weakened the power of capital as a class. At the same time, the expansion of the interventionist state not only ameliorates the position of the working class but, in creating an expanding public employment sector, increasingly unseats the logic of the market and further complicates and differentiates class structure.

Thirdly, since a (reformed) capitalism is capable of growth without crises, and furnishes an increasingly complex class structure, the social democrats argue that further social progress (towards conceptually rather indistinct 'socialist' ends) is best effected, indeed is only possible, through the continued promotion of (capitalist) economic growth.[4]

---

[4] According to the leading turn of the century revisionist Eduard Bernstein, 'the prospects of socialism depend not on the decrease but on the increase of social wealth' (Bernstein, 1909, p. 142).

All of these strategic claims and conclusions rely upon a fourth and decisive element in the social democrats' position. This is their belief in the definitive importance of the winning of mass parliamentary democracy and the changing balance of social forces this occasions between the attenuated economic power (of the owners of industry) and the enhanced political power (of elected governments). The expansion of the franchise within the core societies of developed capitalism in the late nineteenth and early twentieth centuries – which generally corresponded with the rise of social democratic parties – is afforded an unchallenged primacy in social democratic accounts as the key to subsequent social development. Such social development is best explained not by concentrating upon patterns of capitalist development alone, but rather by considering the impact of the expansion of democratic institutions and political rights against a background of economic growth. Of decisive importance is the winning of democracy which brings a new social and political order under which it is *political* authority which exercises effective control over the *economic* seats of power.[5] Buttressed by the increased power of organized labour and the diffusion of the capitalist interest through the 'managerial revolution', the state emerges as the principal directing authority within the advanced capitalist societies. Increasingly, outmoded and irrational direction by the market, responsible to no-one, gives way to the planning and administrative logic of an accountable political authority.

Further, the securing of democratic institutions allows for the *gradual* transformation of both state and society. Before the coming of mass democracy, the exclusion of the mass of the people from within 'the pale of the constitution' justified, indeed necessitated, the call for the revolutionary overthrow of capitalism. However, the winning of parliamentary democracy transformed this relationship, allowing (indeed requiring) that the now-legal mass political and industrial organizations of the working class should effect the gradual transformation of capitalism into socialism by first securing democratic control of the state and then using such state power to effect social and economic transformation. The 'social state' or welfare state – the state which intervenes within the processes of economic production and exchange to re-distribute life chances between individuals and classes – was the principal mechanism for prosecuting such a transformative political strategy.

---

[5] According to Sidney Webb, 'collectivism is the obverse of democracy'; if the working man is given the vote, 'he will not forever be satisfied with exercising that vote over such matters as the appointment of the Ambassador to Paris, or even the position of the franchise . . . he will more and more seek to convert his political democracy into what one may roughly term an industrial democracy, so that he may obtain some kind of control as a voter over the conditions under which he lives' (S. Webb, cited in Hay, 1975, p. 14).

Social Democracy and the Coming of the 'Keynesian Welfare State'

However, this perspective still left practising social democrats with the theoretical 'problem' of the long-term socialization of the economy. As we have seen, early social democrats were distinguished from their more radical socialist opponents not by rejection of the final *aim* of socialization of the economy (which formally, at least, they endorsed) but by their differing (gradualist or evolutionary) *method* for achieving such an end. Neo-classical economics insisted that capitalism required the free play of untrammelled market forces. It seemed that for its socialist (including social democratic) opponents, socialism must by contrast be premised upon some form of centralized and directive planning and investment. However, the social, political and economic costs of transition to such a socialized/planned economy were great, perhaps insurmountable, for social democrats pledged to the introduction of socialism through the medium of liberal parliamentary democracy.[6] The 'solution' to this social democratic dilemma was to be found in the development of Keynesian economic policy in association with the promotion of an expanded welfare state – the so-called *Keynesian Welfare State*. It is in this way that the welfare state comes to assume its familiar centrality in social democratic thinking.

For social democracy, the vital importance of Keynesianism resided in its status as 'a system of political control over economic life' (Skidelsky, 1979, p. 55). Its great strategic beauty lay in its promise of effective political control of economic life without the dreadful social, economic and political costs that social democrats feared 'expropriation of the expropriators' would bring. Though Keynes was not a socialist, he was an opponent of the belief that capitalism was a self-regulating economic system. Above all, it was the neo-classical belief in a self-regulating market mechanism securing full employment that Keynes sought to subvert, indeed to invert.

Say's Law – that under capitalism supply created its own sufficient demand – held true, Keynes claimed, only under the peculiar conditions of full employment. It did not however itself *guarantee* equilibrium at full employment. Such a balance could only be secured *outside* the market, by the state's manipulation of 'those variables which can be deliberately controlled or managed by central authority' (Keynes, 1973, p. 378). The key variables which governments could manipulate were the propensity to consume and the incentive to invest. It was the duty of governments to

---

[6] On the costs and difficulties of revolutionary transition, see Emmanuel (1979), Offe (1985), Przeworski (1985), Przeworski and Sprague (1986).

intervene within the market to generate an enhanced level of 'effective demand', promoting both the propensity to consume and to invest, so as to ensure sufficient economic activity to utilize all available labour and thus to secure equilibrium at full employment. To achieve this, a whole range of indirect measures – including taxation policy, public works, monetary policy and the manipulation of interest rates – were available to the interventionist government.

Keynes's advocacy of a 'managed capitalism' offered a neat solution to the social democratic dilemma of how to furnish reforms for its extended constituency and maintain its long-term commitment to socialism without challenging the hegemony of private capital. It was Keynesian economics that provided the rationale for social democracy's abandonment of the traditional socialist aspiration for socialization of the economy. Keynes himself had famously insisted:

> It is not the ownership of the instruments of production which it is important for the state to assume. If the state is able to determine the aggregate amount of resources devoted to augmenting the instruments and the basic rate of reward to those who own them, it will have accomplished all that is necessary. (Keynes, 1973, p. 378)

In this way, it was possible for social democrats to represent formal ownership of the economy (and the traditional strategy of socialization/ nationalization) as (largely) irrelevant. Economic *control* could be exercised through the manipulation of major economic variables in the hands of the government. The owners of capital could be *induced* to act in ways which would promote the interests of social democracy's wide constituency. At the same time, social democratic governments could shape the propensity to consume, through taxation and monetary policy, as well as through adjusting the level of public spending. They could also rectify the disutilities of the continuing play of market forces through the income transfers and social services that came to be identified with the welfare state. Happily, the raising of workers' wages and income transfers to the poor, a 'vice' in classical economics, suddenly became, given the tendency of lower income groups to consume the greater part of their incomes, a Keynesian 'virtue'. Social democracy was thus able simultaneously to secure the 'national interest' and to service its own constituency.

For traditional social democrats, then, the development of the welfare state institutionalized the successes of social democratic politics. The Keynesian revolution made possible the transition from the (zero-sum) politics of production to what, under conditions of economic growth, were the (positive-sum) politics of (re)distribution. As Berthil Ohlin described it in the 1930s, 'the tendency is in the direction of a "nationalization of consumption" as opposed to the nationalization of the "means of production" of Marxian socialism' (Ohlin, 1938, p. 5). It was a two-fold strategy built upon active government intervention through (1) the macro-management of the economy to ensure economic growth under conditions of full employment and (2) a range of social policies dealing with 'the redistribution of the fruits of economic growth, the management of its human effects, and the compensation of those who suffered from them' (Donnison, 1979, pp.146-50).

Thesis 3

The welfare state is a product of industrial and political mobilization. It embodies the successes of the social democratic political project for the gradual transformation of capitalism.

The Power Resources Model

The power resources model offers a distinctive variant of the social democratic approach. At its heart is a perceived division within the advanced capitalist societies between the exercise of economic and political power, often presented as a contrast between markets and politics. It insists that 'the types of power resources that can be mobilized and used in politics and in markets differ *in class-related ways*' (Korpi, 1989, p. 312; emphasis added). Thus, in the *economic* sphere, the decisive power resource is control over capital assets, the mechanism for its exercise is the (wage labour) contract and its principal beneficiary the capitalist class. However, in the *political* sphere, power flows from the strength of numbers, mobilized through the democratic process, and tends to favour 'numerically large collectivities', especially the organized working class.

Institutionalized power struggles under advanced capitalism are then best understood as a struggle between the logic of the market and the logic of politics and 'this tension between markets and politics is likely to be reflected in the development of social citizenship and the welfare state' (Korpi, 1989, p. 312). The more successful are the forces of the organized working class, the more entrenched and institutionalized will the welfare state become and the more marginalized will be the principle of allocation through the market (Korpi, 1989; Esping-Andersen, 1985; Shalev, 1983; Esping-Andersen and Korpi, 1984, 1987).

In response to his critics, Korpi has insisted that the power resources model is not to be understood as a 'one-factor theory claiming to explain welfare state development more or less exclusively in terms of working class or left strength' (Korpi, 1989, p. 312n). A more complex position – including, for example, the role of confessional parties, party coalitions and pre-emptive conservative reforms – may be developed through the application of a 'games theoretical perspective' to a range of protagonists in the struggle over the welfare state (Korpi, 1989, p. 313). However, to date the principal application of the power resources model has been to underwrite a distinctive left social democratic account of the welfare state as an entrenchment of the power of organized labour and as an avenue of gradual transition towards socialism.

The two core claims of this left social democratic position are succinctly summarized by John Stephens: first, 'the welfare state is a product of labour organization and political rule by labour parties' and secondly, it 'thus represents a first step towards socialism' (Stephens, 1979, p. 72). While recognizing that the welfare state is not universally an expression of the strength of the organized working class, these left social democrats insist that, under the right circumstances, the inauguration and promotion of welfare state policies and institutions has been and can be an effective strategy for the gradual transition from capitalism to socialism. However, their position differs decisively from traditional social democracy in its belief that the coming of democracy, social democratic parties and the welfare state do not transform the social and political nature of the advanced capitalist societies. The logic of Marx's analysis of the contradictions of capitalism and the centrality of class struggle still holds but parliamentary democracy and the interventionist state are seen to provide new media for the prosecution of the class politics of socialism.[7]

Generally, the inception of welfare state policies is seen to follow upon the universalization of the franchise, itself seen as a victory for the organized working class. Initially, social policy may represent an attempt to pre-empt political reform or else to disorganize or demobilize the organized working class. But it is insisted that under wise and far-sighted social democratic governance, welfare state policies can be used both to counteract the dominance of capital that market relationships entail and to reinforce the effective solidarity of organized labour. The left social democrats afford much greater independent importance to political power than do many others in the Marxist tradition, and social democratic governments elected under universal franchise are seen to constitute an effective counter to the power exercised by capital within the privately owned economy. Where social democratic governments become more or less permanently entrenched in office (and this is an essential precondition)

---

[7] In fact, Marxism has always embraced such a radical social democratic wing (with a strategy for socialism built upon incrementalism and parliamentary democracy), perhaps best represented by Karl Kautsky and the Austro-Marxists (Kautsky, 1909, 1910, 1983; Pierson, 1986, pp. 58–83; Bottomore and Goode, 1978).

an effective balance or at least stalemate may be established between the political powers of social democracy and the economic powers of capital. Under these circumstances, some sort of working compromise between capital and labour is likely to emerge, characteristically under the rubric of the welfare state.

But the left social democrats insist that, however longstanding, such a compromise is in essence temporary. Indeed, if the social democrats govern wisely and make the right strategic choices, it is argued that the (Marxian) logic of continuing capitalist development will increasingly tilt the balance of power in favour of organized labour and against private capital. Thus it is suggested that continuing capitalist development will tend to produce an expanding and homogeneous broad working class. Social democratic governments that mobilize this constituency and promote its internal solidarity (through, for example, nationally agreed and uniform salary increases, the support of 'full employment' and the provision of generous unemployment and sickness benefits) can undermine the effectiveness of traditional market disciplines and further entrench their own political power. At a certain point in the strengthening of the powers of organized labour, conditions of balance/stalemate with capital no longer apply. At this point, it is possible for the social democratic movement to advance beyond the 'political' welfare state, with its indirect (Keynesian) influence upon the management of the economy and to engage directly the traditional socialist issue of socialization of the economy.

This process was seen to have attained its highest expression in Sweden. Writing at the end of the 1970s, John Stephens (1979, p. 129) argued that in Sweden, where 'the welfare state has been developed by a strongly organized and highly centralized trades union movement . . . in co-operation with a social democratic government that remained in office for 44 years . . . the welfare state is characterized by high levels of expenditure and progressive financing and thus represents a transformation of capitalism towards socialism' (Stephens, 1979, p. 129).

Summarily, this suggests that the most 'successful' social democratic welfare states will be associated with:

- the extension of the franchise
- the rise of social democratic parties
- a strong (and centralized) trades union movement
- weak parties of the right
- sustained social democratic governmental incumbency
- sustained economic growth
- strong class identity and correspondingly weak cleavages of religion, language and ethnicity.

Thesis 4

The welfare state is the product of a struggle between the political powers of social democracy and the economic powers of capital. Its further development, under social democratic hegemony, makes possible the gradual transition from capitalism to socialism.

WHERE ?!

Commentary: Modernization, Social Democracy and Working Class Power

Some of the weaknesses identified in the industrialism thesis are at least addressed in the literature of modernization and traditional social democracy and in the 'power resources' model of welfare state development. In fact, there has sometimes been a tendency to elide explanations in terms of modernization with those premised upon industrialization. However, Hage, Hanneman and Gargan insist upon the need 'to separate the independent effects of modernization from those of industrialization' and argue that 'the modernization process has much more impact than the industrialization process on the expansion in social welfare expenditures'. Specifically, they isolate urbanization and the increasing density of communication (measured by quantities of mail and electronic/telegraphic communications) rather than industrialization or economic growth as decisive indicators of welfare state growth (Hage, Hanneman and Gargan, 1989, pp. 100–10). Similarly, Peter Flora and Jens Alber prefer the 'vague and ambiguous' but 'multi-dimensional' concept of modernization to either industrialization or democratization as the key to explaining the development of European welfare states (Flora and Alber, 1981, pp. 37–8).

However, the major issue that has divided advocates of modernization and social democratic theses on the welfare state from the claims of industrialism is the independent importance that they attribute to *political forces* in shaping the development of the welfare state. Often, this advocacy of the political causes of welfare state development is simply an inversion of the claims of industrialism. Thus, for example, the burden of Stephens's refutation of Wilensky was to buttress his belief 'that the welfare state is a product of labour organization and political rule by labour parties and thus represents a first step towards socialism' (Stephens, 1979, p. 72; see p. 16 above). Similarly, the purpose of Furniss and Tilton's comparative history of welfare state experience in the USA, Britain and Sweden is to demonstrate 'that a democratic majority, backed by a committed labor movement, can capture and employ political power to create a more decent society along the lines of a social welfare state' (Furniss and Tilton, 1979, p. 93). Christopher Hewitt has also argued that social democratic parties can have a profound influence upon the narrowing of income inequality in advanced capitalist societies largely through the mechanism of government redistribution through the welfare state (Hewitt, 1977, pp. 450, 460; see also Hicks, 1988).

In the 1980s, Walter Korpi was an influential advocate of the view that (social democratic) politics makes a difference. Writing of the post-war experience of Germany, Austria and Sweden, he and Gosta Esping-Andersen argue that 'the relative power position of wage-earners has been of central significance for the development towards an institutional type of social policy' (Esping-Andersen and Korpi, 1984). Assessing survey evidence on the emergence of social rights during sickness in 18 OECD countries since 1930, Korpi finds 'rather unequivocal support for the assumption of the significance of left government participation in the development of social policy'. By contrast, 'while it appears reasonable to assume that the rate of growth of economic resources is of relevance for the opportunities to enact social reforms', he finds 'limited support for this hypothesis'. He concludes cautiously that 'class-based left parties appear to have played a significant role in the development of social rights' (Korpi, 1989, pp. 323–5). Julia O'Connor also claims to have isolated a strong association between left power (in both parties and trades unions) and levels of civil consumption expenditure (O'Connor, 1988).

There is then some (contested) evidence that 'politics makes a difference'. However, we need also to consider *how* it is that 'politics makes a difference'. Much as we found in discussing the evidence brought to support the industrialism thesis, evaluating data in support of modernization and traditional social democratic theses is problematic. Many of the differences in outcomes are the product of the use of differing indices of welfare effort and comparison across differing time periods. In his magisterial review of the evidence, Esping-Andersen, for example, argues that very little difference can be found in the impact of politics upon *levels* of welfare expenditure (a commonly used indicator of welfare effort) but that political forces are crucial in determining differing welfare *policy regimes* (Esping-Andersen, 1990, pp. 35–54; see below, pp. 174–5).

Furthermore, some empirical surveys have found that if politics does matter, it is not necessarily the political impact of social democratic forces that matters most. Castles, for example, identifies the weakness of parties of the right as decisive for the emergence of 'generous' welfare states (Castles, 1978, 1982, 1985), while Hicks and Swank argue that '*all* less business-oriented parties, Christian democratic as well as social democratic, centrist as well as labor, prove about equally supportive of welfare expansion' (Hicks and Swank, 1984, p. 104: emphasis added). Wilensky identifies Catholic rather than left party incumbency as the strongest indicator of welfare expenditure and suggests that *the intensity of party competition* (notably between left and Catholic parties) may itself tend to increase welfare spending effort.[8]

Nonetheless, we can identify some analytic advances in the modernization and social democratic approaches. Most significantly, they do allow that the processes of transformation that create the modern world are simultaneously industrial/technological and political. Correspondingly, weight is given to the expansion of citizenship and the extension of democracy, and attention is also directed to the ways in which the specifically *capitalist* organization of the production process shapes the circumstances of welfare state emergence. Unfortunately, among advocates of modernization and the more traditional variants of the social democratic thesis, these analytic advances are substantially vitiated by the *form* that this revised assessment takes. Thus they have tended to share with industrialism a Panglossian celebration of progress and the imposition of assumptions of 'inevitable' development. Inasmuch as they deal with both historical actors (most notably, the organized working class) and the importance of capitalism, they may be accused of misunderstanding both. Thus, for example, in the influential work of Tom Marshall, the working class is often seen to struggle historically to ensure full political citizenship and to use democracy once achieved to secure social rights under the welfare state. But the very achievement of democracy (and associated welfare state rights) is seen to resolve or at least to accommodate the differences of interest between capital and labour out of which such political struggle might have been seen to arise. The spectre of capitalism, and the deep-seated division of interests it is seen to generate, is raised only to argue that it has been 'tamed' or 'subverted' by the rise of the welfare state.

There are a number of historical objections to this account. First, it is far from clear that the coming of parliamentary democracy does bring the irreversible cessation of class hostilities and a uniform social democratic consensus on the welfare state and the mixed economy. Even where the formal concession of democracy led to the more or less successful incorporation of the working class within the political apparatus of the existing state, this did not lead to the permanent reconciliation of class differences and class hostilities in capitalist societies. Thus it is very uncertain that the spectre of 'the class politics that undermines the need for class politics' is justified by actual welfare state experience.

Secondly, whatever the role of the working class in the later *development* of the welfare state, the earliest welfare state measures were gener-

---

[8] Wilensky (1981, pp. 356–8, 368–70); on differential spending effort related to party competition among the individual United States, see Jennings (1979).

ally introduced by liberal and/or conservative elites and not by the representatives of organized labour. Even, for example, in the Scandinavian social democracies, in which the working class welfare state is often seen to be most effectively entrenched, the origins of the welfare state lay with conservative or liberal political forces and often built upon a multi-class appeal (Esping-Andersen, 1985; Baldwin, 1990). Similarly, there is plenty of historical evidence of organized labour opposition to welfare state measures, often because these were seen as (1) an attack upon the au- tonomy and integrity of trades unions' own forms of mutual support, (2) as a way of depressing wages through welfare subsidization (a repeated argument against family allowances/child benefit), and (3) as a form of state control over the workforce (see below, p. 35).

Thirdly, historical experience suggests that the class analysis of social democracy/modernization theorists is not only too optimistic/uniform but also too crude. Early welfare state measures (of social insurance) were generally limited to particular (very suitable or very vulnerable) trades. Disputes over contributory and non-contributory pensions schemes exacerbated differences of interest between the independent/skilled/respectable' working class (who made limited provision for death and sickness through friendly societies) and the residuum of unskilled (and uninsured) workers. Similarly, there have been differences of interest among employers of labour, between large capital-intensive employers with an interest in a healthy, well-educated and 'regular' workforce, and those in the most keenly competitive, labour-intensive markets whose interest was in securing a mass of unskilled labour at the cheapest possible price (De Swaan, 1988). Such differences of interest among both labour and capital have continued down to the present.

The historical record also shows that the state may have its *own* interest in the promotion of social policy, not least in the securing of a citizenry fit and able to staff its armies. For example, the concern with 'national efficiency' and the physical incapacity of the British working class to defend the empire against the challenge of the Boers has long been cited as a source of British welfare reforms at the turn of the twentieth century (Thane, 1982, pp. 60–1; Fraser, 1973, p. 133; Hay, 1975). This view was echoed by Lloyd George, who argued in 1917 that 'you can not maintain an A-1 empire with a C-3 population' (cited in Gilbert, 1970, p. 15).

Advocates of the traditional social democratic position certainly have good grounds for stressing the importance of citizenship. The idea of a shared status of all members of the community and especially the *right* to varying forms of provision from the state is seemingly a definitive element of the welfare state, and Esping-Andersen insists that 'few can disagree with T. H. Marshall's (1950) proposition that social citizenship constitutes the core idea of a welfare state' (Esping-Andersen, 1990, p. 21). Yet Marshall's unilinear model of expanding citizenship, his qualifications notwithstanding, is unsatisfactory (see pp. 21–2 above). In fact, the nature of citizenship has been, and continues to be, much more consistently contested than Marshall allows. The question of who counts as a citizen, whether full citizenship is gender-specific, what is to count as a citizen's entitlement and under what circumstances welfare rights will be granted and by whom, continue to be daily concerns of contemporary political life.[9] Only the very general process of overall social expenditure growth (often under very varying rules of citizen entitlement) has concealed this continuing struggle over the status of citizenship (Turner, 1986, 1990; Held, 1989).

The 'Keynesian revolution' occupies a similarly problematic place in the traditional social democratic account. Even more explicitly than the winning of citizenship, the emergence of Keynesian forms of economic management, which we have seen to occupy a central place in the justification of the social democratic theory of gradual social transformation, has not been a once-and-for-all change in the governance of capitalist economies. In a number of developed welfare states, perhaps most triumphally in the UK, the formal commitment to full employment and government macro-management of demand has long since been abandoned, and with it goes a substantial part of the theoretical justification of the social democratic position.

These observations on citizenship and the fate of Keynesianism may suggest a need to reorient our understanding of the elements of bipartisanship, consensus and shared citizenship which have been so frequently identified in the post-war period. Certainly, post-war social policy was often institutionally bipartisan and apparently consensual. However, this bipartisanship may have depended in substantial part upon the favourable economic climate that made positive-sum resolutions of distributional conflicts a viable policy. Accordingly, this policy may be better understood in terms of the capacity simultaneously to satisfy a number of (differing) constituencies rather than in terms of a straightforward universalization of citizenship or the coming of consensus. Where reforms did not satisfy these several constituencies, political conflict over social policy could still be acute. Just such an argument has been made about the post-war period in Britain, and both phenomena may also be seen in the violent conflict over the Swedish social democrats' pensions reform of 1958 (see, on Sweden, Esping-Andersen, 1985; on the UK, Taylor-Gooby, 1985; Pimlott, 1988; Deakin, 1987). Thus it is possible that the universal citizenship *form* may have been the medium for promoting interests with a much more traditional class-based political and economic *content*.

Finally, as Esping-Andersen has pointed out, welfare state measures

---

[9] On the feminist critique of conventional conceptions of citizenship, see Pateman (1988), Lister (1993), O'Connor (1996) and the discussion at pp. 69–70 below.

may only properly be seen as securing the overall interests of social democracy's natural constituency in the (broad) working class inasmuch as
they are *market-usurping*, that is, to the extent that they insulate workers
from the discipline of the market.[10] But clearly many welfare state measures, and especially early welfare state social policy, were not market-
usurping but *market-supporting*. Trade unions were, for example, extremely
suspicious of the way in which labour exchanges would be used to recruit
strikebreakers or generally to service employers with non-unionized labour. Social welfare provision was, and still is, criticized as a mechanism
for depressing wages and Pat Thane writes of 'widespread suspicion'
towards Liberal welfare reforms in the UK from a working class which
found them to be 'too limited, too "intrusive", and a threat to working-
class independence both collective and individual' (Thane, 1984, p. 899;
see also Marwick, 1967; Pelling, 1968; Hay, 1978a, pp. 16–21). Many
early recommendations on work/farm colonies, even those supported by
social democratic politicians, were explicitly coercive in intent (Harris,
1977; Gilbert, 1966, pp. 253–65). Terms of entitlement continue to reflect
labour market status and often explicitly 'encourage' labour market participation. Thus, any straightforward claim that the welfare state is an
imposition of working class interests through the medium of parliamentary democracy, which accordingly attenuates the conflict of (class) interests, 'tames' the excesses of capitalism and promotes a national unity
based around common citizenship is unsustainable.[11]

Several of these weaknesses are confronted by the 'power resources'
model. Whilst this approach is still broadly social democratic (premised
upon the pursuit of a reformist path through legal-parliamentary means),
the benign assumptions of an end to class conflict and an irreversible
progress towards an ever-enhanced citizenship is rejected. This is a social
democratic strategy premised upon the historical strength of working
class forces in continuing struggle with the powers of capital. A very
considerable effort is made to show empirically that the effective strength
of working class forces (articulated through labour parties and trades
union organizations) has made a real difference to the patterns of promotion of the welfare state under advanced capitalism.

However, there remain a number of problems with this model. First,
while the more naive evolutionism of traditional social democracy is rejected, elements of a Marxist evolutionism persist. Presumptions about

---

[10] The issue of whether such market-usurpation will prove to be in the *long-term* interests of
the working class will depend upon the place of the national welfare state within the world
economy and other political developments.

[11] There is a case for insisting that it is the capacity of the organized working class to
continue to pursue class-based politics that is the basis for the continued capacity of the
welfare state to represent a practice that is in the interests of that class.

the uniformity of workers' interests, the necessary growth in the proportion of the working class, the weakening of the powers of capitalism in
the face of the collective action of the workers underpin several of the
strategic claims in the 'power resources' model. However, there are good
grounds for doubting that these presumptions about a majoritarian working
class with unified interests are true (Pierson, 1986, pp. 7–30, 58–83;
Przeworski, 1985; Przeworski and Sprague, 1986).

It may also be that the political focus of the 'power resources' model is
too narrow. Middle class support has been crucial to the pattern of welfare state development, particularly in the post-war period, and at strategic times in the historical emergence of the European welfare states, the
attitudes of rural classes have also been a decisive element. Similarly,
parties other than the social democrats (especially the confessional parties of continental Europe) have also played an important historical role
in the expansion of the welfare state, and their position has not always
been one of seeking to minimize levels of social expenditure. This suggests that any understanding of the class politics of the welfare state must
be one that considers the positions of a number of classes (not just capital
and labour) and of a number of parties (not just the social democrats)
and that the decisive element in the success of the social democratic
welfare state project may lie in the capacity of the working class and
social democratic parties to forge long-term, majoritarian *alliances* in
support of its decommodifying form of social policy.

A second criticism of the 'power resources' model is that some of its
optimistic assumptions about the possibilities for successful social democratic strategies arise from its concentration upon experience in a number
of particularly favourable Scandinavian and, more especially, Swedish
examples. As Lash and Urry (1987, p. 10) have pointed out, all of the
favourable corporatist/welfare state examples generally cited in support
of the social democratic model are actually numerically swamped by the
single counter-example of the United States. Still more important is the
diminishing 'success' of these social corporatist states in the 1990s (see
Lane, 1995). Although the 'death of the Swedish model' has been exaggerated, there is no doubt that its status as the exemplar of social democratic welfare state success has been very seriously compromised (with an
unemployment rate which by the late 1990s was almost double that in the
USA).

Three further general criticisms have been raised against the social
democratic perspective. First, there are those who insist that the social
democrats' exclusive concentration on the politics of class neglects the
decisive impact of interest or 'ascribed status' groups or, indeed, of the
state apparatus itself. Secondly, there are those who maintain that all
the social democratic approaches fail to recognize that the most important aspects of power under the welfare state lie in its gender-specific

consequences for women and its 'race'-specific consequences for ethnic minorities. The claims underlying these first two criticisms will be addressed in Chapter 3. A third objection to the social democratic approach is that it underplays the extent to which the welfare state, *even under social democratic auspices*, continues to be, in essence, an instrument of social control of the working population in the interests of capital. This perspective of 'social control' will be considered in chapter 2, in which we turn to criticisms of the social democratic welfare state informed by 'the new political economy'.

2
Capitalism, Social Democracy and the Welfare State II
Political Economy and the Welfare State

In the twenty-five years following the Second World War, it was largely the traditional social democratic outlook that defined the prevailing orthodoxy on advanced capitalism and the welfare state. Buttressed by empirical and programmatic work in social administration, sanctioned by bipartisan support for the expansion of state services and underpinned by continuous economic growth, the social democratic prescription for managed capitalism and social amelioration dominated throughout the advanced industrial world. But from the late 1960s onwards, both the social democratic post-war settlement and its comforting assumptions about the reconcilability of advanced capitalism and the welfare state came under increasing challenge from both right and left. In this chapter, we begin to consider the range of critical responses to the post-war social democratic orthodoxy.

The New Right and the Welfare State

Perhaps the most prominent (and successful) opponent of the post-war orthodoxy has been the New Right, which has argued for a strong identity between social democracy and the welfare state, while insisting that both are inconsistent with the moral, political and economic freedom that only liberal capitalism can guarantee. In common with the other theoretical positions outlined in this study, the New Right does not define a unique set of prescriptions for the welfare state. In fact, it is possible to identify at least two distinct 'strands' in New Right thinking: 'a liberal tendency which argues the case for a freer, more open, and more competitive economy, and a conservative tendency which is more interested in restoring social and political authority throughout society' (Gamble, 1988, p. 29; King, 1987, pp. 7–27). In brief, both elements of the New Right are hostile to welfare state intervention because (1) its administrative and bureaucratic methods of allocation are inferior to those of the market, (2) it is morally objectionable (for both the sponsors and the recipients of state welfare), (3) it denies the consumers of welfare services any real choice and (4) despite the enormous resources devoted to it, it has failed either to eliminate poverty or to eradicate unjust inequalities of opportunity (Gamble, 1988, pp. 27–60). Indeed, the New Right almost invert the common sense of industrialism, modernization and social democratic approaches to insist that the origins of the present social, economic and political problems of advanced capitalist societies lie not in the failure of markets but in the mistaken pursuit of those market-usurping policies identified with the welfare state.

The more interesting and the more important intellectual challenge of the New Right probably comes from its neo-liberal rather than its neo-conservative wing. However, those political movements and ideologies of the 1980s which identified themselves with the New Right, most notably 'Thatcherism' in the UK and 'Reaganism' in the USA, were in practice a potent, if not entirely consistent, mixture of economic liberalization and renascent conservatism. In defiance of the libertarian conclusions drawn by some on the New Right, in the UK and still more prominently in the USA, the 'freeing up' of the economy was associated with the traditionally conservative imperatives of strengthening the 'law and order' state, a more aggressively nationalistic foreign policy, the reversal of minority rights, the glorification of 'traditional family life' and an endorsement of the religious and moral crusade of the moral majority (Nozick, 1974; Gilder, 1982; Stockman, 1986; King, 1987). Some of these conservative elements on the New Right receive fuller attention in chapter 5. Here our attention is more closely focused upon its neo-liberal aspect.

Underlying most neo-liberal assessments of the relationship between capitalism, social democracy and the welfare state is a rehearsal of the sentiments of Adam Smith's advocacy of liberal capitalism (see pp. 7–8 above). It is recognized that Smith wrote under very different circumstances and to a quite different agenda and audience than his latter-day admirers. Yet his was a critique of the interventionist (albeit in his time mercantilist) state and a call for limited government (whether or not democratic). He advocated the spontaneously arising market economy as *the* means of securing both optimum individual and social welfare and the surest guarantee of individual liberty. It is just these prescriptions, and the ways in which social democracy and the welfare state have countermanded them, that lie at the heart of the contemporary neo-liberal view.

In essence, the argument of the New Right is that the impact of social democracy and the associated welfare state represent a usurpation of the sound principles of liberal capitalism. Its political ideal is to achieve a return to what is understood to have been the social and political *status quo ante*. Thus Milton Friedman insists that 'The scope of government must be limited. Its major function must be to protect our freedom both from the enemies outside our gates and from our fellow-citizens: to preserve law and order, to enforce private contracts, to foster competitive markets' (Friedman, 1962, p. 2). Though government intervention beyond this minimum might sometimes be justified, according to Friedman, it is 'fraught with danger' (Friedman, 1962, pp. 2–3; see also Minford, 1987). Certainly, where we have had economic progress, this has been the 'product of the initiative and drive of individuals cooperating through the free market. Government measures have hampered not helped this development' (Friedman, 1962, p. 200; King, 1987, pp. 83–4). Correspondingly, Friedman's advocacy of monetarism is at least in part directed at curtailing the counter-productive interventions of social democratic governments (Friedman and Friedman, 1980; Bosanquet, 1983, pp. 5–10, 22–4, 43–61).

Perhaps the most sophisticated philosophical statement of the neo-liberal view is that developed by Friedrich Hayek in the three volumes of *Law, Legislation and Liberty* (Hayek, 1982). For Hayek, the liberal 'Great Society' championed by Smith can only be secured on the basis of 'catallaxy', the neologism Hayek uses to describe 'the special kind of spontaneous order produced by the market through people acting within the rules of the laws of property, tort and contract' (Hayek, 1982, II, p. 109). Both social democracy and the welfare state seek to undermine this order based on the interlocking of spontaneously emerging markets, and are thus inconsistent with the principles of a free and just society.

In fact, Hayek's Smithian liberalism is tempered by a good measure of Burkean conservatism. As in Burke's critique of the French Revolution, Hayek condemns the '*constructivist rationalism*' of all those, from 1789 onwards, who have sought to recast society in accord with some understanding of the principles of Reason (Hayek, 1982, I, pp. 5, 29–34). Order (and tradition) certainly appeal to Hayek's conservatism but this is the spontaneously generated and in principle unknowable order created by innumerable interactions within a number of interlocking markets – the catallaxy. Indeed, 'it is because it was not dependent on organization but grew up as a spontaneous order that the structure of modern society has attained that degree of complexity which it possesses and which far exceeds any that could have been achieved by deliberate organization' (Hayek, 1982, I, p. 50). In part, this is an issue of philosophical principle, namely, Hayek's belief that every individual should be, insofar as is possible, self-directing. But it also embodies a seemingly compelling sociological argument. As Hayek himself makes plain, in even the most centralized and state-dominated societies, the central political authorities can have only a very tenuous control over the many millions of social decisions made every day within its domain. By contrast, individuals may have a very intimate control as well as an irreducible/irrepressible interest in that much smaller range of *salient* decisions they must make in organizing their own lives. Hayek combines this with something like Smith's own faith in the benevolence of 'the invisible hand' to sustain a distinctive account of the promotion of welfare. Thus, he argues, 'a condition of liberty in which all are allowed to use their knowledge for their purposes, restrained only by rules of just conduct of universal application, is likely to produce for them the best condition for achieving their aims' (Hayek, 1982, I, p. 55)

Hayek ascribes a correspondingly limited role to the state. The duty of the public authority is not to pursue its own ends but rather to provide the framework within which 'catallaxy' may develop. Those functions for which the state may properly raise taxation are limited to these:

- provision of collective security against the threat of external assault;
- preservation of the rule of law where law is in essence confined to the impartial application of general rules of property, contract and tort;
- provision for (though not necessarily the administration of) those collective or public goods which the market cannot efficiently provide; for example, protection against (internal) violence, regulation of public health and the building and maintenance of roads.

To these duties of the minimal state, Hayek adds the following:

- provision of 'a certain minimum income for everyone', more precisely for 'those who for various reasons cannot make their living in the market, such as the sick, the old, the physically or mentally defective, the widows and orphans – that is all people suffering from adverse conditions which may affect anyone and against which most individuals cannot alone make adequate provision but in which a society that has reached a certain level of wealth can afford to provide for all' (Hayek, 1982, III, p. 55).

However, Hayek is insistent that this last duty to relieve destitution is not to be identified with the welfare state. Relief is not a statutory right of citizenship, but needs-based and discretionary. Least of all is such relief to be understood as part of an attempt to manufacture 'social justice'.

Hayek's model may be completed by a brief consideration of his views on democracy. Although Hayek would doubtless have considered himself a democrat, he was perhaps still more an advocate of individual freedom, and certainly he was an opponent of the ideas of sovereignty and unlimited government frequently associated with the rise of democracy. 'Only limited government can be decent government', he insisted, 'because there does not exist (and cannot exist) general moral rules for the assignment of particular benefits' (Hayek, 1982, II, p. 102). Where parliament is sovereign, governments become the plaything of organized sectional interests. Principles and 'the national interest' are abandoned in the attempt to mobilize a majority-creating coalition of particular interests against the *genuinely* common or public interest.

The welfare state and the political agenda of social democracy are seen by Hayek to be at odds with almost every aspect of this model of the liberal capitalist ideal. First, social democrats set out to adjust the spontaneous order of catallaxy, a project which Hayek depicted as hopeless given the impossibility of adequate centrally organized knowledge of the infinity of market-like decisions. Interventions in the market will *always* have suboptimal outcomes and *always* lessen general social welfare. Secondly, the welfare state represents a break with Hayek's insistence that the law must be confined to rules of 'just conduct of universal application'. Social democracy prescribes particularistic legislation, most notably to confer privileges upon its allies in the organized labour movement, and governments under its auspices seek not only to negotiate general and market-usurping agreements between labour and capital but even to intervene on a day-to-day basis in the conduct of particular transactions within the marketplace. Not only is this an invasion of individual freedom and a usurpation of the proper role of the law, it is also bound to fail, given the opacity of the spontaneously generated catallaxy.

Thirdly, the welfare state is also the principal institutional vehicle of the misconceived aspiration for 'social justice' (Hayek, 1982, II, p. 1). Justice, Hayek insists, is strictly *procedural* and can only refer to the proper enforcement of general rules of universal application without regard to its particular results. No set of human arrangements, no cumulation of particular actions (however unequal its outcomes) can be described as just or unjust. 'The mirage of social justice' which the social democratic welfare state pursues is, at best, a nonsense and, at worst, pernicious and itself unjust. It means undermining the justice of the market, confiscating the wealth of the more successful, prolonging the dependency of the needy, entrenching the special powers of organized interests and overriding individual freedom. Indeed, 'distributive justice [is] irreconcilable with the rule of law' and in seeking to press state intervention beyond its legitimate minimum, the social democrats have been the principal offenders in 'giving democracy a bad name' (Hayek, 1982, II, p. 86).

Public Choice Theory

Hayek's writings may be newly prominent but they are certainly not new. His arguments against the welfare state date back at least half a century. But in recent years, this longstanding (and largely philosophical) case has been supplemented with arguments drawn from social science sources and particularly from work in public choice theory. The latter is often seen to give enhanced empirical and logical rigour to the moral and philosophical case against the welfare state.

Public choice theory, located on the boundaries between economics and political science, has traditionally been concerned with collective or non-market forms of decision making. In the hands of the New Right, it is taken to show that under liberal democratic procedures, collective choice through state actions, beyond that necessary minimum advocated by both Smith and Hayek, will always tend to yield outcomes that are less efficient or desirable than outcomes determined by private choice through markets. Public choice writers sympathetic to the New Right seek to show that the welfare state project is flawed both logically and sociologically.

The great weakness of decision-making procedures under liberal democratic arrangements within which the welfare state has developed is that it encourages both governments and voters to be fiscally irresponsible. The individual making a private economic choice within the market has always to weigh costs against benefits in making a decision. Public choice theorists argue that in the political 'market' both voters and governments are able to avoid or at least to deflect the consequences of spending decisions and thus to seek benefits without taking due account of costs. Within the rules of the liberal democratic game, it is then possible for both governments and voters to act rationally but through their collective action to produce sub-optimal or even positively harmful consequences. This, it is suggested, may be shown in a number of ways.

First, it may not be rational for individual voters carefully to consider the full range of a prospective government's public policy, still less to consider the overall consequences of such policies for the 'national interest'. The marginal impact of a single voter's decision is so limited that the opportunity costs of a well-considered decision would be unreasonable (Downs, 1957; Olson, 1982). Under these circumstances, rational actors will not normally press their consideration beyond a crude calculation of how the incumbent government has benefited the voter. Given this, it is in the interests of a government seeking re-election to ensure that the pre-election period is one in which as many voters as possible feel that they are prospering under the current regime. Government will then, it is suggested, seek to manage the economy in the run-up to an election so as to lower inflation and unemployment and to maximize incomes (perhaps through lowering personal rates of taxation). In this way, a political business cycle may be established, with governments manipulating economic variables in the prelude to an election. Not only will this give misleading signs to the electors, but it will also undermine the long-term stability of the economy and will tend to increase the state's indebtedness (through an imbalance of spending and taxation). Under circumstances of adversary politics, such fiscal irresponsibility is unlikely to be challenged by the opposition who are more likely to 'bid up' the electorate's expectations, promising 'more for less' in the attempt to unseat the existing government (Downs, 1957; Alt and Chrystal, 1983).

Clearly in a private economic market such overbidding would be constrained by the threat of bankruptcy. A corporation that sold goods and services at less than their cost of production would soon be forced out of business. But governments do not face this same constraint (at least in the short and medium term). By increasing the public debt, governments may defer the costs of their present spending upon future governments (and/or generations). This may have a damaging effect on the medium-term prospects for the economy – by encouraging inflation, squeezing out private sector investment or whatever – but while this runs against the overall public interest, it is not rational for either particular governments or particular voters to seek to stop it. Indeed, Olson argues that economic growth becomes a 'public good' for most interest groups. It is more rational to seek to extract a greater proportion of the national budget (through political pressure) than to seek to enhance the overall growth of the economy (Olson, 1965, 1982; Rose and Peters, 1978).

In a number of other ways, this logic of collective action can be seen to furnish sub-optimal outcomes. Governments that are seeking to maximize their electoral appeal are driven to support the particularistic claims of well-organized interest groups and to satisfy the claims of special interests. The costs of meeting the claims of the well-organized are discharged upon the unorganized generality of the population. The politics of voter-trading and political activism tend to lead to an expansion of government beyond that which is either necessary or desirable (Tullock, 1976).

This oversupply of public services is further exacerbated by the nature of the public bureaucracy. First, the public bureaucracy is itself a powerful interest group and public bureaucrats have a rational interest in maximizing their own budgets and departments. Secondly, the public bureaucracy does not normally face competition, nor indeed any of the economic constraints of acting within a marketplace. Where costs are not weighed against benefits and where the utility maximization of bureaucrats is dependent upon the maximization of their budgets, the public choice theorists insist that there will be a chronic tendency for the public bureaucracy to oversupply goods and services (Niskanen, 1971, 1973;

Tullock, 1976). This problem becomes still more acute when the mono-polistic powers of the public bureaucracy are strengthened by an expan-sion of white collar trade unionism, as happened, for example, in the much expanded British Civil Service in the period after the Second World War (Bacon and Eltis, 1978).

This complex is seen broadly to describe the political circumstances of the modern welfare state. Under liberal democratic and adversarial po-litical arrangements, and without some sort of constitutional constraint upon the action (and spending) of governments, politicians, bureaucrats and voters *acting rationally* will tend to generate welfare state policies which are suboptimal, indeed, in the long run, unsustainable.

The New Right and the Welfare State: a Summary

The case of the New Right against the welfare state, which, in the hands of its academic advocates, often took an abstract and technical form, achieved its present polemical status largely as a response to a series of social and political problems in the advanced capitalist world of the 1970s. Accordingly, further comment upon these New Right theses is deferred to the more appropriate context of chapter 5. Here we can conclude our consideration of the general New Right case, by briefly summarizing the main substantive claims to which it has given rise:

- *The welfare state is uneconomic.* It displaces the necessary disciplines and incentives of the marketplace, undermining the incentive (of capi-tal) to invest and the incentive (of labour) to work.
- *The welfare state is unproductive.* It encourages the rapid growth of the (unproductive) public bureaucracy and forces capital and human resources out of the (productive) private sector of the economy. Monopoly of state provision enables workers within the public sec-tor to command inflationary wage increases.
- *The welfare state is inefficient.* Its monopoly of welfare provision and its creation and sponsorship of special/sectional interests lead to the inefficient delivery of services and a system which, denuded of the discipline of the market, is geared to the interests of (organized) pro-ducers rather than (disaggregated) consumers. Generally, as govern-ments extend the areas of social life in which they intervene, so policy failures mount.
- *The welfare state is ineffective.* Despite the huge resources dedicated to it, welfare state measures fail to eliminate poverty and deprivation. Indeed, they worsen the position of the poorest by displacing tradi-tional community-based and family-based forms of support and en-trap the deprived in a 'cycle of dependence'.

- *The welfare state is despotic.*   It constitutes a growth in, at best, the enervating hand of bureaucracy and, at worst, social control of individual citizens and, in some cases, whole communities, by an overweening state. In many such cases the victims of state control and manipulation are those same deprived citizens that it is claimed the welfare state exists to assist.
- *The welfare state is a denial of freedom.*   Its compulsory provision of services denies the individual freedom of choice within the welfare sector, while its heavy and progressive tax regime can be represented as 'confiscatory'.

Thesis 5

The welfare state is an ill-conceived and unprincipled intrusion upon the welfare-maximizing and liberty-maximizing imperatives of a liberal market society. It is inconsistent with the preservation of freedom, justice and real long-term welfare.

Marxism, Neo-Marxism and the Welfare State

A second general account of the irreconcilability of capitalist and welfare state imperatives, and thus a rejection of the social democratic orthodoxy, has come from the Marxist and neo-Marxist left. It is a much-cited paradox of this Marxist analysis of the welfare state and welfare capitalism that it seems to share much in common with the politically quite opposed New Right. This is not perhaps so surprising, given the status of Marx's definitive study of *Capital* as 'a critique of political economy'. Just as Marx took the work of the classical political economists and sought to press their premises to radically new conclusions, so do contemporary Marxist writers find much to endorse in the New Right's morphology of the problems of welfare capitalism, while seeking quite different explanations pressed to very different conclusions. What they share is a common belief that the 'steady-state' welfare capitalism of traditional social democratic analysis is untenable. Both have sought out contradictions within the welfare state/welfare capitalism, the one to label them 'the excesses of democracy/socialism', the other to style them 'the contradictions of capitalism'. In essence, the impasse of social democracy and the welfare state is seen to lie in the impossibility of reconciling the imperatives of capitalism with the requirements of authentically democratic arrangements or the furnishing of 'genuine' social welfare.

Twentieth Century Marxism and the Welfare State

In chapter 1, we saw that the essence of Marx's view was that even if limited social reform could be forced by organized labour, the securing of widespread state welfare for the majority of the population was inconsistent with the demands of capital accumulation. Down to the Second World War, mainstream classical Marxists saw little reason to amend this account of welfare provision under capitalism. Though these were the years in which many formative welfare states emerged, provision was seen to be minimal and in the 1930s rising unemployment and falling benefits were seen to express the dominance of the (crisis) logic of capital over the wishful thinking of welfarist social democrats. By contrast, in the halcyon years of social democracy after 1945, it was the social democrats who had little time for 'outmoded' Marxist analyses of (a now transformed) capitalism. Marxism, with its outdated appeal to the class war, belonged to a bygone era of working class poverty, mass unemployment and class privilege. While post-war societies were not egalitarian, under the impact of Keynesian economics and extensive social welfare provision, systematic differences of class no longer carried their pre-war resonances. Meanwhile the Marxist left, demoralized by the experience of the Hungarian uprising, the (limited) exposure of Stalinism and the seemingly uninterrupted growth of the post-war economy, increasingly directed its attention towards alienation and the cultural consequences of capitalism. Marcuse's *One Dimensional Man* depicted organized capitalism as a system of total administration in which the working class was lost as the revolutionary agent of social change. Even opposition was now co-opted within an all-embracing system of structured irrationality (of which the welfare state was an important component). Consciousness of the need for radical change was confined to marginal groups on the periphery of society – students, ethnic minorities and *déclassé* elements. The provision of welfare to the working class became not an avenue for their gradual advance towards socialism but the means by which workers were controlled, demoralized and deradicalized. According to Marcuse, 'the prospects of containment of change . . . depend on the prospects of the welfare State . . . [as the embodiment of] a state of unfreedom' (Marcuse, 1972, pp. 51–2).

However, by the end of the 1960s – especially under the impact of the events loosely and graphically associated with 1968 – the image of unproblematic post-war social democratic consensus began to crack. A period of uninterrupted political and industrial unrest also saw a re-emergence of academic interest in Marxist and other radical/socialist thinking. It is from this period that we can date the emergence or possibly renaissance of Marxist theories of the (welfare) state.

Neo-Marxist Analysis of the Welfare State

Although others, and most notably Antonio Gramsci, might lay claim to initiating Marxist study of the welfare state, the origins of this renaissance are widely seen to reside in the much-rehearsed debate between Ralph Miliband and Nicos Poulantzas (Gramsci, 1971; Miliband 1969; Poulantzas, 1973, 1978). These more recent accounts have instituted a number of changes from classical Marxist thinking on the state. Without entering upon this extended debate here, we may note the following significant amendments in more recent accounts:

Proposition 1
That the state enjoys *relative autonomy* from the capitalist class; the possibility of the state acting in the general interests of capital is dependent upon its distance from particular capitals.

Proposition 2
That the state articulates the general needs of capital accumulation – and this may involve paying an *economic* price for securing the *political* compliance of non-ruling class interests.

Proposition 3
That the state is not straightforwardly unitary; it is, as Poulantzas has it, 'constituted-divided' by the same divisions that characterize capitalist society more generally.

Neo-Marxism I: the Welfare State as Social Control

In fact, (neo-)Marxist responses to the welfare state have been remarkably varied. We have already seen that advocates of the power resources model have interpreted the welfare state (under specified conditions) as a strategic element in the transition to socialism. Others, drawing on Propositions 1 and 2 above, continue to regard the welfare state as predominantly an instrument for the social control of the working class, acting in the long-term interests of capital accumulation. Within the broadly neo-Marxist camp, this is the view that is perhaps closest to the classical Marxism of Marx, Engels and Lenin. It confronts quite explicitly the traditional social democratic perspective of a benign and progressive welfare state but also challenges the claims of the 'revisionist' power resources model.

We have seen that one of the core claims of the classical Marxist position was that in any epoch, the state mobilizes exclusively the interests of a single ruling class. Thus, in contrast to the social democratic view (and Proposition 3 above), it is insisted that, under capitalism, 'the functioning and management of state welfare remains part of a *capitalist* state which is fundamentally concerned with the maintenance and reproduction of capitalist social relations' (Ginsburg, 1979, p. 2). Above all else, the welfare state is involved in securing the production and reproduction of labour power under capitalist forms. The benefits of the welfare state to the working class are not generally denied, but they are seen to be largely the adventitious by-product of securing the interests of capital. Here there is characteristically an echo of Marx's commentary on an earlier series of reforms, the Factory Acts, which, while a gain for the working classes thus protected, arose from the 'same necessity as forced the manuring of English fields with guano' – that is, the need to preserve from total exhaustion the sole source of future surplus value (Marx, 1973a, p. 348).

Thus, Norman Ginsburg maintains:

> From the capitalist point of view state welfare has contributed to the continual struggle to accumulate capital by materially assisting in bringing labour and capital together profitably and containing the inevitable resistance and revolutionary potential of the working class . . . the social security system is concerned with reproducing a reserve army of labour, the patriarchal family and the disciplining of the labour force. Only secondarily and contingently does it function as a means of mitigating poverty or providing 'income maintenance'. (Ginsburg, 1979, p. 2)

This principal thesis is defended through a number of more specific rebuttals of the social democratic position:

- Social provision under the welfare state is characteristically geared to the requirements of capital, not the real needs of the working population.
- Many welfare policies were originated not by socialists or social democrats but by conservative or liberal elites. Their intention was to manage/regulate capitalism and to discipline its workforce, not to mitigate the social hardship of the working class.
- Social policy has long been recognized by these elites as the 'antidote' to socialism. As British Conservative Prime Minister Arthur Balfour insisted in the 1900s, 'social legislation . . . is not merely to be distinguished from Socialist legislation, but it is its most direct opposite and its most effective antidote' (cited in Marshall, 1975, p. 40).
- Changes in social welfare regimes reflect the changing accumulation needs of capital: for example, (1) the shift from extensive to intensive exploitation of labour (and the correspondingly greater need of a

healthy, docile, disciplined and educated workforce), (2) the need of fit men to staff the armies of the imperialist capitalist nation states (and of women to replace them in the sphere of industrial production); (3) the rise (and perhaps the fall) of mass production and scientific management.

- The funding of welfare state measures has often been regressive and/ or associated with an extension of the tax base; at best, welfare state spending has been redistributive within the working class or across the life cycle of the average worker.

- The compulsory state management of welfare has deprived the working class of the self-management of its own welfare (through friendly societies and trade unions); the *form* of welfare services has characteristically been bureaucratic and anti-democratic.

- Social legislation has often enhanced the intrusive powers of state professionals within the everyday life of individual citizens and concentrated surveillance and discretionary power in the hands of agents of the state.

- The ameliorative impact of state relief and the ideology of a welfare state in which each member of the community is guaranteed a certain minimum of welfare provision has demobilized working class agitation for more radical economic and political change.

Thesis 6

The welfare state is a particular form of the developed capitalist state. It functions to secure the long-term circumstances for the continued accumulation of capital.

Commentary: Neo-Marxism I: the Welfare State as Social Control

A number of commentators have complained that it is extremely difficult to 'operationalize' Marxist theses on the welfare state (Pampel and Williamson, 1988, p. 1450; Korpi, 1989, pp. 315–17). However, there is a good deal of historical evidence to support the social control thesis. First, welfare state measures often developed in tandem with a traditional Poor Law whose intent was explicitly coercive (as in the UK down to 1948). Secondly, the conditions that are placed upon state benefits (a record of regular employment, 'willingness to work' clauses, a qualifying period and cut-off points for payment of benefits) are often oriented not to the meeting of recipients' needs but rather to the requirement not to under-mine the dynamics of the labour market. Thirdly, the administration of benefits by the state has placed considerable discretionary, investigative and directive powers in the hands of state officials. Thus, Piven and Cloward argue that the intent of welfare provision in the USA has always been one of 'regulating the poor', allowing for more generous provision at times when mass mobilization (rather than mass need) pressed upon the prevailing order, but then reimposing tighter labour market disci-plines upon recipients (by moving them off welfare rolls) once the imme-diate threat of disorder has been demobilized. This, for example, was their verdict on the New Deal social security reforms:

> The first major relief crisis in the US occurred during the Great Depres-sion. By 1935, upwards of twenty million people were on the dole. But it would be wrong to assume that this unprecedented volume of relief-giving was a response to widespread economic distress, for millions had been unemployed for several years before obtaining aid. What led government to proffer aid . . . was the rising surge of political unrest that accompanied this economic catastrophe. Moreover, once relief-giving had expanded, unrest rapidly subsided, and then aid was cut back – which meant, among other things, that large numbers of people were put off the rolls and thrust into a labour market still glutted with unemployment. But with stability re-stored, the continued suffering of these millions had little political force. (Piven and Cloward, 1971, p. 45)

Further support for the social control thesis may be found in the evidence of early working class hostility to the state provision of welfare. Such hostility (from trade unions and friendly societies) can be understood not simply as 'respectable' working class conservatism but rather as a fear that the state would replace working class self-administration with forms of social welfare that would serve the interests of capital. There is further historical evidence that many early social work/public health initiatives – for example, the activities of Charitable Organization Societies on both sides of the Atlantic or the introduction of schools' medical services – were immediately concerned with the production of a literate, docile, 'regular' and 'fighting fit' workforce. According to Elizabeth Wilson, 'the literature of social work *is* the ideology of welfare capitalism' (Wilson, 1977, p. 28; Ginsburg, 1979; Taylor-Gooby and Dale, 1981; Langan and Lee, 1989). Again, much of the earliest US welfare legislation was con-cerned with rehabilitation which would bring the economically inactive off benefits and into work. Often states' welfare legislation was commended precisely because of the financial benefits which would accrue to business and taxpayers. Meanwhile, the severest punitive measures were reserved for those who could not or would not respond to their 're-education' and remained unemployable (see, for example, Katz, 1986).

Yet, despite all this evidence, it is difficult to sustain the argument that the growth of the welfare state was exclusively or even preponderantly in the interests of the capitalist class. It is certainly true that early public welfare measures were parsimonious, often introduced under conservative/dual monarchy regimes and with an explicitly anti-social democratic or anti-trade union intent. Yet, the more liberal reforming regimes were often driven by a radical/social democratic wing; they were a response to new working class electors and they frequently sought to outmanoeuvre the electoral appeal of social democratic parties by offering public welfare for the working classes. Similarly, while early public welfare measures often had a coercive and disciplinary element, they still represented an improvement in the basic circumstances of many members of the working class. Thus, for example, even though early pensions were minimal and means-tested, this represented an improvement upon reliance on the Poor Law and the workhouse. Again, while there were, for example, attempts to restrict welfare to non-unionized labour, state management of welfare was probably less antagonistic to labour than was the administration of welfare by employers (though less in the working class interest than self-management through trades unions or friendly societies). Where such measures were introduced on a social insurance rather than a public assistance basis, an (albeit circumscribed) *right* to public welfare was also established. While such early gains were often extremely limited, they were not generally conceded without a struggle. While parliamentary democracy and the welfare state might have come to constitute part of the apparatus for the political incorporation of the working class and the deradicalization of labour, the view that accordingly such measures were willingly embraced by enlightened and sophisticated conservative elites proves to be historically quite exceptional.

Contemporary fears among elites (and the pattern of early take-up of social insurance) also suggest that social insurance might indeed lessen the stranglehold of the market upon the working class. Even very limited compensation for unemployment or sickness did lessen the drive for workers to return to the market to undergo the disutility of labour. Thus although public welfare has often been fiscally regressive (based on a payroll tax and [re]distributing benefits to the better-off and longer-lived), inasmuch as programmes were based on (or subsidized by) general tax revenues this could be expected to have a mildly redistributive effect. Similarly, fears that the expenditure incurred could lead to a fiscal crisis of the state can, in fact, be retraced to the very origins of the public welfare system. Indeed, the escalating cost of earlier systems of public assistance was one of the major spurs to welfare reform – in Britain, for example, both in the 1840s and again in the 1900s.

One response to this evidence is to suggest that such improvements as the working class did enjoy under the welfare state were simply the adventitious benefits of capital's interest in a more productive source of surplus value. In this sense, the evidence is just a vindication of Marx's understanding of the contradictory logic of capitalism. The capitalist class could not have a healthier, better educated, reliable (and thus more profitable) source of surplus value without improving the health, education and housing of the working class. It may also reflect the importance of the working class as a source of consumption under difficult circumstances for the valorization of capital. Yet this does not lessen the material improvements secured by the working class and it was the case that these services were generally being provided by the state rather than in a potentially more coercive and partisan way by the owners of industry themselves. Furthermore, the *unintended* consequences of welfare state legislation might significantly strengthen the defensive powers of the working class. The experience of the early introduction of sickness insurance in Britain was of a greater than expected take-up and of a lower return to work by recuperating workers (Gilbert, 1966). As we shall see in chapter 5, the ways in which social insurance (even if self-financed) were to distort the labour market was to become a very major concern of those who argued that the post-war welfare state was undermining the very bases of the capitalist economy.

Neo-Marxism II: Contradictions of the Welfare State

This view of the welfare state as primarily the instrument of capitalist social control continues to attract some support. More typically, however, the renaissance in neo-Marxist thinking has followed Proposition 3 above and concentrated upon contradictions *within* the welfare state itself. It has also become increasingly oriented around the apparent *crisis* experienced in the welfare state following twenty-five years of seemingly unproblematic growth in the post-war period. Indeed, it is difficult to isolate a *general* statement of this (neo-)Marxist view from the context of a perceived *crisis* of the welfare state. This is most clearly the case with James O'Connor's path-breaking work on the *Fiscal Crisis of the State*, which is considered in some detail in chapter 5 (O'Connor, 1973, 1987). It is also a concern of Ian Gough's classic study of *The Political Economy of the Welfare State*.

Locating the welfare state in terms of the overall structure of welfare capitalism, Gough is profoundly critical of those social democratic accounts of welfare which have sought to isolate economy and polity or to reduce welfare to the study of discrete social problems and particular institutions. He himself defines the welfare state 'as the use of state power to modify the reproduction of labour power and to maintain the non-working population in capitalist societies' (Gough, 1979, pp. 44–5). Such modification is effected through the taxation and social security systems, regulation of the provision of certain 'essentials' (for example, food and housing) and the provision of certain services in kind (most notably, health and education). He views the development of this welfare state as essentially *contradictory*. Thus, it 'simultaneously embodies tendencies to enhance social welfare, to develop the powers of individuals, to exert social control over the blind play of market forces; and tendencies to repress and control people, to adapt them to the requirements of the capitalist economy' (Gough, 1979, p. 12). On the one hand, welfare state institutions are seen to be consonant with the interests of capital. They represent a response to changes undergone in capitalist development – for example, periodic unemployment, technological change, the need of a skilled and literate workforce – and to the new requirements these changes generate in the area of social policy. On the other, the origins of the welfare state lay in organized working class struggle and the ameliorating response of organizations of the ruling class to the threat this was seen to pose. This means that the welfare state cannot be seen as straightforwardly 'functional for capital' – as simply a means of exercising social control over the working class and subsidizing capital's profit making. At least a part of the prodigious growth of the post-war welfare state may be seen as a response to the defensive economic strength of the organized working class and the labour movement. Yet, at the same time, 'paradoxically . . . it would appear that labour indirectly aids the long-term accumulation of capital and strengthens capitalist social relations by struggling for its own interests within the state' (Gough, 1979, p. 55).

The welfare state, then, is a 'contradictory unity', exhibiting both positive and negative features for both capital and labour. Correspondingly, the long-term consequences of the welfare state for the continued accumulation of capital are themselves ambivalent. Although the welfare state may serve to subsidize some of the costs of capital, its strengthening of the defensive powers of the working class may in the long run undermine the reproduction of suitable conditions for profitable capital accumulation. The welfare state's institutionalization of income support and full employment will tend to strengthen the defensive power of the organized working class and thus the capacity of labour to protect real wage levels and to resist attempts to raise productivity. Under the (perhaps consequent) circumstances of sluggish economic growth, it will prove ever more difficult to finance the growing state budget without increasing inflation or further weakening growth or both. For the funding of the welfare state could be neutral for capital accumulation only if the whole of the tax burden of funding it could be met within the household sector and thus preponderantly by the broad working class. However, in reality, the distribution of the burden of taxation between capital and labour – and indeed the scale and distribution of welfare services themselves – is itself a matter of class struggle and reflects the prevailing balance of social forces. Under these conditions, the circumstances for long-term capital accumulation may be imperilled. The outcome is likely to be inflation, a slow down in economic growth and, for developed welfare states operating within a world market, the potential loss of international competitiveness.

The Welfare State as 'the Crisis of Crisis Management': Offe

Perhaps the most developed account of the welfare state as the contradictory and contested product of continuing capitalist development within the neo-Marxist or, more properly, 'post-Marxist' literature is that developed by the German political theorist Claus Offe. Offe follows classical Marxism in arguing that the 'privately regulated capitalist economy' is innately crisis-prone. However, this crisis is not best understood as predominantly *economic*. In fact, the welfare state emerges as an institutional/administrative form which seeks to 'harmonize the "privately regulated" capitalist economy with the [contradictory] processes of socialization this economy triggers' (Offe, 1984, p. 51). The welfare state is that set of political arrangements which seeks to compromise or 'save from crisis' what classical Marxism had identified as the central contradiction of capitalism – that between social forces and private relations of production. The welfare state arises then as a form of systemic crisis management.

For Offe, the structure of welfare capitalism can be characterized in terms of three subsystems as in Figure 2.1. According to his account, the economic subsystem of capitalism is not self-regulating and has dysfunctional consequences for the legitimation subsystem. The state has to intervene in and mediate between the other two subsystems to secure on the one hand, continued accumulation and, on the other, continued legitimation. Correspondingly, the state under welfare capitalism is to be seen as a form of crisis management – and for twenty-five years following the Second World War a remarkably successful one. But this process of reconciliation under the welfare state proves in the long run to be impossible, as the welfare state is subject to a particular crisis logic of its own. Three manifestations of this underlying contradiction of the welfare state are of particular importance:

1 *The fiscal crisis of the welfare state.* The state budget required to fund strategies of recommodification tends to grow uncontrollably and to become increasingly self-defeating, occasioning (through high

taxation and welfare provision) both a 'disincentive to invest' and a 'disincentive to work'.

2 *Administrative shortfall.*   The welfare state repeatedly fails to live up to its own inflated programmatic-administrative claims, a failure variously attributed to the ineffectiveness of the indirect instruments of public policy, to struggles *within* the state and to the external imperatives of public accountability, democratic representation and short-term political expediency.

3 *Legitimation shortfall.*   Under these circumstances of fiscal crisis and administrative shortfall, state intervention is seen to be increasingly particularistic and *ad hoc* and this undermines the political norms of 'equality under the rule of law', leading to a short-fall of mass loyalty/ legitimacy.

This makes the focus of Offe's analysis *the crisis of crisis management* (Offe, 1984, pp. 57–61).

Under advanced capitalism, Offe argues, *economic* contradictions of capital accumulation increasingly express themselves in a *political* crisis of the welfare state. Offe's economic subsystem is characterized by the production and exchange for profit of privately owned commodities. The success of this capitalist economy based upon private ownership is indis-

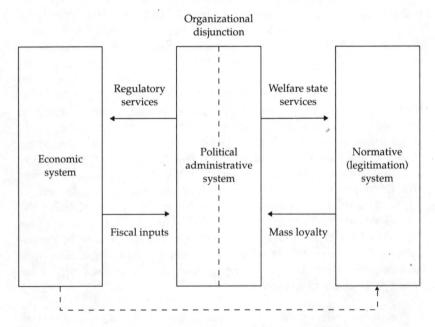

Figure 2.1   Three subsystems and their interrelationship
Source: Offe, 1984, p. 52.

pensable to the long-term viability of the welfare state, both because it is the ultimate source of that state's fiscal viability (through taxation and borrowing) and because consequently it is the basis of mass loyalty and legitimacy for the state (through the funding of welfare services, the securing of 'full employment' and so on). The key problem for the crisis management strategy of the welfare state is that, in practice, 'the dynamics of capitalist development seem to exhibit a constant tendency to paralyse the commodity form of value', and thus to imperil the state's primary source of revenues (Offe, 1984, p. 122).

Offe suggests that, if unregulated, the development of the capitalist economy tends systematically to exclude elements of labour power and capital from productive exchange (through the underemployment of labour or the underutilization of capital). The state cannot itself generally restore effective and profitable commodity exchange by intervening directly in the accumulation process, as this would both undermine the normative basis of the private-exchange capitalist economy and engender the risk of an (anti-nationalization) capital investment strike.[1] Since the state is prevented from intervening directly in the economy, it has to proceed indirectly, through essentially Keynesian means, to re-establish the conditions under which capital and labour will be drawn into profitable commodity exchange, through regulations and financial incentives (corporate tax concessions, special development areas, interest-free industrial loans, subsidizing energy costs), public infrastructural investment (training and retraining, recruitment services, subsidized transport facilities), and the sponsoring of neo-corporatist arrangements (between trade unions and employers). Offe calls this strategy 'administrative recommodification'. The intention is to promote the fuller utilization or *commodification* of both capital and labour through indirect, administrative means. Its vitiating weakness is that, in practice, it promotes a process of *decommodification* – that is, it undermines the circumstances for the fuller utilization of capital and labour. Thus the strategies which are supposed to encourage *more* effective commodity exchange in fact place ever greater areas of social life *outside* of the commodity form and *outside* the sphere of market exchange. The principal contradiction of the welfare state then is that strategies of *recommodification* effect a widespread process of *decommodification* (Offe, 1984).

Similar issues are raised by Claus Offe's distinguished countryman, Jürgen Habermas. He argues that the nature of this crisis in the developed capitalist state is a crisis not so much of capitalism as of the reactive aspirations and strategies of its opponents. Sociologists of all persuasions

---

[1] Corporatism may represent a partial attempt to realize such a policy. Elsewhere, Offe discusses the nature of state interventions of this kind (Offe and Wiesenthal, 1985).

have tended to present *abstract labour* as the key explanatory variable in
industrial societies and the utopia that has inspired most socialists is that
of 'a labor-based social organization of free and equal producers'. But,
Habermas insists, within the advanced capitalist societies, labour no longer
enjoys this definitive centrality nor can production and growth any longer
provide the basis for a utopian view of a future society. Thus, the 'utopian idea of a society based on social labor has lost its persuasive power'.
The great import of this discovery is that, for Habermas, it was precisely
this utopia of 'free and equal producers' which inspired the development
of the welfare state. Since the mid-1970s such a model has been rapidly
losing its authority. What Habermas calls the 'new obscurity' (the incapacity of progressive forces to decide how or whither we should progress)
'is part of a situation in which a welfare state program . . . is losing its
power to project future possibilities for a collectively better and less en-
dangered way of life' (Habermas, 1989, pp. 53–4).

'The welfare-state compromise and the pacification of class antagonisms'
were to be achieved by 'using democratically legitimated state power to
protect and restrain the quasi-natural process of capitalist growth'. The
status of employee was to be complemented by social and political citizenship, on the presupposition 'that peaceful coexistence between democracy and capitalism can be ensured through state intervention' (Habermas,
1989, p. 55). For a period following the war this strategy was successful
within the expanding economies of advanced capitalism, but from the
early 1970s it became increasingly problematic, not least because of contradictory elements within the welfare state itself.[2]

The first of these contradictions turned upon the familiar question of
the reconcilability of capitalism and democracy and the incapacity of the
state to intervene directly to organize the accumulation process. Accordingly, Habermas argues the more successful is the welfare state in securing the interests of labour, the more will it come to undermine the
conditions for its own continuing success and the conditions for its long-
term viability. Those voters on whom the social democrats or 'welfare
state parties' relied in the post-war years, and who benefited most from
the development of the welfare state, may increasingly move to protect
themselves against the more underprivileged and excluded.

Habermas also identifies a second and less familiar contradictory principle within the welfare state. The pioneers of the welfare state directed
themselves almost exclusively towards the taming of capitalism, as if the
state power they used to effect such control was itself neutral or 'inno-
cent'. But while their interest lay in the emancipation of labour, the day-

---

[2] Though Habermas does recognize other extrinsic sources of difficulty for the welfare state
from the mid-1970s (Habermas, 1989).

to-day practice of the welfare state has increased state control over the individual worker. In the promotion of welfare legislation programmes, 'an ever denser net of legal norms, and of governmental and para-governmental bureaucracies is spread over the daily life of its potential and actual clients'. Habermas concludes:

> In short, a contradiction between its goal and its method is inherent in the welfare state project as such. Its goal is the establishment of forms of life that are structured in an egalitarian way and that at the same time open up arenas for individual self-realization and spontaneity. But evidently this goal cannot be reached via the direct route of putting political programs into legal and administrative form. (Habermas, 1989, pp. 58–9)

In part because of its former successes in securing the basic needs of the mass of the population, the welfare state is subject to increasing discontent and defections among a more affluent population dissatisfied with the bureaucratic and alienating way in which its 'services' are delivered.

Thesis 7

The welfare state is a particular form of the developed capitalist state. It embodies the essentially contradictory nature of developed capitalism and is chronically liable to the logic of fiscal and administrative crises.

Post-Fordism and the Decline of the Keynesian Welfare State

In the end, the 'crisis' of the welfare state failed to resolve itself in quite the dramatic way that Offe and others had anticipated. Rather, welfare states appeared to be subject to a process of what has come to be called '*structural adjustment*': a series of gradual but deep-seated reforms which were designed to make social policy more consonant with a quite new (international) political economy.[3] Perhaps the most sustained effort to understand these changes from within a broadly neo-Marxist theoretical framework has come from those working under the rubric of *post-Fordism* (see Burrows and Loader, 1994). Broadly speaking, Fordism describes

---

[3] This process is extensively discussed in chapter 5 below.

that form of capitalism (and its attendant social and political institutions) which predominated in the West in the period between the end of the Second World War and the end of the 1960s. This was the epoch of full (male) employment, sustained economic growth and 'managed' capitalism. The welfare state under Fordism was a response to both the accumulation needs of capital (including mass *consumption* as an important component in the valorization of capital) and the defensive strength of the organized working class. For a time, it facilitated not only the class basis for mobilization behind the welfare state (the massification of collective labour), but also the corporate basis (in the rise of organized labour and organized capital) and the institutional basis (with the rise of the interventionist state). The social and economic turbulence of the late 1960s and early 1970s, however, was an expression of the exhaustion of this Fordist regime, and its characteristic welfare state form, as a framework for sustainable capitalist economic growth. Stability (security plus predictability), which had been a positive feature in the immediate postwar years, had descended into rigidity or, to use a much-favoured medical analogy, sclerosis. The institutions of Fordism and the Keynesian Welfare State, which had once secured the grounds for capital accumulation by sustaining effective demand and managing the relations between capital and labour, had now become a barrier to further economic growth. The crisis of Fordism was thus about finding and institutionalizing a new social and economic regime (a *post*-Fordist regime) which could restore the conditions for successful capitalist accumulation and thus economic growth.

The watchword of post-Fordism is *flexibility*. At the global level, flexibility can be seen in the deregulation of international markets, the abandonment of fixed exchange rates and the introduction of new financial institutions which give (especially financial) capital much greater international mobility, freed from tutelage to particular nation states. In the world of industry, Fordist mass production of standardized goods, typified by the assembly line and the minute division of semi-skilled labour, increasingly gives way to batch production of diversified products, a growth in small-scale service industries and increased 'flexibility in the use of machines, materials, and human beings as well as in the inter-firm relations of production' (Albertsen, 1988, p. 348). The demands of batch production and 'niche marketing', taken together with the production possibilities afforded by the application of new technologies, favour a 'demassification' of the workforce. At its simplest, employment becomes polarized between a 'core' of well-paid, secure and qualified wage-earners with polyvalent skills and a 'periphery' of poorly paid, casualized and unskilled workers who may move in and out of a category of still more marginalized 'welfare dependents'. There is a growth in subcontracting, in 'non-standard' employment and in work within the 'informal' economy (with its attendant lack of rights). Most significantly, the division in the workforce between a skilled employed core and an unskilled and partially employed periphery and the prospect of 'jobless growth' means that those 'who are most desperately dependent on the welfare state's provision of transfers and services are, however, politically most vulnerable' (Offe, 1987, pp. 529–34). The 'core' working class no longer has any reason to adopt the material interests of this disadvantaged 'surplus class' as its own. Meanwhile, trade unions, especially at the national level, lose much of the power that they exercised when industry was based upon the typically unionized semi-skilled worker of Fordist mass production.

Two changes in the general transition towards post-Fordism are seen to be of especial importance in recasting welfare state policy. First, there are the ways in which 'flexibilization' of the *international* political economy has undermined the pursuit of Keynesian policies at a *national* level. Thus the deregulation of international financial institutions has tended to weaken the capacities of the interventionist state, to render all economies more 'open' and to make national capital, and more especially national labour movements, much more subject to the terms and conditions of international competition. In as much as the Fordist welfare state truly was a *Keynesian* welfare state, those changes in the international economy which have precipitated a decline of Keynesianism may be seen to have had a very material effect on the welfare state. The prospects for sustaining long-term corporatist arrangements within particular nation states (including the institutionalization of a 'social wage') will seem even less promising in a deregulated international economy. For many of its sponsors, the commitment to sustain full employment through government-induced demand was an indispensable element in the welfare state regime. Yet it is unclear now that *any* government can redeem this pledge and insofar as the deregulation of the international economy and its consequences lie outside the scope of even the most powerful governments, it represents a challenge to national welfare state settlements, *irrespective* of the varying political aspirations of national governments.

A second challenge to the bases of the traditional welfare state comes from changes in the labour process and the organization of employment associated with flexibilization under post-Fordist imperatives. Changes in patterns of employment and corresponding class formation bring with them modification in both the patterns of dependency and the patterns of political support within a post-Fordist welfare state. It has been argued for some time that, partly as a result of the growth of the welfare state itself, the advanced industrial societies in which Fordism was most effectively entrenched have seen the emergence of a new line of political cleavage between those dependent for their consumption respectively upon the public and private sectors (Dunleavy, 1980). The post-Fordist epoch is one in which the political power base of the public sector is increasingly outpowered and outvoted by the interests of the private sector. There is a consequent erosion of the basis of political support upon which the Fordist welfare state was built. For other commentators, it seems likely that divisions in the workforce between 'core' and 'periphery' will accelerate the transition from a 'one nation' welfare state built around the objective of providing 'a high and rising standard of benefit . . . for all citizens as of right', towards a 'two nations' or 'Americanized' welfare state, in which there is 'a self-financed bonus for the privileged and stigmatising, disciplinary charity for the disprivileged' (Jessop, 1988, p. 29, 1991, pp. 151, 154; Lash and Urry, 1987, pp. 229–31). At worst, it may lead to a wholesale residualization of state welfare, as the securely employed middle classes defect from public welfare, leaving the state to provide residual welfare services for an excluded minority at least possible cost to a majority who are now sponsors but not users of these public services.

A third aspect of post-Fordist reform is the greater subservience of social policy to the imperatives of economic competitiveness (and, in its neo-Marxist variants at least, to the interests of global capital). In Jessop's account, for example, the attempt to install a distinctive post-Fordist social policy is summarized in terms of a transition from the Keynesian Welfare State (KWS) towards a *Schumpeterian Workfare State* (Jessop, 1994). Under this new formation, the state's social policy interventions are directed towards the twin goals of sponsoring innovation and technological know-how amongst its 'own' players in an open international market economy (the element loosely identified with Schumpeter), whilst sublimating social protection ever more explicitly to the needs of 'competitiveness' and a transformed labour market (workfare in intent if not always in practice). In Jessop's words, 'it marks a clear break with the KWS as domestic full employment is de-prioritised in favour of international competitiveness and redistributive welfare rights take second place to a productivist re-ordering of social policy' (Jessop, 1994, p. 24). Similarly, Phil Cerny's account (1990, 1995) identifies a general move from 'the welfare state to the competition state' with 'a shift in the focal point of party and governmental politics from the general maximisation of welfare within a nation . . . to the promotion of enterprise, innovation and profitability in both private and public sectors' (Cerny, 1990, p. 179).

Globalization

In fact, these arguments about post-Fordism and the welfare state are properly seen as part of a still broader account of fundamental changes in the character of welfare states arising from the multiple processes of *globalization*. The idea of globalization has been called upon to do an extraordinary amount of explanatory work in accounts of recent social and political change and, as such, it has generated a vast literature and a great deal of disagreement. At one extreme are those who believe that nation states are increasingly losing their powers, as ever more perfectly integrated international markets articulate the sovereignty of the global consumer across what is rapidly becoming a 'borderless world' (Ohmae, 1990). Sceptics, by contrast, doubt that there really is a new phenomenon of 'globalization', insisting that nation states have always faced powerful transnational forces and that, in spite of these, they retain significant governing capacities and policy discretion (Hirst and Thompson, 1996). Unremarkably, the truth probably lies somewhere between these two perspectives (Perraton et al., 1997).

Globalization is clearly a multi-faceted phenomenon – an 'open-ended process' rather than a given 'end state' in Perraton et al.'s (1997) treatment – but its most significant impact upon the welfare state arises from two sources. First, at least since the 1960s, there has been the emergence of a 'new international division of labour' which has seen the transfer of manufacturing activity (and the semi-skilled jobs that go with it) from the developed economies of the North to newly industrialized countries (especially on the Pacific Rim). With new developments in transport and communication technologies, newly industrializing economies are able to offer a low wage, low tax environment which draws investment away from traditional developed economies, presenting these economies with the twin problems of rising unemployment and a fiscal shortfall (see Martin, 1997). A second difficulty lies in the consequences of a seemingly exponential growth in transnational economic activity: increasing trade, rising foreign direct investment (FDI) and, perhaps above all, a rapid intensification of international financial movements. In Robert Cox's account

> The two principal aspects of [economic] globalisation are (1) global organisations of production (complex transnational networks of production which source the various components of the product in places offering the most advantage on costs, markets, taxes, and access to suitable labour, and also the advantages of political security and predictability); and (2) global finance (a very largely unregulated system of transactions in money, credit, and equities). These developments together constitute a *global economy*, i.e. an economic space transcending all country borders, which co-exists still with an *international economy* based on transactions across country borders and which is regulated by inter-state agreements and practices. (Cox, 1993, pp. 259–60)

This process affects different states in differing ways but generally, 'economic globalisation has placed constraints upon the autonomy of states' and, increasingly, 'states must become the instruments for adjusting national economic activities to the exigencies of the global economy' (Cox,

1993, pp. 262, 260). In a context in which it makes increasingly little sense to talk of distinct 'national economies', it is less and less possible for individual states to regulate the economic activity that goes on within and across their borders.

This loss of governing capacity is peculiarly consequential for traditional welfare state strategies. Facing the heightened international mobility of capital, governments find themselves exposed to a 'permanent referendum' upon their capacity to pursue what 'the markets' judge to be 'sound economic policy' and competition to attract capital encourages governments to establish a favourable climate for investment – which includes flexible labour markets, low social costs and low taxation (on capital, at least). Governments which defy international market opinion and seek to pursue expansionary economic policies (to increase levels of employment and/or to raise standards of social provision) face the prospect of catastrophic disinvestment (and an unsustainable accompanying rise in their welfare budget). Newly industrialized countries, with much more rudimentary welfare states and much lower wages, are at a considerable advantage in the competition for job-creating employment (though behind the NICs trail a series of still less developed states with still lower wages and worse employment conditions). If more developed states (such as Britain) are not able to compete by offering technically more proficient workers (and their advantages in this area are vulnerable to rapid advances in the transmissibility of information and in computer literacy), they face the danger of a 'race to the bottom' in terms of social protection and/or the creation of a permanent 'underclass' of unskilled unemployables.

There are a number of ways in which established welfare states might respond to the challenge presented by globalization. They may, for example, modify their funding arrangements so that more of the costs of social provision fall upon the users of services or upon employees (rather than employers) with a consequent reduction in social costs for capital. Secondly, they may tighten eligibility for benefits (raising the retirement age or increasing qualification periods) or increase targeting (by, for example, means testing income maintenance). Thirdly, they can make their social provision more 'market-supporting', by tying benefits to training or sponsoring more vocational education. The twin focus of such reforms is upon reducing costs (particularly those costs levied upon capital) and increasing the flexibility and productivity of labour (without raising its cost to employers).

Few serious commentators on social policy accept the globalization story in its simplest and most draconian form. Not all capital is, after all, perfectly mobile and investors are searching for something more (and other) than the lowest possible wage costs. At the same time, there remains a persistent diversity in states' tax and spending profiles which defies any straightforward account of 'convergence at the bottom'. Nonetheless, there is a good deal of evidence to support the view that states have been obliged to recast their social policies under the imperatives of global economic forces. Further commentary on the plausibility of the globalization thesis is delayed until we have had an opportunity to review some of the evidence of recent changes in the political economy of welfare states in chapter 5. We have also though to consider criticisms of the social democratic orthodoxy that have their origins in the political theory of the 'new social movements', and it is to these that we turn next.

Thesis 8

Changes in the global political economy are undermining traditional forms of national social policy and moving us increasingly 'from the welfare state to the competition state'.

3
Capitalism, Social Democracy and the Welfare State III
New Social Movements and the Welfare State

In the Introduction, I indicated that recent years have seen the emergence of a distinctive critique of the social democratic welfare state from the perspective of several new social movements. These have generally been concerned with those costs and consequences of welfare provision which have escaped the vision of the political economists. In this chapter, we consider the distinctive contributions of the feminist, anti-racist and green critiques of welfare state arrangements. In the final section of the chapter, we consider the claims of those who are sceptical about *all* of those generalizing theories of welfare state development which we have so far considered and who insist upon a much closer examination of the individual historical records of a range of quite differing welfare states.

Feminism and the Welfare State

The burgeoning of distinctively feminist writing on social policy in the last twenty years cannot be seen to define a single and unified perspective on the welfare state.[1] There are, however, a number of shared features of feminist accounts of welfare state development which help to distinguish them from all of the 'mainstream' approaches so far considered. First, feminist writers concentrate upon the gender-specific consequences of the welfare state. Secondly, they broaden their evaluation of welfare beyond the formal or monetarized economy, to consider production and reproduction within the domestic sphere. Thirdly, they register that the welfare

---

[1] For comprehensive surveys, see Sainsbury (1994) and O'Connor (1996).

state is largely *produced* and *consumed* by women, though typically under the control of, and in the interests of, men. There is disagreement as to whether the welfare state is primarily to be explained in terms of *patriarchy* (the systemic oppression of women by men) or *capitalism* (the systemic oppression of labour by capital), but characteristically feminist approaches have represented the welfare state as organized in the interests of men and of capital, at the expense of women. While there have been those who have understood the welfare state as overwhelmingly explicable in terms of the dominance of men or of capital, possibly the most fully developed account (at least during the 1980s) was that Marxist-feminist view which represents the welfare state as an expression of *both* patriarchal and capitalist oppression.[2]

Such analyses begin from the recognition that, left to themselves, markets are unable to secure the circumstances for the successful long-term accumulation of capital. Particularly within advanced capitalism, the state must intervene within the economy and society to guarantee conditions for sustained capital accumulation. It is in this context that the development of the welfare state must be understood. For the welfare state describes all those state interventions which are required to ensure the production and reproduction of labour power in forms which will sustain capitalism's profitability. However, given the (ideological) imperatives of maintaining the family, in which labour power is reproduced, as a 'private' sphere, the state typically intervenes 'not directly but through its support for a specific form of household: the family household dependent largely upon a male wage and upon female domestic servicing' (McIntosh, 1978, pp. 255–6). Thus, the profitability of capitalism is sustained not just through the state-sanctioned oppression of labour under the wage contract but also through the oppression of women within the state-supported form of the 'dependent-woman family' (Weir, 1974).

This state-sponsored family form is promoted through a range of taxation and benefit provisions (differential arrangements for men and women, and for single and married women) and omissions (the absence of statutory nursery places or collective cooking/laundry facilities). It secures the interests of capital in three main ways:

1 It lowers the costs of the reproduction of labour power. A major determinant of the wage costs of capital is the reproduction (on a day-to-day and generation-to-generation basis) of labour power. These costs are substantially cut where they can be displaced upon either the state (public education, public health care), or upon women's unpaid

---

[2] Among those who see the principal opponent/beneficiary as men are Firestone (1979) and Delphy (1984). For a classification of feminist approaches to the welfare state, see Williams (1989, pp. 41–86).

domestic labour (cooking, washing, childcare, care of dependent relatives).

2 It provides employers with a 'latent reserve army of labour'. Married women are a source of potential cheap labour (given the prioritization of the male 'family wage') to be drawn into employment in times of labour scarcity and to be redeployed towards their 'natural' role in the home when jobs are scarce.

3 Where 'caring'/reproduction services are performed within the waged sector of the economy, the definition of such employment as 'women's work' enables it to be provided at comparatively low cost.

A number of important qualifications have been appended to this briefly outlined position. First, it has been suggested that such accounts tend to underestimate the specific impact of *patriarchy*. It is argued that greater weight must be given to the way in which the welfare state serves the interests of (especially white and skilled) working class men. Some commentators suggest that the welfare state has an *economic* cost for capital (in privileging male wages) but that this is outweighed by the *political* benefits of the gender division of interests within the general category of wage labour which it sustains (Barrett, 1980, p. 230). Secondly, greater attention has been directed towards the ideological construction of women's subordination under welfare state capitalism. The capacity of the welfare state to organize the interests of capital in the ways indicated relies upon pre-existing forms of oppression of women by men which the state is able to shape and exploit but not to create. More weight is given to the deep-seated ideology of men's and women's 'natural' roles, which are seen to be crucial in underpinning the structures of patriarchal capitalism. Greater attention is thus directed towards the specifically patriarchal aspects of women's oppression under the welfare state. Thirdly, there has been a re-evaluation of the nature of women's work in the welfare state. Women do not function straightforwardly as a reserve army of labour. In fact, the dependent-female, male-waged household is increasingly untypical within modern economies, while labour markets are heavily sex-segregated, so that expanding women's employment does not typically mean supplementing or replacing a male workforce.

Finally, it is argued that while the expansion of the welfare state has often meant the replacement of women's unpaid labour in the home with women's underpaid 'caring' work in the public sector, state provision of such services can represent a strengthening of women's position (Quadagno, 1990, p. 27; see also Balbo, 1987, p. 204). It does, for example, represent the recognition of a public/state responsibility for those forms of care which were previously defined as exclusively a private (and woman's) responsibility. The welfare state has afforded an avenue of (otherwise blocked) career mobility for some women (Rein, 1985). It has offered (albeit very limited) childcare provision and healthcare services. These are not to be exhaustively understood as securing the long-term interests of capital, but rather as forms of provision which constitute a 'second-best' strategy for both women *and* capital. According to Brenner and Ramas, 'the welfare state is a major arena of class struggle, within the limits imposed by capitalist relations of production. Those limits can accommodate substantial reforms'. Yet this establishes a context in which women have to choose 'between a welfare state which assumes the male-breadwinner family and no state help at all' (Brenner and Ramas, 1984, pp. 66, 68).

Sheila Shaver has argued of this Marxist-feminist paradigm that, in general, 'Marxism's categories were too little questioned, and feminism's too superficially applied'. She calls for a more historical approach grounded in 'the day-to-day legislative and bureaucratic politics of the welfare state', recognizing that the structure of the welfare state is simultaneously 'gendered' and 'classed' (see Shaver, 1989, pp. 91–3). This is reflected in a more general shift in the focus of recent feminist writing on the welfare state. There has, for example, been a wealth of new and detailed historical writing on women and the welfare state (see Skocpol 1992; Pedersen, 1993; Gordon, 1994) which shows women to have been very actively involved (albeit not from a position of strength) in the generation of early social policy regimes. There has also been a major growth of case studies and cross-national surveys which show that not all welfare states are the same in their treatment of women (see Lewis, 1992; Sainsbury, 1994; Hill and Tigges, 1995; O'Connor 1996). This has reinforced Hernes' (1987) emphasis, grounded in Scandinavian experience, upon the positive opportunities for working towards a 'woman-friendly state' in which 'injustice on the basis of gender would be largely eliminated without an increase in other forms of inequality such as among groups of women' (Hernes, 1987, p. 15). In general, there has been a shift away from a narrow focus upon the position of women as an issue within the welfare state towards much more extensive evaluations of social policy regimes which are understood to be profoundly and comprehensively gendered (Lewis, 1992; Orloff, 1993).

The newer literature has also developed a more nuanced reading of the salience of key welfare terms such as 'dependence' and 'care', whose ambiguous meaning is seen to have a very clearly gendered inflection (see Fraser and Gordon, 1994; Maclean and Groves, 1991). Especial attention has been focused upon the key welfare category of 'citizenship'. An essential term in traditional welfarist advocacy (above all in Marshall), citizenship is seen by critics such as Pateman (1988) to be profoundly gendered. Classically, citizenship has been seen overwhelmingly to belong in a public domain which has itself been predominantly populated by men. Indeed, the individual with which classical liberal theory has concerned itself is already gendered: 'the public character of civil society/

state is constructed and gains its meaning through what it excludes – the private association of the family' (Pateman, 1988, p. 236). Under more contemporary forms of social citizenship, so Pateman argues, a similar logic of exclusion obtains. In societies based on market economies, 'paid employment has become the key to citizenship' (Pateman, 1988, p. 237). Access to the more generous system of contributory social rights, as well as self-esteem, seems to turn upon one's record in employment. But the work that has counted towards citizenship is paid work in the public sphere of the formal economy. Under the Beveridgian welfare state in the UK, for example, women were quite explicitly given a secondary status and welfare rights which derived from their presumed marriage to a male breadwinner. Beveridge (1942, p. 53) recognized that 'housewives as mothers have vital work to do' – but it would largely be as unpaid carers and mothers in the home. Even in an economy which looks less and less the way that Beveridge imagined it to be, women's practical experience of welfare citizenship (because of differing patterns of employment, lower lifetime earnings, greater responsibility for dependents and so on) is different from that of men (Lister, 1993). According to Pateman, 'if an individual can gain recognition from other citizens as an equally worthy citizen only through participation in the capitalist market, if self-respect and respect as a citizen are "achieved" in the public world of the employment society, then *women still lack the means to be recognised as worthy citizens*' (Pateman, 1988, pp. 246–7; emphasis added). The universalization of social citizenship, then, cannot simply be about expanding the number who enjoy its status but must also be about changing the character and nature of social citizenship itself.

The precise configuration of the feminist view of the welfare state continues to develop. What this work seems unquestionably to have established, however, is (1) that the domestic sphere of production and reproduction in which most welfare is secured has been systematically ignored in more traditional 'mainstream' accounts and (2) that the more public systems of formal economic and state welfare cannot be understood except in the context of their relation to welfare within the family-household system.

Thesis 9

The welfare state is comprehensively constituted through, and divided by, gender. It is heavily dependent upon arrangements outside the formal economy and/or public provision through which women provide unwaged/low-waged welfare services.

Commentary: The Feminist Critique of the Welfare State

There is a good deal of evidence to support the broad bases of the feminist argument, and one of the clearest indicators of the gendered structure of inequality under the welfare state is given by the differential vulnerability of men and women to poverty. While poverty has nowhere been eliminated under the welfare state, its incidence and distribution has altered. In preparing his Report for Britain in the 1940s, Beveridge found that the insufficiency of wages to support children explained up to a quarter of all poverty (Beveridge, 1942, p. 7). Thirty years later, over half of the lowest quintile group of income by family type were pensioner households. While low pay and pensioner status remain important sources of poverty (especially for women) these causes of poverty have been in part attenuated by economic and social policy changes. What these changes have in their turn exposed, particularly over the last twenty years, is a process of *the feminization of poverty* (Bane, 1988; Goldberg and Kremen, 1990). While some commentators insist that 'it is not so much that women are more likely than before to be poor, but that their previously invisible poverty is becoming increasingly visible', it is possible to identify at least a *statistical* feminization of poverty in recent years (Glendinning and Millar, 1987, p. 15).

Thus, in the USA, for example, in the late 1980s more than 81 per cent of households receiving public assistance were headed by women, more than 60 per cent of families receiving food stamps or Medicaid were headed by women, and 70 per cent of all households in publicly owned or subsidized housing were headed by women (Fraser, 1989, p. 107). According to the US Bureau of the Census (1996), more than half of all poor families in the USA in 1995 were female-headed, a figure that had increased from a little over a third in 1970. Nearly a third of female-headed households were living in poverty (with rates closer to a half for those families headed by black and Hispanic women), compared with a rate in the general population of about one in ten. Lone parent families headed by a woman were twice as likely to be living in poverty as those that were headed by a man. In the UK, Millar (1997, p. 100) notes that in 1995 'just over one million lone mothers were receiving income support, including almost 650,000 who had been in receipt for at least two years'. In 1994/5, average weekly household disposable income was about £300 in the UK, but for lone parents it was just £150.

While the poverty and welfare status of these lone mothers has attracted particular attention in recent years, not least because of the 'explosive' growth in this family form especially among blacks in the USA, elderly women and particularly lone elderly women have continued to be a group particularly vulnerable to poverty. In the UK, for example, Walker notes that in 1987:

> More than one in three older women (35 per cent) were living on incomes on or below the poverty line ... compared with less than one quarter of older men (23 per cent). Just under half of lone older women compared with just under two-fifths of single older men had incomes on or below the poverty line. In all, more than three out of five older women were living in or on the margins of poverty. (Walker, 1992, p. 178)

In May 1995, in the UK 'there were almost 1.2 million single women aged over 60 receiving income support, including just over half a million women aged 80 and over' (Millar, 1997, p. 99). Over three times as many women pensioners as men are dependent on income support (Oppenheim, 1993, p. 68). In the USA, Jill Quadagno notes that while by 1980 over 80 per cent of the elderly population was covered by old age survivors and disability insurance, average monthly benefits ranged from $432 for white males, to $351 for black males, $279 for white females and $235 for black females. She concludes that 'women and minorities have been unable to share fully in the economic rights of citizenship' (Quadagno, 1988a, p. 2).

Thus in the most basic area of income maintenance, the welfare state has probably failed women more comprehensively than any other group. However such failure is not simply to be explained in terms of inadequate levels of benefits. Rather, it must be connected to the evidence supporting the several other claims of the feminist critique.

One aspect of this is the *formal* inequality of welfare rights for men and women. While welfare states have always treated the claims and needs of men and women differently, there has, in fact, been considerable progress in the last twenty-five years towards eroding *formal* differences of entitlement on the basis of gender. There has been some movement away from taxation and social security provision based on the (male-headed) *family* towards a system based on the individual (male or female). Some formal differences do remain: for example, in unequal pensionable ages, in the allocation of survivor's and dependant's benefits within public insurance schemes and in assessments of the availability for work (OECD, 1985b, p. 139). In practice, such differences in the formal provision of services and benefits, while significant, are probably much less important than the consequences of applying 'gender-neutral' rules to social and economic institutions which are themselves strongly sex-segregated. For example, women's lower lifetime earnings and intermittent employment patterns mean that they are much less likely than their male counterparts to have access to occupational pensions or contributory social security benefits. However, as we shall see, the welfare state does more than simply 'reproduce' existing patterns of sexual (and racial) inequality. It also reconstitutes and reorganizes the process of impoverishment and patterns of inequality.

A further major element in the feminist critique concerns the ways in which women's unpaid domestic labour – both in the social reproduction of the workforce and in caring for unwaged dependants – subsidizes those economic costs which would have otherwise to be met by capital, through the direct provision of services, increased taxation or an increase in workers' wages. It has long been recognized that housework – principally 'cleaning, shopping, cooking, washing up, washing, and ironing' – has been work that is overwhelmingly unpaid and done by women. Though difficult to quantify, a number of studies have estimated housework to be in excess of fifty hours per week in an average household (Oakley, 1974; Hartmann, 1981; Piachaud, 1984). A second aspect of such unpaid domestic labour is the work of caring for dependents – the sick and disabled, the elderly and, perhaps above all, children. (The *British Social Attitudes* survey in 1991 (Jowell, 1991) found that 60 per cent of women looked after children when sick compared to 1 per cent of men!) Because much of such care is informal and within the private or domestic sphere, it is difficult to establish how much care is being given by how many carers. Official figures in the UK suggested that in 1991 almost one in seven adults provided care for an elderly or disabled person. Overall, women are more likely to be carers than men (17 per cent compared with 12 per cent) and spend more time in the provision of care (41 per cent of women spent over 50 hours a week caring for someone living with them compared to 28 per cent for men) (Corti and Dex, 1995).

Attempts to redirect welfare provision from the state to 'the community' have intensified the demands upon women to provide unpaid care. According to Finch and Groves,

> Both demographic change and the 'restructuring' of the welfare state have been grafted on to a pre-existing situation in which women have been defined as the 'natural' carers and also as the dependants of men. These alleged characteristics of women make them especially attractive as potential providers of unpaid care, in the private domain to which they have traditionally been assigned. (Finch and Groves, 1983, p. 5)

State policy is particularly explicit in regarding the provision of child care as 'women's work'. Drawing upon a series of presumptions about the 'natural' dispositions of motherhood, the welfare state is often quite explicit in affording differential status to mothers and fathers (for example, in rights to paid and unpaid leave from work, in the payment of children's allowances and in the right to claim unemployment benefits). The clearest, if indirect, measurement of the differential costs of child care for men and women can be seen in their differing patterns of participation in paid employment. As Graham observes, 'caring for young children is typically a full-time and unpaid job and most women withdraw from full-time paid work to do it' (Graham, 1987, p. 223). Throughout the developed capitalist economies, male labour force participation rates have fallen over the past twenty to thirty years, while female participation rates have increased (OECD, 1985b, pp. 12–13). Yet labour force participation rates of women (though not men) with (especially young) dependent children are still low (reflecting a paucity of childcare provision). In the UK, in 1993/4, fewer than one in six women with children under five were in full-time employment (Oppenheim and Harker, 1996, pp. 105–6).

For most women then, childrearing implies economic dependency, whether upon a male partner's income or, failing this, upon the state. Lone parenthood and dependence upon state benefits are, as we have seen, major and growing sources of poverty. In 1994, more than a million lone parents were reliant on income support (Oppenheim and Harker, 1996). Nor are the disadvantages to women of their responsibility for child care confined solely to dependence and loss of present earnings. First, because of the characteristic break in career which childrearing entails, most women who return to full-time employment do so on less advantageous terms than their male peers who have had no break in employment. Secondly, many forms of welfare provision, especially retirement pensions, are based on long-term contributions whilst in paid work. This includes not only public entitlements, but also, for example, rights under increasingly important private or company pension schemes, which are much less generally available to those with intermittent or part-time work records.[3] In summary:

> the differential distribution of the rewards received from entitlement programs reflects their eligibility rules. Although these are technically gender-neutral, they are modelled on male patterns of labor force participation. By rewarding continuous attachment to the labor force, long years of service, and high wages, these rules disadvantage women whose shorter and more irregular work histories make it more difficult for them to obtain full benefits. (Quadagno, 1990, p. 14)

These disadvantages are further exacerbated by the tendency of women (especially those with continuing responsibility for dependants) to return to work on a part-time basis. The growth of part-time work has been a secular trend in most OECD countries, particularly pronounced over the

---

[3] Figures for membership of UK employers' pension schemes for 1987 show that among full-time workers, 62% of men and 51% of women were included. When coverage of both full-time and part-time workers is considered, the figures are 59% for men and 33% for women (OPCS, 1989, pp. 75, 146).

last twenty years, though perhaps showing some tendency to level out in the most recent period (OECD, 1985b, p. 16; Ermisch, 1985, p. 64). Although there is significant international variation, part-time work is disproportionately carried out by women. In the mid-1980s, the proportion of female workers among part-time employees in the OECD ranged from 63 per cent in Greece to more than 94 per cent in the UK (OECD, 1985b, p. 16). Thus, much of women's enhanced involvement in paid work has been on a part-time basis. So, for example, 53 per cent of working women in Norway and 45 per cent in the Netherlands were part-time employees, though in Finland, Greece, Ireland and Italy, the figure remained below 10 per cent (OECD, 1985b, p. 16). While such patterns of partial employment may enable women to reconcile their caring and domestic responsibilities with paid employment, a number of disadvantages flow from part-time employment. Not only is remuneration lower, but part-time workers also tend to receive lower rates of pay, enjoy less security of employment or prospect of promotion and have weaker welfare and employment rights. It often means working anti-social hours (as, for example, in much hospital-based nursing). It also helps to explain a pattern in which women's average earnings continue to be about two-thirds those of men (EOC, 1985, p. 39). Because of a lack of state provision of child care, many women wishing to return to work are forced to make ad hoc arrangements, often with (female) relatives or friends. Where such work is paid, especially within the 'informal' child care economy (for example, the work of unregistered childminders), it is carried out by women on low wages with few welfare or employment rights (Jackson and Jackson, 1979).

This leads on to a final element in the feminist critique, that is the claim that women, in part because of their dependent status and their domestic responsibilities, offer employers a potential pool of cheap and adaptable labour. In fact, any straightforward version of the 'reserve army' thesis is probably unsustainable, because the very pronounced sex segregation of the labour market means that women's labour is not usually directly replacing the work of men. This does not, however, mean that women are not a source of cheap labour. Whatever its salience in the wider economy, in terms of employment *within* the welfare state, women are the principal and comparatively cheap source of labour power. Thus, the nursing profession, which is often seen to replicate women's 'natural' and 'caring' role in the home within paid employment, is almost 90 per cent female. Ancillary workers, responsible for much cleaning and catering work in Britain's National Health Service, are predominantly female and disproportionately drawn from ethnic minority populations (Williams, 1989, p. 170; Beechey and Perkins, 1987, pp. 86–90; Cook and Watt, 1992). Similarly, the teaching of young children is predominantly a female profession (with the partial exception of Germany). In both health and education, however, women are systematically underrepresented in the more senior and decision-taking levels of the profession. In the UK, for example, while women make up more than 90 per cent of all staff nurses and auxiliary nurses, less than one in five senior managers are women (Steering Group on Equal Opportunities, 1988).

At the same time, in the UK, 'the state is the largest employer of women workers and most of these women work in the welfare services of health, education and the social services' (Williams, 1989, p. 181). Though this concentration of women in what Rein calls 'the social welfare industry' (SWI) varies between countries, he finds decisive evidence of (growing) segregation in employment between men and women. Looking at four developed capitalist countries, he found that the concentration of women in the SWI ranged from 66 per cent in Germany to over 80 per cent in Sweden. Furthermore, the SWI was the major area of women's increased labour force participation over the past thirty years and an especially important avenue of career mobility for professionally trained women (Rein, 1985, pp. 36–47; on the USA, see Kemp, 1994; on the UK, see Oppenheim and Harker, 1996). Although there have been significant changes in the distribution of paid work between men and women in recent years, occupational segregation persists and much of the growth in women's employment has been in part-time work (which is still overwhelmingly done by women).

Of course, these patterns are subject to change. Historically, women have been overrepresented in the welfare professions but, at the same time, these have offered greater opportunities for career mobility than working in the private sector. Again, whilst welfare states have often treated women less favourably than men, Hills estimates that UK welfare provision probably represents an average lifetime transfer of resources from men to women of about £50,000 at 1991 prices (Hills, 1997, p. 21). Some changes may favour women (perhaps growing employment opportunities in the private sector) but welfare reforms which lower both taxes and benefits will generally work against the interests of women.

The 'Anti-Racist' Critique of the Welfare State

In the non-institutional politics of the new social movements, a parallel has frequently been drawn between the disadvantaged position of women and the disadvantaged position of ethnic minorities. Such a parallel has, to a very limited extent, been applied to discussions of the welfare state (Williams, 1989, 1993; Cook and Watt, 1992). In fact, the anti-racist critique, as Williams' survey reveals, is less clearly delineated and less fully elaborated than the critical positions adopted by feminist writers. However, as Jill Quadagno (1994, pp. 3–15) makes clear, in the USA, at least, 'race' is crucial to any understanding of the politics of the welfare state (see also Block et al., 1987; Murray, 1984; Moynihan, 1965) and it has attracted increasing attention amongst commentators in the UK (Oppenheim and Harker, 1996, pp. 115–33).

Few commentators deny that 'simple' racial prejudice amongst white people against black people is an important constituent of the latter's disadvantaged position within the welfare state. At the same time, very few suppose that individual racism can adequately explain the levels and persistence of such disadvantage. In seeking a more systemic explanation, and paralleling the discussion of 'patriarchy' and 'capitalism' in the feminist critique, there is some disagreement among commentators as to whether the disadvantages experienced by ethnic minorities under existing welfare state arrangements are primarily to be explained in terms of the interests of the majority community or else by the interests of international capital. However, there is widespread agreement with the core proposition that ethnic minorities face a 'double process' of disadvantage under the welfare state. First, their economically and socially less privileged position tends to make them more reliant upon provision through the welfare state. Secondly, this welfare state upon which they are peculiarly dependent treats them on systematically less favourable terms than members of the majority community. This core claim has been developed in a number of directions.

First, ever since its inception, the welfare state has been underpinned by a conception of nationhood and it has been counted as one of its strengths that it institutionalizes and strengthens claims based upon the equality of citizenship. However, not all those living within a given national territory have counted equally as 'members of the nation' or as citizens, and not everybody has enjoyed the same rights of access to the welfare state. In fact, some sort of residence qualification for relief is a commonplace of public welfare which long predates the coming of the welfare state (Webb and Webb, 1927; De Swaan, 1988; see p. 102 below). Thus a whole series of disqualifications from access to the welfare state have been enacted against migrant workers, their families and their descendants. These divisions have been reinforced where the immigrant community can be further identified by differences of colour, language or religious background. Amongst those who see the welfare state as a form of class compromise, it is argued that this compromise represents a *rapprochement* between capital and a white, male, metropolitan and organized working class, secured largely at the expense of other groups of workers.

This dovetails with a second claim, that immigration has served as a source of cheap labour to be employed (albeit intermittently) either by capital or indeed within the welfare state itself. Here again, ethnic minority and immigrant workers are seen to parallel the role feminists attribute to women as a 'reserve army of labour', introduced in times of labour scarcity to do poorly paid work and to act as a constraint upon rising wages. Similarly, and particularly for black women, those areas of a highly segregated labour market to which they most readily gain access are in low-skilled 'caring' or 'servicing' occupations. Indeed, Williams, writing of employment within the National Health Service in the UK, insists 'that the racist image of the *Black woman as servant* is as strong as that of *carer* in the acceptance of Black women in domestic, nursing and cleaning roles' (Williams, 1989, p. 72; Carby, 1982, p. 215). Bhavnani (1994, pp. 78–9) reports that black women in the NHS are overrepresented in ancillary and lower nursing grades and within the less prestigious areas (of mental health and geriatrics). Because of their lower levels of sanctioned skills and of unionization, their lack of accumulated employment rights and political clout, in periods of economic downturn, ethnic minorities are subject to differentially high levels of unemployment. Just as for both state and employers, the 'ideal' solution to the problem of unemployment in the case of women was to define them out of the workforce, so the 'optimum' solution in the case of migrant workers may be to repatriate them. Where this is not possible, these displaced workers are still more likely than others to find themselves dependent upon the residual provision of state benefits.

A further parallel with the feminists' argument is to be found in the role attributed to ethnic minority labour in reducing the costs of the reproduction of labour power. First, immigrant workers may not enjoy the same rights to housing, unemployment benefit and health care as 'indigenous' workers. Secondly, immigration laws may explicitly seek to exclude from citizenship, or indeed from residence, dependent relatives of the immigrant worker. Thirdly, the costs of education and training of immigrant workers will generally have been met by their country of origin, while the 'guest' worker approaching retirement age may be 'encouraged' to 'go home'.

Critics also argue that the welfare state itself performs a role in the reproduction of these disadvantages of ethnic minority labour. An educational system in which ethnic minorities systematically underachieve, or a system of housing allocation in which ethnic minorities are confined to the poorest quality public stock, are seen to reinforce across generations disadvantages which were originally experienced by an immigrant population. Finally, it is argued that access to more generous forms of welfare provision – for example, Social Security in the USA or earnings-related pensions in the UK – is tied to an individual's previous employment record. This 'achievement'-oriented welfare state is constructed around characteristically white and male patterns of permanent, full-time and (more or less) continuous employment. Even within a gender-blind and colour-blind welfare system, characteristic differences in economic opportunities and rewards for women and blacks means unequal rewards from the welfare state.

Clearly, there are important similarities between the feminist and anti-racist critiques of the welfare state. But there are also substantial differences. For example, the ideology of 'promoting healthy family life' may have very different, if similarly unattractive, consequences for white women and black men. Again, the patterns and consequences of exclusion of women and ethnic minority men from the employed workforce may be quite different. Perhaps the single most important issue raised in this context is the status of ethnic minority women. Thus, Williams writes of a black feminist critique of other schools of feminism arising from 'the use of the concept of "patriarchy", from the omission of Black women's struggle against slavery, colonialism, imperialism and racism in the writing of feminist history (or "herstory"), and from the tendency to see racial oppression and sex oppression and the struggles against them as parallel but separate forms' (Williams, 1989, p. 70). Williams argues that 'Black women have a qualitatively different experience of the welfare state compared with white women' and if ethnic minority women are 'doubly disadvantaged' within the welfare state, this does not straightforwardly represent a process of *reinforcement*, but rather a *reconstitution* of their experience (Williams, 1989, pp. 78–9).

Thesis 10

The welfare state is a characteristic form of the developed capitalist state securing the interests of capital and of white people (and especially men), at the expense of ethnic minorities (and especially women).

Commentary: The 'Anti-Racist' Critique of the Welfare State

Turning to the evidence which is cited in support of the 'anti-racist' perspective, we can again identify important similarities with (as well as some significant differences from) the feminist critique. The first point to note is that while *ethnicity* is seen as an appropriate way of describing people's differing and largely self-ascribed cultural identities, *'race'* is widely rejected as a spurious and largely ideological term. Claims that 'races' and 'racial differences' have some biological basis, and often that they form some sort of evolutionary hierarchy, are denied. The rhetoric of race – of, for example, 'the British race' or 'the white races of South Africa' – is seen simply as a device for mobilizing prejudice in the interests of one (often ethnically diverse) group over others.

Characteristically, the idea of 'race' is associated with 'insiders' and 'outsiders' or members and non-members. Historically, it was perhaps most often used in the context of imperialism and colonialism to justify the dominance of a (generally white-skinned) minority over an (often brown- or black-skinned) majority. Within the welfare state, it is more typically a majority population that constitutes the 'insiders' and a minority or minorities that make up the 'outsiders'. Such accounts rest upon an extremely selective history. In fact, the whole of human history is marked by patterns of migration and many of the most developed industrial societies (and amongst them, some of the most developed welfare states), are largely immigrant societies (Australia, New Zealand, Canada and the United States, for example).

The experience of these immigrant societies demonstrates that it is not always the indigenous population that successfully sustains the claim to constitute the 'true' basis of the nation. Thus in North America and Australasia, the *truly* native population was effectively marginalized by more powerful incomers. The USA, as is well known, was itself made up of successive waves of immigration. Following the English and other northern Europeans, the Irish, southern and eastern Europeans, and Hispanics found themselves to be successively and temporarily the newest and the most economically and socially disadvantaged sections of the US population. This history of successive waves of immigration was itself entwined with the forced importation of black Americans and their subsequent and continuing struggle for formal and substantive equality. This experience of the American blacks also illustrates the ways in which the dynamics of population in the welfare state have been affected by *internal* migration (as, for example, in their shift from southern agriculture to northern industrial cities). Though less dramatic and less long-distance, migration has been and continues to be an important element in the histories of the developed welfare states of Western Europe (Grammenos, 1982, pp. 30–2; Paine, 1974, pp. 5–36; Piore, 1979; Rosenblum, 1973; Skellington, 1996). In 1995, immigration accounted for nearly 75 per cent of the total increase in the population of the European Union, with only Ireland and Portugal reporting net emigration (Eurostat, 1996a, p. 7).

In practice, the experience of racism within the welfare state is not, of course, confined to immigrants or ex-immigrant populations as the experience of Maoris, Aborigines and native Americans attests. (Indeed, the aboriginal peoples of Australia have a health and welfare status which is vastly inferior to that of the rest of the population; Jones, 1996, pp. 9–10.) Yet this has been the principal focus of the anti-racist critique and it is an experience which makes their claims particularly clear. Furthermore, it is a part of the disadvantaged experience of non-immigrant ethnic minorities to find themselves *treated like immigrants*. Correspondingly, the focus here is on the immigrant experience of the welfare state.

A crucial background condition for this immigrant experience is the fact that welfare states have always been *national* institutions based upon some conception of *national* citizenship. While we have seen that welfare as the right of a citizen has something to commend it as an alternative to welfare as the charitable relief of the destitute pauper, it clearly marginalizes the position of those resident within a national territory but not enjoying the full rights of citizenship. Exclusion from full citizenship is a frequent concomitant of immigrant status, and exclusion from full citizenship will often mean exclusion from full participation in the welfare state (Freeman, 1986, p. 51). Correspondingly, formal differences in *legal* status are perhaps more important in the anti-racist than in the feminist critique. Of course, exclusions from access to the welfare state on the basis of citizenship are not necessarily racist, nor are they necessarily unjustified, if one understands the welfare state to be funded by the accumulated efforts and abstinence from immediate consumption of a given national population.[4] However, if the ways in which citizenship is granted and withheld, or the ways in which welfare rights are implemented, are themselves racist, this qualification is nullified.

In practice, different types of migrants, enjoying different legal status, are differentially excluded from rights of access to the welfare state (Hammar, 1990). The most disadvantaged group in this sense is likely to be made up of illegal immigrants. As workers, illegal immigrants tend to be almost wholly without employment rights. Normally, they have no rights to the provision of health care or to housing, no rights to welfare protection or pensions and no entitlement to social provision for their dependants. Living under constant threat of deportation, they remain largely on the sufferance of their employers and often find themselves 'super-exploited' in intermittent work on low wages, under poor and unregulated conditions, often, for example, in the building trade or in domestic service (Grammenos, 1982, pp. 17–18; OECD, 1985b, pp. 101–5). There are some indications that, as official migration to the developed countries has been increasingly restricted over the last twenty years, illegal immigration may have been rising (Maillat, 1987, p. 55).

Rather less marginal is the position of 'official' migrant workers. Facing a labour shortfall in a period of sustained economic growth in the 1950s and 1960s, a number of European countries sought to supplement their labour supply by 'inviting in' migrant workers from less developed countries. Those countries with an extensive colonial past (for example,

[4] For an interesting discussion, see Carens (1988).

the Netherlands and the UK), tended to turn to their former colonies, sometimes because such workers were seen to be cheaper to the host country than immigrants from extra-colonial sources (Joshi and Carter, 1984, p. 58). Others, such as West Germany, took workers from the less developed areas of southern Europe (initially from Italy, later from Yugoslavia and Turkey). While such migrant workers enjoyed certain welfare rights (for example, limited access to housing and health care, and the statutory protection of health and safety legislation), they did not enjoy the same rights as indigenous workers. They did not, for example, enjoy the same entitlement to unemployment benefit nor, very often, the right to bring in dependants with the same rights of access to housing, education and health care as the dependants of indigenous workers. Nor did they always enjoy the same rights upon *leaving* the workforce (Brubaker, 1989, pp. 155–60). As Grammenos points out, while migration before 1945 was largely 'one-way', in the post-war period, migration more commonly took the form of 'rotation' (Grammenos, 1982, pp. 30–1). Under such 'two-way migration', workers (ideally young, skilled, educated and free of dependants), work temporarily in the host economy, meeting pressing labour demands and leaving when the labour market slackens. West Germany's *Gastarbeiter* or 'guest worker' system, largely based on temporary Turkish migrant labour, is often seen as the archetypal expression of this system. The warmth of the welcome for such visiting workers, as for other 'guests', is contingent on the recognition that their stay will be temporary and, as Freeman points out, 'the problem with the guest-worker system from the point of view of the host state is that it tends to break down' (Cashmore and Troyna, 1983, p. 52; Grammenos, 1982, p. 30; Freeman, 1986, p. 60).

A third category of migrant worker is defined by those accepted for permanent settlement and/or incorporation into full citizenship. Formally, such a group may enjoy full equality with members of the indigenous population. However, where welfare practice is discriminatory, this formal equality of citizenship may not result in actual equality of treatment or of condition. Thus, as has been the experience of those with Afro-Caribbean and Asian backgrounds in both the USA and the UK, formal equality of citizenship has not ended discriminatory practices in the provision of health, housing or personal social services. Perhaps most importantly, it has not ended discrimination in what is for most people the single most important source of welfare, that is, the labour market. Fully to appreciate this, we need to move on to consider how racism is seen to service the interests of the welfare state capitalist economies.

In discussing the feminist critique of the welfare state, we saw how women's subordinate position was said to serve the capitalist economy in three ways: (1) by providing a source of cheap labour, (2) by providing a 'reserve army' of labour to be drawn in and out of active participation in response to the changing needs of the labour market, and (3) by reducing the costs of the reproduction of labour power. We can trace these same elements in considering the anti-racist critique of the economic consequences of existing welfare state arrangements.

Occasionally, the welfare state has been seen to be directly complicit in securing the supply of cheap labour within a racist regime. Writing of attempts at reform in the USA in the 1970s, Jill Quadagno argues that for 'more than a century, blacks had been excluded from welfare in the South because the welfare system was an instrument of social control, a part of the local racial caste system' (Quadagno, 1990, p. 24). Both Alston and Ferrie (1985) and Quadagno (1988a, 1988b, 1990, 1994) argue that the structure of the welfare state in the American south from the 1930s to the 1970s was principally shaped by the interests of white southern planters in the preservation of a poor and dependent black population. When federally supported old age assistance was first introduced in the 1930s, the white Southern Democrats who controlled the southern political machine resisted all attempts to increase the levels of support to poor southern black families and thus the threat to the availability of the black population to perform low paid and irregular work. In the cotton belt of the south, average monthly benefits were systematically lower than in the north and west (standing in 1938/9, for example, at $7.06 in Mississippi, $21.79 in New York and $30.54 in California). Rates were lower for blacks than whites throughout the cotton belt south and, within this region, lower within the cotton counties than the non-cotton counties (Quadagno, 1988b, pp. 244–5). Through their control of the local welfare state, 'southern landholders ... were able to prevent the payment of significant benefits to their tenants, croppers, and wage workers under the Social Security Act, and thereby assured themselves a continued supply of cheap, loyal labor' (Alston and Ferrie, 1985, p. 117).

Although this particular form of the racial welfare state in the southern USA was eventually to be rendered obsolete by changes in agricultural technology, black migration and black political empowerment, Quadagno identifies much the same process at work in the south in the 1970s. Reviewing President Nixon's unsuccessful welfare reform proposals aimed at securing a guaranteed annual income for the working poor (the Family Assistance Plan), a reform which promised significantly to raise the wages of black workers in the South and threaten its traditional low-wage economy, Quadagno found 'the Southern power elite' to be amongst its most vocal and committed opponents. As Georgia Representative Phillip Landrum protested: 'There's not going to be anybody left to roll these wheelbarrows and press these shirts' (Quadagno, 1990, pp. 23–5).

More usually, the 'complicity' of the welfare state in the supply of cheap labour is less direct. It is a process which is particularly well illustrated by the experience of immigrant labour. In fact, the long-term economic consequences of immigration for the receiving countries have been much discussed (see, for example, Paine, 1974, pp. 12–23). Some have suggested that, in the longer term, immigration may detract from capital accumulation by delaying technological innovation or increasing social infrastructural costs. Yet the predominant economic view, and certainly the motivation of those welfare states which encouraged migration in the 1950s and 1960s, was that the importation of migrant workers (especially on a temporary basis) would improve circumstances for capital accumulation. Under conditions of near full employment, there is likely to be a shortfall in the availability of indigenous labour, which will put upward pressure on wages and lead to difficulties in filling lower paid and unskilled jobs. Under these circumstances in the 1950s and 1960s, many of the Western European welfare states turned to migrants as a source of comparatively cheap labour to fill unskilled positions. For the migrants themselves, coming from less developed countries with high unemployment and much lower wages, there was clearly an economic incentive to take what were, by Western European standards, poorly paid and unattractive jobs. In the host countries, under conditions of near full employment, the use of such immigrant labour was not only in the interests of capital but also of native workers. Migrants were not competing with native workers, but, in fact, creating more skilled jobs for nationals by filling those unskilled positions which were needed to support higher levels of general economic activity. Thus migrant workers were generally introduced to perform unskilled jobs at low wages and heavily concentrated in particular sectors of a highly segregated labour market (Maillat, 1987). In Germany, in 1968, for example, while the national average male wage was DM 5.81 per hour, the rate for male migrants from southern Europe was DM 4.51 per hour (cited in Paine, 1974, p. 99). Such disadvantages are not confined to temporary migrants. In the UK (Sly, 1995), the average hourly pay of Pakistani/Bangladeshi men in 1994 was 68 per cent of the rate for white men. The comparable figure for black men's earnings was 81 per cent (although the same survey reported black women's earnings at 106 per cent of their white equivalents). In the USA, in 1993, the median annual income of two-parent families with children stood at $48,630 and $36,670 for blacks (US Bureau of the Census, 1996). From several countries there is evidence of 'an ethnic minority labour market which seems to be in some respects quite different from that of white workers' (Brown, 1984, p. 293). In France in 1980, 56 per cent of migrants were either manual workers or employed in the domestic service sector, compared with 26.5 per cent in the general population (cited in Grammenos, 1982, p. 19). The situation is now more complex, with 'the position of minority ethnic groups . . . becoming more differentiated both *between* and *within* minority groups', but these populations are still overrepresented amongst less skilled and lower paid occupations and underrepresented (with the partial exception of some Asian men) in professional and managerial positions (Oppenheim and Harker, 1996, pp. 123–4).

In turning to the status of migrants and ethnic minorities as a 'reserve army of labour', we again find a pattern of disadvantage which is rather different from that experienced by women. First, that migrant labour should act as a reserve pool of labour, to be taken up in times of heightened activity and stood down in periods of economic recession, is not seen as a regrettable economic 'accident'. It is entrenched as *an element of governments' economic policy*. The intention of bringing in temporary migrant labour is precisely to meet a *temporary* excess of labour demand. When demand no longer exceeds supply, the policy imperative is to shed labour by returning migrants to their countries of origin. This policy intention (however flawed its realization) was quite clear in the Western European welfare states following the economic downturn of the early 1970s.[5] In West Germany, new restrictions were placed on rights of entry for dependants of foreign workers; in France, family reunions were suspended for a time in the late 1970s (Grammenos, 1982, p. 29). In the UK, rules governing right of entry and entitlement to state support have been repeatedly tightened, most recently in respect of those seeking political asylum (Oppenheim and Harker, 1996; Bloch, 1997). In practice, the effects of recession on migration, integration and repatriation have often been very different from those that governments of the 1970s had anticipated (Hammar and Lithman, 1987). But they have done little to improve the economic marginality of immigrant workers. Maillat concludes that:

> In the final analysis, the differences in the unemployment rates of nationals and foreigners are indicative of the insecure nature of the jobs held by foreigners. Reasons for this vulnerability of foreign workers relate to their concentration in sectors in crisis, the high proportion of unskilled workers among them, their lack of any real negotiating power, and the fact that they are often the first in line in the event of redundancies. (Maillat, 1987, p. 51)

This disadvantage in terms of employment also extends to resident ethnic minority populations. In the UK in the mid-1990s, a period of falling unemployment, levels of joblessness were more than twice as high among blacks as among whites. Among those under 25, male unemployment for black and other ethnic minority populations was running at 37 per cent

---

[5] Despite governments' policy intentions, the effects of recession in terms of migration, integration and repatriation have often been perverse (Hammar and Lithman, 1987).

(compared with 18 per cent in the equivalent white population). Long-term unemployment was also higher among the black and ethnic minority population, with six out of ten black people without work being long-term unemployed (Oppenheim and Harker, 1996, pp. 115–16). In the USA in 1997, when unemployment amongst the white male population had slipped below 5 per cent, the rate amongst young black men still stood at 22.6 per cent (US Bureau of Labor, 1997).

The problems of migrants and ethnic minorities are further aggravated by their generally lower levels of formal qualifications and acquired skills, their lack of accumulated employment and welfare rights and, in the case of migrants, the unwillingness of state and employers to invest in a 'temporary' resource.

A third element indicated in the anti-racist critique is the role of immigrant and ethnic minority workers in lowering the reproduction costs of labour. Here again, for migrant labour at least, this is a conscious intention of various governments' economic policy. The preponderance of the young, single, healthy and economically active among migrants means that they make very limited demands on the most expensive elements of the welfare state – health, education and pensions. There are also elements of transfer income, for example, unemployment benefit, from which they may be effectively excluded. At the same time, migrants help to finance the welfare state through direct and indirect taxation. Although migrant and ethnic minority populations are often represented as a drain upon welfare state resources, Grammenos argues that they may be very substantial net contributors to the public exchequer. He cites evidence for West Germany which shows 'that savings on child-rearing and education resulting from immigration come to at least 19 per cent of net investment for the period 1969 to 1973' (Grammenos, 1982, p. 31). Grammenos also argues that the fact that 'the host country receives young healthy workers without having to educate them or support them as children' led to savings in West Germany in the period 1957–73 which 'would have generated additional capital of 27.721 billion DM at 1973 prices' (Grammenos, 1982, p. 37; Blitz, 1977, p. 496). The economic consequences of a permanently settled immigrant population are less clear cut. The demographic make-up of this population will be different from that of the established population. In time (as the immigrant community aged), one would expect it to make greater demands on the social infrastructure. However, in the UK experience, the comparative growth of the (ex-)immigrant population and its historically high levels of labour force participation challenge the popular claim of the later 1970s that ethnic minorities are a drain upon both the productive economy and the welfare state (see Golding and Middleton, 1982). In fact, a defraying of the costs of labour power may occur very directly through the dependence of the welfare state upon the low paid labour of (especially women) workers from the ethnic minority population (see above pp. 75–6).

One final element in the anti-racist critique concerns the ways in which the welfare state itself *reproduces* the disadvantages of ethnic minority populations. In part, this simply echoes the observation made by the feminists (p. 74) and by Jill Quadagno, that a welfare state which relates entitlements to previous labour market performance militates against all those, notably women and ethnic minorities, whose lifetime's earnings and employment are below the white male average. In part, it concerns racial discrimination on the part of those officials responsible for allocating public housing, adjudicating claims for benefits or making decisions about the educational destinations of children. Although patterns of welfare inequality are complex, and differ in important ways between different ethnic minority populations, evidence of unequal welfare outcomes is clear.

In the UK, the 1985 Committee of Inquiry into the Education of Children from Ethnic Minority Groups, established by the government under the chairmanship of Lord Swann, echoed earlier findings in identifying systematic educational underachievement among the West Indian school population (Swann, 1985; Brown and Madge, 1982). The Swann committee cited evidence showing that low examination performance among sixteen-year-old working-class children stood at 20 per cent among white children and 21 per cent among Asians, but rose to 41 per cent among West Indians. It also noted that while 1 per cent of West Indian pupils went on to full-time degree courses in further education, this compared with a figure of 5 per cent amongst Asians and 'all other leavers' (Swann, 1985, pp. 60–2). The committee argued that

> A substantial part of ethnic minority underachievement . . . is the result of racial prejudice and discrimination on the part of society at large, bearing on ethnic minority homes and families, and hence, *indirectly*, on children. [The rest] . . . is due in large measure to prejudice and discrimination bearing *directly* on children, within the educational system, as well as outside it. (Swann, 1985, pp. 89–90)

More than a decade on from Swann, the picture is more complex. Evidence suggests that many Asian pupils are significant 'overachievers' compared with the rest of the school-age population but Afro-Caribbean pupils are more likely to be excluded from school for bad behaviour and are underrepresented amongst those going on to university (T. Jones, 1993; Skellington, 1996, pp. 176–201). The latest Policy Studies Institute survey points to significant variation in the educational performance of differing groups *within* the Asian population (Modood and Berthoud, 1997).

The provision of housing is another area of the welfare state which reflects an ethnically divided access to resources and reveals a pattern of disproportionate disadvantage among ethnic minorities, as deprivations based upon social class and economic status are reinforced by patterns of discrimination. Patterns of household tenure among different ethnic groups are complex (with much higher levels of owner-occupation in the Asian population). The PSI survey of 1994 found that Indians and Africans were now as likely to be in detached or semi-detached accommodation as whites, but these levels were still much lower among Pakistani, Bangladeshi and Caribbean families. Although the general incidence of overcrowding has declined in the past decade, it is still more significant amongst Pakistani and Bangladeshi families than for all other groups (Madood and Berthoud, 1997, pp. 218–23). The *Family Resources Survey* for 1993/4 indicated that twice as many black as white households were in receipt of housing benefit (DSS, 1995). There was evidence that, as responsibility for 'social' housing moved from local authorities to housing associations, families from ethnic minorities faced discrimination in this sector (Skellington, 1996, p. 139).

Explanations of these patterns are very varied and not all support the claims of the anti-racist critique. Yet it is possible to identify a very broad agreement about the existence of *prima facie* evidence of discrimination and inequality along ethnic lines within the welfare state.

Finally, it is worth remarking upon the peculiar position of ethnic minority women. This population is seen to be disadvantaged in terms of both feminist and anti-racist critiques of the welfare state. Thus, Cook and Watt insist that 'Black women in Britain have to face . . . the dual oppressions of racism and sexism which impinge on their opportunities and consign them to low-paid and lower-status jobs' (Cook and Watt, 1987, p. 69). A 1985 OECD study, *The Integration of Women into the Economy*, found that immigrant women were often the single most economically disadvantaged group within the population. Typically, they have 'more dependants but fewer family resources; they have a greater need for gainful employment but run a higher risk of unemployment' (OECD, 1985b, p. 92). However, this 'double disadvantage' is not simply cumulative. Thus, for example, while black women are disadvantaged economically both as blacks and women, the nature of this disadvantage is also shaped by the fact that they are married to (economically disadvantaged and more marginally employed) black men or, particularly in the USA, that they are disproportionately likely to be at the head of (frequently impoverished) single-parent families (Wilson, 1987). This may yield distinctive patterns of, for example, employment participation or welfare dependency. Correspondingly, the experience of black women under the welfare state is something other than the cumulative consequence of being black and being female (Cook and Watt, 1992).

The Green Critique of the Welfare State

Insofar as we may speak of a single Green perspective on the welfare state, it is principally to be derived from a characteristic concern with the harmful consequences of unsustainable economic growth and bureaucratized welfare services. While there is a conservative wing to the Green perspective, which argues against the welfare state and in favour of traditional (and sometimes pre-democratic) forms of religious, community and family life, the mainstream Green critique of the welfare state can be seen as an attack 'from the left'. Broadly, Green commentators identify the welfare state with the political programme of traditional social democracy, and see both as inevitably implicated in the logic of advanced capitalism. In varying ways and to differing degrees, they reject all three (Dobson, 1995).

We may summarize this Green critique of the welfare state under two major headings: the welfare state and the logic of industrialism, and the welfare state as social control.

The Welfare State and the Logic of Industrialism

The welfare state is embedded in an industrial order which is itself premised upon economic growth. We have seen that such economic growth was a core component of social democratic strategy under the Keynesian Welfare State. It was the engine of economic growth that was to fund the welfare state, which in turn would adjust patterns of distribution in society, so as to offset the inegalitarian consequences of growth under capitalist forms. For the Greens, this perspective of open-ended growth is untenable: 'an economy and society premised and organised on the basis of ever increasing levels of economic growth is impossible ("unsustainable") within the finite ecological parameters of human societies' (Barry, 1998). Theirs is a protest 'not against the failure of state and society to provide for economic growth and material prosperity, but against their all-too-considerable success in having done so, and against the price of this success' (cited in Poguntke, 1987).

According to Jacobs (1996), the 'dominant model' of economic growth underpinning improving social welfare no longer works. In part, this is an expression of familiar Green arguments about the environmental 'limits to growth' (global warming, poisoning of the oceans, loss of biodiversity) but there is also an insistence that economic growth no longer generates improvements in the quality of life for most people. Rising Gross National Product (GNP) is not an index of improving well-being for the general population (indeed, the index of Sustainable Economic Welfare, which many Greens prefer, has been moving steadily *downwards* over the past twenty years).

Raising the rate of economic growth, given its current patterns, will not improve people's well-being. These patterns are generating the social costs – inequality, crime, environmental degradation, insecurity, the decline of public services and public goods – which are reducing people's perceived quality of life. (Jacobs, 1996, p. 83)

The trade-off between inequality and efficiency on which the social democratic view of the welfare state was premised (that economic inequality is justified *if* it both promotes economic growth and allows the state to compensate the losers through welfare redistribution) no longer works. We live in societies of rising income inequality in which the poorest have been left behind. The existing welfare state is not a viable long-term political arrangement because the costs of economic growth (upon which it relies) are too severe for the natural and human environment, and are eventually counter-productive.

Greens also insist that the welfare state is one of the most important sites of the dominance of technological rationality or technocracy in contemporary societies. Rejection of the attempt to subjugate all forms of human and social conduct to the logic of rational domination has a long history in the New Left/Western Marxism. Retraceable at least to the writings of Horkheimer and Adorno is the view that the attempt to dominate and exploit nature (which industrialism has represented) will always enjoin the subjugation and exploitation of humankind-in-nature. It was Marcuse who described the welfare state as a 'state of unfreedom' built upon 'technological rationality' and 'administered living' (Marcuse, 1972, pp. 51–2). For the Greens, the welfare state is inextricably involved in surveillance, control and the creation of social capital, to the detriment of the human(e) development of the population it administers.

This subservience to both economic growth and technical rational domination are to be understood as a part of the logic of developed capitalism. Gorz, for example, follows more traditional Marxists in arguing that 'the two main functions of the institutions and policies of the welfare state [are] *the production of order **and** the production of the right type of demand* needed for capitalist development' (Gorz, 1985, p. 14). The welfare state, even if it emerges in response to the mobilization of the working class, is a way of discharging the social costs of capitalist development upon the general public. It also serves to represent collective problems and needs as individual ones, which may be responsive to marketable goods and services. For most Greens, real social needs could be met more efficiently through greater public provision (preventative rather than curative healthcare, public rather than private transport), but this is not consonant with the interests of capital. The welfare state has also to respond to the surplus production of social need that is generated by capitalist forms of industrial organization (for example, nervous disorders and alcoholism generated by the stress of work under capitalist imperatives). The welfare state is a part of capitalism which is itself unavoidably tied to the corrupt logic of economic growth. Neither is consistent with the support of sustainable and humane forms of social life.

Green commentators also charge that the social democratic commitment to the welfare state as a compromise based on the encouragement of capitalist economic growth means 'bracketing out' a whole range of radical issues (including socialization of production, workers' control, quality of life, the planned use of resources) which were a part of the traditional ideological baggage of pre-welfare state socialism. Its commitment to, and association with, the capitalist welfare state makes social democracy an impossible vehicle for radical social change. Finally, the welfare state represents a national rather than a global response to the problem of reconciling general social welfare with economic growth. As such, it depends upon displacing the dysfunctions of economic growth upon the Third World, offering a national political solution which makes global problems of welfare still more severe. The lack of real social security is expressed not only in the scale of absolute poverty across the globe (especially in sub-Saharan Africa) but also in attendant problems of military conflict, displacement of populations and international drugs trafficking which redound upon the developed world (see Jacobs, 1996, pp. 41–64).

The Welfare State as Social Control

The Greens' critique of the welfare state is also intimately concerned with its implications for the exercise of 'micro-power' or social control by the state over the individual. Thus the history of the rise of the welfare state is simultaneously the history of the rise of the 'disabling professions' (Illich, 1977). In reducing the citizens of the democratic state to the clients of the welfare state, welfare institutions, under the guise of the 'helping' or 'caring' professions, exercise ever greater control over the personal lives of individuals. Far from 'enabling' or 'empowering', welfare state professionals – doctors, social workers, teachers, housing administrators – much more characteristically 'disable' their clients, stripping them of the competence (and often the legal right) to make their own decisions and making them increasingly dependent upon the state and its paid professionals. For Lasch, 'the expansion of welfare services presupposed the reduction of the citizen to a consumer of expertise' (Lasch, 1978, p. 224). According to Illich, 'industrial welfare systems . . . incapacitate people's autonomy through forcing them – via legal, environmental, and social changes – to become consumers of care' (Illich, 1978, p. 41). Pluralistic self-reliance, focused on communal and individual initiatives grounded in native knowledge and competences, is displaced by the legalized monopoly of standardized state management of state-defined needs in a subject and dependent clientele.

As a consequence, the welfare state is necessarily anti-democratic. What should properly be the subject of choices made by individuals or collectivities becomes the province of professionals, whose credentials are state-certified and whose interventions are state-legitimized. Choosing to give birth at home or without medical supervision, building one's own home to one's own specifications, educating one's own children at home are all choices or forms of self-help proscribed or strongly discouraged by the state. Furthermore, even the best-intentioned and 'enabling' of welfare state interventions are undermined by their bureaucratic form. Even where the welfare state is predominantly the product of working-class agitation to counter-balance the despotic control of capital, it cannot avoid itself becoming a form of domination over its subject population. Even those more 'moderate' Greens who see a continuing role for governments and markets (and, indeed, scope for continued economic growth) wish to see much greater scope for self-production, voluntary and co-operative activity and a 'social economy' independent of state and capitalist markets. Insofar as social welfare is a response to real needs – and not simply to the 'false needs' created by the requirements of industrial capitalism – these can best be met by small-scale, co-operative, 'bottom-up' self-production and self-management.

Thesis 11

The welfare state is a particular form of the industrial capitalist state. Even under social democratic auspices, it is vitiated by the logic of unsustainable economic growth and alienating bureaucratic forms.

We shall return to a consideration of the Green perspective and its agenda for change in the closing chapter.

The Historical Uniqueness of Welfare States' Development

All of those positions considered thus far have tended to identify one or more mobilizing principles underlying welfare state development. But I have already observed that not all commentators are persuaded that the development of welfare states can be most effectively explained in terms of these kinds of metatheoretical principles. In particular, and in response to the accounts of both left and right, criticism has increasingly been directed towards (1) the persistent functionalist or derivationist elements in such accounts, (2) the dominance of society-centred over state-centred explanations and (3) the dominance of class to the exclusion of other social forces in the generation of social policy. In a variety of ways, such critics have called for a greater concentration upon the *historical uniqueness* of particular welfare states' development and an emphasis upon multiple sources of social policy initiatives. In the final sections of this chapter, I turn to a brief assessment of this theoretically more sceptical approach.

Interest-Group Politics and the Welfare State

Given this theoretical scepticism, those who, for example, stress the importance of interest-group activity in the emergence of welfare states do not represent this as the definitive guiding principle of welfare state development. Nor do they seek to isolate some particular social force or movement as the prevailing fact of such evolution. Indeed, in contrast to the major positions already outlined, they insist upon (1) the independent importance of the political processes through which welfare state policies emerge, (2) the importance of existing state formations for the structure of (early) welfare states and (3) the historically unique configurations of social and political forces which shaped welfare state development in different countries. Advocates of this position[6] do not argue that the process of welfare state development is wholly indeterminate (and that industrialization, urbanization and democratization have no independent effect upon the emergence of welfare regimes) but they do maintain:

- that prevailing accounts give too much weight to such determining societal prerequisites;
- that a more accurate understanding of the substantial differences between welfare states requires a closer investigation of their particular and peculiar historical circumstances;
- that many existing accounts overstress the salience of social class as a source of welfare state development, to the neglect of other social forces – based, for example, upon age or gender structures – and other social groups, for example, professional associations, civil servants and veterans' organizations;
- that the competing social forces at the fount of the welfare state must be understood to have been mobilized and accommodated within the comparatively new media of mass democratic political organization.

[6] Pampel and Williamson (1988, 1989); Pampel and Stryker (1990); Weir, Orloff and Skocpol (1988b); Baldwin (1990); Skocpol (1992).

The intent of the interest group politics approach is above all a procedural or methodological rather than a substantive one, calling for a clear interrogation of the historical record to be used to discipline the rather grander generalizations of some other approaches. However, a number of substantive claims can be identified with this perspective.[7] Among the most important of these are:

- that economic and demographic change affect the structure of group resources and demands for welfare spending and that the existence of democratic institutions facilitates the realization of these group interests;
- that non-class, ascriptive groups (notably, the retired and the aged) are central to the growth of the welfare state;
- that democratic political procedures (voting participation and electoral competition) are important for explaining the translation of group demands into higher spending;
- that where (working) class organization is poorly developed, mobilization for public welfare measures is likely to be by other subordinate forces, for example, by the unemployed or ethnic groups;
- that sectoral interests (for example, those of agriculture), professional interests (doctors), and business interests (private insurance companies) may have a decisive effect in shaping the particular character of welfare legislation;
- that within any given, broadly defined group, there may be a diversity of interests for and against the welfare state. Thus, for example, differing levels of the medical profession may have a differing attitude to compulsory health insurance (UK in 1911); differing groups of workers may have differing attitudes to state provision of welfare (where, for example, trade unions offer health insurance as a collectively bargained 'fringe benefit') (US in 1930s); employers in monopoly and competitive sectors of the economy may also have quite differing approaches to, and interests in, the state provision of welfare (Germany in 1930s); or their attitude may change through time (employers in the UK and Germany in the late nineteenth and early twentieth centuries).

---

[7] Piven and Cloward (1971, 1977, 1985); Block et al., (1987); Ashford (1986a, 1988b); Ashford and Kelley (1986); Gilbert (1966, 1970); Berkowitz and McQuaid (1980); J. Hay (1975); R. Hay (1977, 1978a, 1978b); Mommsen (1981); Ritter (1985); Lash and Urry (1987); De Swaan (1988); Hennock (1987); Skocpol (1980, 1992); Ullman (1981); Foot (1975); Klein (1983); Gale Research Company (1985); Pierson (1994).

State-centred approaches to the Welfare State

Again, what have been labelled 'state-centred' approaches to welfare state development do not generally deny the salience of the sorts of issues raised in the major theoretical positions outlined above. They recognize the importance of industrialization, urbanization, democratization and class interests. However, they do insist that all these influences are mediated in practice by the independent effects of state organization. That is, the relationship between the 'macro' causes of welfare state development and actual social policies and practices is shaped by the differing configuration of historically unique nation states. Characteristically, Theda Skocpol, one of the leading advocates of 'bringing the state back in', criticizes both pluralist and Marxist accounts of social change and welfare state development as being too *society*-centred: 'State formation, political institutions, and political processes (understood in non-economically determinist ways) must move from the penumbra or margins of analysis and towards the center' (Skocpol, 1992, p. 40; see also Nordlinger, 1981).

This point is pursued by Douglas Ashford in *The Emergence of the Welfare States* (Ashford, 1986a). He insists that 'the many forms of the contemporary welfare state are the manifestations of the complex and diverse compromises forged by political leaders and administrative officials over many years' (Ashford, 1986a, p. 2). Thus, 'Political, institutional and even constitutional issues affected the transition from liberal to welfare state as much as economic and social realities' (Ashford, 1986a, pp. 3–4).

Abram de Swaan is still more explicit:

> Social security was not the achievement of the organized working classes, nor the result of a capitalist conspiracy to pacify them. . . . The initiative for compulsory, nationwide and collective arrangements to insure workers against income loss came from reformist politicians and administrators in charge of state bureaucracies. (De Swaan, 1988, p. 9)

The perspective of the welfare state emerging fully formed and wholly determined from a set of pre-existing social prerequisites is a misconception based upon historical hindsight. The growth of the welfare state was 'a gradual and often uninformed process propelled as much by ambitious politicians and rather visionary civil servants as by an abstract notion of a crumbling social order or of fears of major social unrest' (Ashford, 1986a, pp. 3–4).

To see the (welfare) state as simply a response to the needs of capital or else as the product of industrialization is inadequate. What is required is an account of the process by which social issues move onto the policy agenda, what policy proposals are accepted, which rejected (and why), and how and by whom such policies are implemented. Correspondingly, state-centred accounts tend to stress *the growth of states' competence*. The growth of the state's capacity to act is a subtype of the more general evolution of bureaucratic forms of organized action. Thus, to an extent, the development of the welfare state is a product of the expanded techniques of information processing, communication and surveillance which make the nation state (and, especially important in the welfare field, the overcoming of localism) possible (Berkowitz and McQuaid, 1980).

Such accounts also stress the independent importance of the state's *learning capacity*. This is an approach most fully developed by Hugh Heclo. Reviewing the varying sources of social policy development, he concludes that 'while parties and interest groups did occasionally play extemely important parts, it was the civil services that provided the most constant analysis and review underlying most courses of government action'. Furthermore, the politics of such social policy initiatives is not best understood as the exercise of power but rather through the idea of 'politics as learning'.

> Governments not only 'power' ... they also puzzle. Policy-making is a form of collective puzzlement on society's behalf; it entails both deciding and knowing. The process of making pension, unemployment, and superannuation policies has extended beyond deciding what 'wants' to accommodate, to include problems of knowing who might want something, what is wanted, what should be wanted, and how to turn even the most sweet-tempered general agreement into concrete collective action. (Heclo, 1974, p. 305)

The principal agency and location of this political learning process has been the public bureaucracy.

The general tenor of the state-centred approach is effectively summarized by Skocpol and Ikenberry:

> the ideas for modern social insurance and welfare policies came from domestic experimentation and transnational communication, and they were put into effect by sets of political executives, civil administrators, and political party leaders who were looking for innovative ways to use existing or readily extendable government administrative capacities to deal with (initially key segments of) the emerging industrial working class. Pioneering social insurance innovations, especially, were not simply responses to the socioeconomic dislocations of industrialism; nor were they straightforward concessions to demands by trade unions or working-class based parties. Rather they are best understood ... as sophisticated efforts at anticipatory political incorporation of the industrial working class, coming earlier (on the average) in paternalist, monarchical-bureaucratic regimes that hoped to

head off working-class radicalism, and coming slightly later (on the average) in gradually democratizing liberal parliamentary regimes, whose competing political parties hoped to mobilize new working-class voters into their existing political organizations and coalitions. (Skocpol and Ikenberry, 1983, pp. 89–90)

State-centred accounts of social policy development have tended to criticize prevailing explanations for their neglect of the (indeterminate) process of policy formation and the (uncertain) practice of policy implementation. Correspondingly, they do not themselves produce a firm list of expectations to which the actual history of all welfare states can be expected to correspond. They do, however, recognize important similarities between actual welfare states. These tend to be addressed in terms of (1) the international diffusion of social policy patterns ('policy transfer'), (2) the similarity of bureaucratic development and (3) the ubiquity of the challenges to which social policy makers must respond. But greater emphasis is placed upon the *uniqueness* of differing welfare states,[8] particularly around:

- the nature of state-building (federal/absolutist past, imperialism, period of state formation)
- the nature of the civil service and its reform (period at which formed/ reformed; meritocratic or appointed/nepotic)
- the nature of the state (period at which democratized; federal or unitary)
- the relationship of the state to powers in civil society (incorporation or isolation; attitude to organized labour and/or organized capital).

Thesis 12

The (partially indeterminate) development of welfare states must be understood in a comparative and historical context. Among the most important sources of this development are the actions of interest groups, nationally unique political configurations and varying patterns of state organization.

---

[8] Orloff and Skocpol (1984); Quadagno (1984, 1987, 1988a, 1994); Skocpol (1980, 1992); Weir, Orloff and Skocpol (1988a); Orloff (1988); Skocpol and Amenta (1986); Amenta and Skocpol (1989); Amenta and Carruthers (1988); Baldwin (1990); Pierson (1994); Leibfried and Pierson (1995).

Conclusion

Both interest-group and state-centred approaches are concerned less with the generic development of the welfare state than with the historically unique development of differing welfare states. Indeed, if we are to make an informed evaluation of the multiplicity of theoretical claims outlined in these opening chapters, and of the likely prospects for change in the future, it is essential to consider these historical patterns of welfare state development. It is to just such a consideration that we turn in chapter 4.

4
Origins and Development of the Welfare State 1880–1975

For many people, the welfare state is a product of the period immediately following the end of the Second World War. In the Anglo-Saxon world, it is widely identified with the (partial) implementation of the recommendations of Sir William Beveridge's celebrated Report on Social Insurance in the first years of the post-war British Labour Government. The very term 'welfare state' is widely associated with Archbishop Temple's wartime contrast between the *power state* of Nazi Germany and the *welfare state* which was to be the ambition and promise of post-war Allied reconstruction (Temple, 1941, 1942; Zimmern, 1934).[1] This common understanding may well be justified inasmuch as most of the developed capitalist world saw a quantitative and, at times, qualitative leap in the public provision of welfare in the twenty-five years following the war. Yet, while the world was profoundly altered by the experience of world war, after 1945 as after 1918, there were important elements of continuity with the pre-war order, not least in the provision of public welfare. In recent years, there has been a growing recognition that if we are to understand the experience of the 'Golden Age' of the welfare state after 1945 and the epoch of 'crisis' after 1970, we shall need to consider their common origins in a much earlier period of public welfare innovation. Correspondingly, this chapter offers a synoptic reconstruction of the history of the welfare state which runs from its origins in the last third of the nineteenth century through to the period of its much accelerated growth after 1945.

---

[1] Ashford (1986a) attributes the first use of 'welfare state' to A. Zimmern (1934). It is sometimes suggested that the term 'welfare state' was already in common usage in the UK by the late 1930s. For a differing explanation, see Hayek (1960), p. 502.

Before the Welfare State

In fact, welfare states are little more than a hundred years old and mass social democratic movements little older. Significantly, welfare states tended to emerge in societies in which capitalism and the nation state were both already well-established and these pre-existing economic and state formations have themselves prescribed the limits of subsequent welfare state development. Capitalism in its many forms has a relatively long history, stretching across several centuries and touching upon, if not penetrating, almost every quarter of the globe. This longevity and ubiquity of capitalism has often been seen to predominate over the comparatively modern and (territorially limited) influence of welfare administered through the state. A similar logic applies to the relationship between the welfare state and pre-existing state forms. Normally, the welfare state was a product of already existing (nation) states, which were themselves intimately related to the rise of capitalism. Accordingly, prior elements of state formation (territoriality, monopoly over the legitimate use of violence, underwriting of the rule of law) have often been seen to predominate over the commitment to welfare even within the more highly developed welfare states.

While it is the case then that most welfare states emerged under (liberal) capitalism and its corresponding state forms, this does not define the first or original relationship between state, economy and welfare. Pre-capitalist societies subscribed to quite different views of the responsibility for social welfare. In fact, the theorists of nascent liberal capitalism had considerable success in sustaining the belief that the laws of capitalism corresponded with the laws of nature and chimed with people's 'natural instincts'. [2] The brilliance of these accounts should not, however, blind us to the fact that liberal capitalism was not naturally given but historically created and often, if not universally, historically imposed. Taking up this argument, C. B. Macpherson insists that the pre-modern notions of 'fair prices', 'fair wages' and 'just distribution' – sustained by the external sanction of church or state – themselves arose as a defence of the pre-existing order against the novel encroachment of market relations (Macpherson, 1987). They endorsed the subjugation of economic relations to social and political ends *under which all previous human societies had operated*. Similarly, the mediaeval idea of a 'Christian duty to charity', while more honoured in the breach than in the observance, reflected a view of the nature of welfare which was quite different to the maximizing individualism of the advocates of liberal capitalism. Furthermore, if

---

[2] Definitively in Smith (1895, 1976), though Smith famously had his reservations about this belief.

we move forward to the early capitalist period itself, it was not the views of Adam Smith but those of the mercantilists, of whom he was so critical, that defined the prevailing view of state, economy and welfare. Under this mercantilist doctrine, the state was seen to have an active role to play in the promotion of national prosperity and a responsibility for the labouring poor, as the principal source of this national wealth. This, as seen, for example, in the Elizabethan reform and codification of the Poor Law, expressed itself in an almost modern disposition to coercion and control (Webb and Webb, 1927; Fowle, 1890; Fraser, 1981). Thus, the liberal capitalist view of an extremely limited entitlement to public welfare did not arise primordially from the state of nature but had, as Gaston Rimlinger and before him Karl Polanyi noted, itself to be created and sanctioned by the 'liberal break' in states' practice (Rimlinger, 1974; Polanyi, 1944). That is, the non-intervention of the state under liberal capitalism did not arise from a pre-ordained 'state of nature' but had consciously to be created by the state's *disengagement* from previous patterns of intervention in the securing of social welfare (albeit that the pre-modern state and its interventions were wholly different from those of its modern counterparts).

Nor did the 'minimal' nineteenth century state 'stand off' from involvement in the economy and the provision of welfare. Victorian Britain, sometimes depicted as the very essence of *laissez-faire* liberal capitalism and the 'nightwatchman' state, saw the implementation of a wide range of measures on the control of factory work, the quality of housing, the securing of public health, the provision of public education, the municipalization of basic services and compulsory workers' compensation following industrial accidents (Roberts, 1960; Mommsen, 1981; Ensor 1936; Evans, 1978). Even the definitively liberal USA made federal provision in the nineteenth century not only for public education, but also for the public support of the blind, dumb, insane and insane/indigent, as well as for public boards of health (Trattner, 1988; Katz, 1986). Other states, with a more paternalistic and activist state tradition saw still more and more intrusive public regulation of welfare. Thus, the prelude to Bismarck's innovative welfare legislation in a newly unified Germany was a tradition of (sometimes compulsory) welfare and insurance legislation in nineteenth century Prussia.[3] Again, states with a colonial background were often developmentally precocious in their welfare legislation. This in part explains the rapid and early development of the welfare state in Australia and New Zealand (Castles, 1985).

---

[3] See Tampke (1981, pp. 72–5); Rimlinger (1974, pp. 102–15); Ritter (1985) argues that 'the 1854 law on miners' provident societies was of central importance in influencing the design of Germany's later social insurance legislation of the 1880s' (p. 22).

In practice, most of the developed capitalist countries considered here have institutional arrangements for the provision of public welfare dating back several centuries. Most had legislated some form of poor law, under which specified (generally local) public authorities were charged with the responsibility for raising and disbursing (often under pain of some civic penalty for the recipient) limited funds for the relief of destitution (Webb and Webb, 1910; Bruce, 1968; Henriques, 1979; Samuelsson, 1968, pp. 129–30; Axinn and Levin, 1975; Fowle, 1890). The concern of these earlier states was primarily with the maintenance of public order, the punishment of vagrancy and the management of the labour market, rather than the well-being of the poor.[4] With the increasing spread of industrialization, a number of nineteenth century states provided for the maintenance of public health, the regulation of conditions of employment and limited public education. These states also showed a growing interest in the day-to-day surveillance and management of their national populations (Giddens, 1985, pp. 172–97; Mitchell, 1975; Foucault, 1975).

Origins of the Welfare State

Abram De Swaan has argued that 'the development of a public system of social insurance has been an administrative and political innovation of the first order, comparable in significance to the introduction of representative democracy' (De Swaan, 1988, p. 149). Yet for all its importance, it was an innovation that was both gradual and rather mundane, and there are considerable difficulties in defining with any precision the dates at which national welfare states became established. The implementation of some measure of public control over welfare is hardly a sufficient criterion for such a definition, and few would want to characterize even the most developed of these nineteenth century capitalist states as welfare states. But identifying a point along a continuum of expanding public provision as *the* threshold of the welfare state is itself somewhat arbitrary. A substantial difficulty is that those traditional accounts through which 'the welfare state' moved into common usage have tended to describe it in terms of that state's *intentions*, that is, as a state principally concerned to realize the welfare aspirations of its subjects (see, for example, Hall, 1952). One obvious objection to this approach is that such an aspiration can *not* be taken to define the intention or purpose of the welfare state. A still more fundamental objection is that attributing a

---

[4] Graphically Fowle (1890) insisted that 'in England, France, Spain, and the German Empire, we read the same dismal tale of whipping, branding, the pillory, burning the ear, cropping the ear, couples chained together to cleanse sewers, long terms of imprisonment, and, finally, death itself, in hundreds every year in every country' (p. 43).

global *intentionality* to the state and seeking to define it in terms of this intention is itself unsustainable (Weber, 1968, p. 55). At the same time, there is clearly a qualitative difference between a comparatively tiny nineteenth century bureaucracy devoting a few hundred thousand pounds each year to the provision of poor relief and a modern state directing as much as half of its massively enhanced expenditure to the provision of social welfare. While offering no definitive resolution, in this study the origins of the welfare state are isolated around three sets of criteria:

1 *First introduction of social insurance* This is a widely used indicator of welfare state development. Although very modest by contemporary standards, in both breadth and depth of coverage, these are the programmes which have developed into the major institutional (and financial) elements of the welfare state. They entail the recognition that the incapacity to earn a living through contingencies such as old age, sickness or unemployment is a normal condition in industrialized market societies and that it is legitimately the business of the state to organize for collective provision against the loss of income arising from these contingencies (Flora and Heidenheimer, 1981; Flora, 1986; see also the reservations of Jones, 1985).

2 *The extension of citizenship and the depauperization of public welfare* The legitimization of social insurance means also a change in the relationship of the state to the citizen and of both to the provision of public welfare. First, the interest of the state in public welfare is extended beyond the traditional concerns with the relief of destitution and the maintenance of public order (albeit that these remain major elements within even the most developed welfare states). Secondly, the provision of social insurance is increasingly seen as a part of the assemblage of rights and duties which binds the state and the (expanding) citizenry. Thirdly (and correspondingly), the receipt of public welfare becomes not a *barrier* to political participation but a *benefit* of full citizenship.[5] Simple indices of this extension of citizenship are the dates of the inauguration of male and universal suffrage and the date at which the receipt of public welfare ceases to be a bar to full citizenship (i.e. no longer entails disenfranchisement).

3 *Growth of social expenditure* One of the most important aspects of the developed welfare state is the sheer quantity of public spending that it commands. Throughout the twentieth century (at least until the 1970s), the welfare state has commanded a sometimes rapidly growing proportion of a much enhanced national product. Clearly there is no critical threshold figure at which the welfare state may be

---

[5] On the importance of claims to welfare as rights, see R. Goodin (1988).

said to have begun, but as an indicator of this important quantitative aspect of welfare state development, we may take a social expenditure of 3 per cent of GDP as a notional indicator of the *origins* of the welfare state. It may be useful to compare this threshold with the date at which social expenditure exceeds 5 per cent of GDP.

The Birth of the Welfare State: 1880–1914

Cross-national evidence of these developments is varyingly approximate. We may be reasonably certain about dates for the extension of suffrage and for the first introduction of various measures of social insurance. However, these last cover programmes of very varying range, expenditure and funding criteria which may mask important differences in the social and political impact of seemingly similar initiatives. Of these differences, perhaps the most important was whether provision was tax-funded or contributory. These figures may also conceal the extent to which alter-

Table 4.1   Introduction of social insurance (OECD) countries

	Industrial accident	Health	Pension	Unemployment	Family allowances
Belgium	1903	1894	1900	1920	1930
Netherlands	1901	1929	1913	1916	1940
France	1898	1898	1895	1905	1932
Italy	1898	1886	1898	1919	1936
Germany	1871	1883	1889	1927	1954
Ireland	1897	1911	1908	1911	1944
UK	1897	1911	1908	1911	1945
Denmark	1898	1892	1891	1907	1952
Norway	1894	1909	1936	1906	1946
Sweden	1901	1891	1913	1934	1947
Finland	1895	1963	1937	1917	1948
Austria	1887	1888	1927	1920	1921
Switzerland	1881	1911	1946	1924	1952
Australia	1902	1945	1909	1945	1941
New Zealand	1900	1938	1898	1938	1926
Canada	1930	1971	1927	1940	1944
USA	1930	–	1935	1935	–

These figures include schemes which were initially voluntary but state-aided as well as those that were compulsory.
Sources: Flora (1987a, pp. 144, 210, 433, 559, 627, 777; 1987b, vol. 1, p. 454); Flora and Heidenheimer (1981, p. 83); Dixon and Scheurell (1989, pp. 151, 245, 192).

Table 4.2 Welfare state innovators: first introduction of major welfare state programmes

	First	*Second*	*Third*
Industrial accident insurance	Germany (1871)	Switzerland (1881)	Austria (1887)
Health	Germany (1883)	Italy (1886)	Austria (1888)
Pensions	Germany (1889)	Denmark (1891)	France (1895)
Unemployment	France (1905)	Norway (1906)	Denmark (1907)
Family allowances	Austria (1921)	New Zealand (1926)	Belgium (1930)
Male suffrage	France (1848)	Switzerland (1848)	Denmark (1849)
Universal suffrage	New Zealand (1893)	Australia (1902)	Finland (1907)

Sources: Flora (1987b, vol. 1, p. 454); Flora and Heidenheimer (1981); Dixon and Scheurell (1989).

native policies (for example, public works or retraining rather than unemployment compensation) represent a society's commitment to the public redress of the consequences of market disutilities by other means. However, these cautions having been sounded, the figures do reveal a striking historical pattern (see tables 4.1 and 4.2).

In the thirty years between Germany's initiation of health insurance in 1883 and the outbreak of war in 1914, all the countries cited, with the exception of Canada and the USA, had introduced some state-sponsored system of workmen's compensation. Even within the USA, considerable advances were made towards the end of this period in individual *states'* provision (Axinn and Levin, 1975, p. 131; Reede, 1947; Kudrle and Marmor, 1981).[6] In the same period, eleven of the thirteen European countries had introduced measures to support health insurance and nine had legislated for old aged pensions (as had Australia and New Zealand). Although compensation for unemployment was generally the last of the four initial measures of social insurance to be introduced, by 1920 ten of

---

[6] Kudrle and Marmor (1981) cite evidence that about 30 per cent of the US workforce was covered by workmen's compensation legislation by 1915.

Table 4.3   The expansion of citizenship

	Male universal suffrage	Universal adult suffrage
Belgium	1894	1948
Netherlands	1918	1922
France	1848	1945
Italy	1913	1946
Germany	1871	1919
Ireland	1918	1923
UK	1918	1928
Denmark	1849[a]	1918
Norway	1900	1915
Sweden	1909	1921
Finland	1907	1907
Austria	1907	1919
Switzerland	1848	1971
Australia	1902[a]	1902[a]
New Zealand	1879[b]	1893[b]
Canada	1920	1920
USA	1860[b]	1920

[a] with significant restrictions.
[b] largely restricted to Europeans/whites.
Sources: Flora (1987b, vol. 1); Mackie and Rose (1982); Taylor and Hudson (1983).

the European countries had acknowledged some form of state responsibility for protection against the consequences of unemployment. What table 4.2 also shows is that for most countries family allowances belong to a 'second generation' of welfare legislation. Only one third of the states cited had legislated for family allowances by the outbreak of the Second World War.

Turning to *the expansion of citizenship*, there is a strong correspondence (though, as we shall see, no straightforward causal link) between the coming of *male* universal suffrage and the earliest development of social insurance. In the quarter century between 1894 and 1920, eleven of the seventeen countries achieved (more or less) universal male suffrage (table 4.3). Notably, those that had achieved full male suffrage earlier (including Germany, France, Denmark and New Zealand) were also among the most precocious of welfare innovators. We might also note that New Zealand which was 'a generation early' in extending the vote to women (while restricting this right to Europeans) was also 'a generation early' in introducing family allowances. It is also towards the end of this period that we see the abolition of rules disenfranchising those who had been in receipt of public welfare. As late as 1894, universalization of the suffrage in Belgium explicitly excluded 'les mendiants et vagabonds internés dans une maison de refuge . . . par décision des juges de paix' (Orban, 1908, p. 24). However, many countries extending their suffrage in the early twentieth century reversed this disqualification of paupers from voting. The enfranchisement of paupers was effected during this period in, for example, the UK (1918), Norway (1919) and Sweden (1921) (Flora, 1987b, vol. 1; Rawlings, 1988, p. 98). This is an important indicator of the transition from public welfare as an *alternative* to citizenship to public welfare as one of the *rights* of citizenship. As we shall see later, this evidence does not, however, justify the unqualified claim that it was democratization that created the welfare state.

Figures for *the growth of social expenditure* in this early period must be approached with especial caution. Differing national criteria in defining 'social expenditure', differences in the calculation of national income, difficulties in aggregating national and subnational expenditures and the unreliability and paucity of figures before 1945 mean that these expenditure thresholds must be seen to be very approximate. Certainly, they should not be taken to define some international sequence of rising ex-

Table 4.4 The growth of social expenditure

	Social expenditure 3% + GDP	Social expenditure 5% + GDP
Belgium	1923	1933
Netherlands	1920	1934
France	1921	1931
Italy	1923	1940
Germany	1900	1915
Ireland	1905	1920
UK	1905	1920
Denmark	1908	1918
Norway	1917	1926
Sweden	1905	1921
Finland	1926	1947
Austria	1926	1932
Switzerland	By 1900	1920
Australia	1922	1932
New Zealand	1911	1920
Canada	1921	1931
USA	1920	1931

Sources: Flora (1986, 1987a, 1987b); Mitchell (1975); Taylor and Hudson (1983); US Department of Commerce (1975, Part 1, p. 340); Urquhart (1965); Commonwealth Bureau of Census (1910–); *New Zealand Official Year Book* (1882–).

penditure. Yet the overall figures do give compelling expression to the modest but consistent growth in social expenditure throughout this period. With the possible exception of Germany and Switzerland, it appears that none of these countries had reached social expenditure levels of 3 per cent by 1900. Yet by 1920, more than half had reached this threshold and by 1930 all had passed the 3 per cent figure. Indeed, about a third of these states passed the 5 per cent threshold during the 1920s and most of the others were to follow in the early and middle years of the 1930s (years in which increasing demands upon social insurance funds had often to be met from a *falling* national product under circumstances of depression).

Welfare States 1920–1975: The Epoch of Growth

In fact, this experience of the expansion of social budgets in the inter-war years helps to isolate the most consistent and remarkable feature of the welfare states in the whole of the period down to the mid-1970s, that is, the ubiquitous dynamic of *sustained growth*. By the 1970s, all of the welfare states we are considering were quite different from what they had been at the end of the First World War. Much else in the advanced capitalist societies had changed with, and sometimes because of them. Furthermore, the core institutions of the welfare state are now so commonplace that we are perhaps inclined to forget the sheer scale of the transformation wrought between 1920 and 1970. In fact, throughout this period, the pace of growth varied between differing phases, differing programmes and different countries. Here, as elsewhere, caution is required in talking about the generic experience of *the* welfare state. Yet so substantial and striking are the developments of this period that at least some generalizations are warranted.

The Growth of the Social Budget

First, there is the sheer scale and ubiquity of growth in the social budget. In 1914, only seven of the countries in table 4.4 had reached social expenditure levels of 3 per cent of GDP. By 1940, nearly all had reached social expenditure levels in excess of 5 per cent. In the early 1950s, this figure ranged between 10 per cent and 20 per cent. By the mid-1970s, among the European welfare states, between one quarter and something more than a third of GDP was devoted to social expenditure. Even the most 'reluctant' welfare states saw a wholesale transformation of their public budgets. In the USA, total social expenditure rose from 2.4 per cent of GDP in 1890 to 20.2 per cent in 1981. Even in Japan, where an exceptional proportion of welfare is organized and delivered through private corporations, the social budget has expanded from 1.4 per cent of

GDP in 1890 to 16.2 per cent in 1985 (Flora, 1986, vol. 1, p. xxii; Maddison, 1984; Minami, 1986, pp. 332ff; Oshima, 1965, pp. 368–71; OECD, 1985a, 1988; US Bureau of Statistics, 1975).

Much of the remarkable overall growth in public expenditure of the twentieth century can be attributed to the growth of the social budget, and this rapidly growing proportion of national wealth devoted to social welfare must be set against the background of a sevenfold increase in average per capita output in the cited countries over the past 100 years (Maddison, 1984, p. 59).

Incremental Growth and Demographic Change

A substantial source of this remarkable and general growth in the social budget was the maturing of rights and claims as pensions legislated in the take-off period came 'on stream'. This was substantially an incremental and inertial development which was the more pronounced because of certain demographic changes which were common to most of the advanced capitalist societies. The most important of these changes were the continuing increase in life expectancy and the decline in mortality rates. For example, life expectancy at birth of females rose between 1900 and 1967 from 49.4 to 74.1 (England and Wales), from 47 to 75 (France) and from 46.6 to 73.5 (West Germany). Crude annual death rates fell in the same countries between 1900 and 1950 from 18.2 (per thousand) to 12.5 in England and Wales, from 21.9 to 12.7 in France and from 22.1 to 10.5 in West Germany (Winter, 1982; Mitchell, 1975, pp. 104–24). What did constitute an authentically *political* intervention was the common practice of introducing (contributory) pensions *before* sufficient premiums had been collected to fund these on an actuarially-sound basis. The electoral call for 'pensions now' was a powerful one, even in the characteristically insurance-minded USA (Quadagno, 1988b; Fraser, 1973, p. 213; Rimlinger, 1974, p. 234).

It is possible that the severest demographic challenge to the welfare state lies in the future, but the growing aged population in advanced capitalism has certainly hugely extended the costs of the welfare state, not just in the provision of pensions, but in those other costly areas where the elderly are disproportionate users of services, as in public health provision. The proportion of the population aged 65 or over in the OECD countries has risen from 9.7 per cent in 1960 to 12.7 per cent in 1985, and is projected to increase further to 18.0 per cent by 2020 (OECD, 1988, p. 11). Meanwhile, Heikkinen notes that 'the use of [health and social] services among the aged is 3–4 times that expected on the basis of proportion of the population' (Heikkinen, 1984, p. 162).

In fact, the demographic structure of the several welfare states has varied. For example, the disproportionately youthful structure of the early twentieth century New Zealand and Australian populations (as 'new', immigrant-based nations), afforded unusually favourable circumstances for their early expansion. In other countries, notably in France, social policy initiatives have been related to the demographic consequences of the Great War (especially in the number of war pensions and later in the structure of natalist policy).[7] But overall, the number of aged in the population has grown throughout the industrialized world as life expectancy has increased. In the 1880s, only 5 per cent of the population was over 65. One hundred years later, the elderly constitute some 13 per cent of the population and a still higher proportion of the electorate. In Western Europe, the percentage of people aged 65 and over in the population is predicted to rise from 13.3 per cent in 1985 to 14.9 per cent in 2000 (Heikkinen, 1984, p. 162; OECD, 1984, pp. 3–6, 1986a, pp. 3–10). Still more importantly, the ratio of the economically inactive to the economically active section of the population (out of whose productive labour 'pay-as-you-go' pensions must be funded) is rising and set to continue to rise. Dependency ratios (the proportion of people aged 0–14 years plus the proportion of people aged 60 years and over to the proportion aged 15–59 years) actually *fell* in Western and Northern Europe in the 1980s because of the declining numbers of young people. But they are set to rise from 59.2 to 66.8 per cent in Western Europe and from 64.4 to 66.2 per cent in Northern Europe between 1990 and 2000. The UK Treasury estimates that whereas there were 2.3 economic contributors to each pension claimant in the UK in 1985, by 2025 this number will have fallen to 1.8 contributors to each pensioner (Heikkinen, 1984, p. 169; DHSS, 1985, p. 15). Overall, the OECD estimates that the old-age dependency ratio will have doubled by 2040 (OECD, 1988, p. 35).[8]

Sequential Growth of Welfare State Programmes

Most of the welfare states considered here have also expanded their social welfare provision in terms of a broadly shared sequence. Certainly, there have been differences between 'early' and 'late' adopters in terms of the comparative stage of industrialization at which social welfare was introduced, the sorts of funding regimes established and the generosity of initial coverage. There is some disagreement as to whether the spread of the welfare state is best explained in terms of *prerequisites* (with state welfare initiatives being a response to endogenous national developments) or *diffusion* (a process of international imitation of welfare state innovators). In

---

[7] The First World War saw losses of approximately 1.3 million among the French population and an equally large 'birth deficit' (McEvedy and Jones, 1978, p. 56). See also McIntosh (1983), esp. pp. 43–57; Ashford (1986a, pp. 112–13); Dyer (1978); Glass (1940).

[8] This demographic challenge to the welfare state is extensively discussed in chapter 6.

the period before 1908, the spread seems to have been from less industrially developed and more authoritarian regimes towards the more developed and democratic. In the period between 1908 and 1923, the principal determinant of innovation appears to have been geographical proximity to an existing welfare state rather than the level of industrial development. After 1923, there is a tendency for countries to adopt welfare state measures at a lower level than their own economic development, (with the notable exception of the USA). Paralleling the pattern of the spread of industrialization, 'late starters' have tended to develop welfare state institutions earlier in their own individual development and under more comprehensive terms of coverage (Collier and Messick, 1975, p. 1301; Schneider, 1982; Alber cited in Flora, 1986, vol. 1, p. xxiv; Alber, 1982; Kuhnle, 1981).

Wherever welfare states have emerged, the order of adoption and expansion of programmes has been broadly similar. We can identify three sequential patterns. In terms of *programmes*, workmen's compensation for industrial accidents was generally the first measure to be adopted. This was followed by sickness and invalidity insurance, (old age) pensions and finally unemployment insurance. Though some provision for maternity occurred quite early, family allowances were generally introduced rather later and were widely viewed as an 'endowment of motherhood' rather than as insurance against the contingency of having children. Secondly, *coverage* also followed a shared pattern. Initially, coverage was limited to workers in particularly strategic industries or in peculiarly dangerous occupations. Mining, for example, was often one of the first industries to be covered (Tampke, 1981, pp. 72–3). Legislation was subsequently extended to cover all industrial workers, thence to rural/ agricultural workers and so to dependants and survivors of insured workers. Latterly, coverage was extended to the self-employed and thence characteristically to the generality of the population (or at least to all those recognized as citizens) without further discriminating criteria.

Thirdly, there were broadly similar patterns in the *expansion* of programmes. Earlier extensions tended to be built upon broadening of criteria of eligibility (making for more beneficiaries) and the legislating of more generous benefits. Characteristically, later enhancements were built upon the less restrictive application of definitions of eligibility and from the late 1950s and 1960s onwards upon the transition from flat-rate to earnings-related benefits. There was also a general tendency for programmes to proceed from voluntary to compulsory provision.

The Periodization of Welfare State Growth

In fact, it is possible to think of not just a sequential but indeed of a shared historical pattern in the development of the welfare states of advanced capitalism. Clearly this is not a uniform pattern. The USA lacked basic federal provisions for social insurance down to 1935 and still lacks comprehensive measures for health care or family allowances. Some welfare states emerged early and then stagnated (e.g. Australia), some developed early and expanded before 1940 (e.g. New Zealand) while others were marginal before the Second World War but expanded rapidly after 1945 (e.g. Finland). Yet a significant historical pattern may be identified.

1918–1940: 'Consolidation' and Development

The period between the wars has often been described as a rather uneventful one for the welfare state, falling between the extensive innovations of the preceding twenty-five years and the period of remarkable growth immediately after 1945. Hamilton characteristically describes this period in the British experience as one of 'steady and purposeful social advance' (Hamilton cited in Bruce, 1968, p. 255).

Yet more recent commentators have tended to see the 1920s and 1930s as the seed-bed of post-war welfare state development. For Douglas Ashford, this was the period in which serious obstacles to 'the complete nationalization of social policy' were removed, making the expansion of the welfare state after 1945 comparatively uncontentious:

> First, the liberal refuge of private or charitable assistance proved totally inadequate. Second, the private insurers learned . . . that many serious social problems exceeded the capacity of actuarially sound insurance. Third . . . professional groups were gradually co-opted into national social security programmes. Fourth, the agricultural sector first received the protection of the state . . . before substantial aid went to urban dwellers. (Ashford, 1986b, p. 107)

In Britain, Sweden and the USA, for example, this is seen as the decisive epoch in establishing the institutions and practices of that more interventionist form of government in which the post-war welfare state was grounded. It also saw governments facing new choices about the macromanagement of the economy and the possibility of the active and interventionist pursuit of full employment. Thus Middlemas, in his study of *Politics in Industrial Society*, argues that it was in the inter-war years that a new system of 'managerial collective government', built upon the negotiation and compromise of the interests of the state, organized capital and organized labour, first emerged in the UK. This was a system oriented around the amelioration of class conflict and the avoidance of systemic crisis through, among other media, the promotion of social policy

(Middlemas, 1979).[9] As we shall soon see, in both Sweden and the USA, the Great Depression of the early 1930s triggered new forms of government intervention in social and economic life, new relationships between state, employers and trades unions and a process of political realignment which established new political forces at the heart of the state (Korpi, 1979, 1983; Weir and Skocpol, 1985).

Certainly in terms of coverage and cost, the inter-war welfare state often dwarfs provision in the period of innovation. As the figures for social expenditure indicate, while the period between 1880 and 1920 is properly understood as the epoch of *legislative* innovation in the welfare state, it is only after 1920 that the *fiscal* consequences of these initiatives become clear. Many of the early systems of social insurance offered, like Lloyd George's old age pensions in the UK, extremely modest benefits to 'the very poor [and] the very respectable' (Thane, 1982, p. 83).[10] Many programmes, notably those in Germany, envisaged a strictly limited financial involvement by the state, expecting benefits to be drawn from the premiums of potential beneficiaries or their employers (Alber, 1986, pp. 40–1). However, the growth of social expenditure in the 1920s and the early 1930s is what we might have expected as the legislative innovations of the pre-1914 period yielded to the maturing of insurance and pension claims in the post-war age. In fact, this tendency for innate or incremental growth of social expenditure – growth not through legislative or executive initiative but through the maturing of pension rights or demographic change – has been a marked feature of the whole period of the welfare state.

In many countries, this process was accelerated by the consequences of the Great War. First, it led to a major expansion of pension, health, housing and rehabilitation demands from those millions incapacitated or bereaved as a consequence of the armed conflict. In Australia in 1922, for example, war pensioners outnumbered old age and invalid pensioners in a proportion of more than two to one.[11] Secondly, it conditioned politicians, bureaucrats and tax-payers to new levels of public expenditure, from which there was no wholesale retreat once the immediate demands of wartime had passed (the 'displacement effect' described by Peacock

---

[9] Although primarily concerned with the UK, Middlemas comments that his 'propositions have an importance not only for modern Britain, but most western industrialized societies' (Middlemas, 1979, p. 23).

[10] New Zealand's innovative old age pensions, for example, cost £197,292 in 1900 rising to £362,496 in 1910 (*New Zealand Official Year Book*, 1919).

[11] In 1922, in Australia, there were 225,372 war pensioners, 110,278 claiming old age pensions and just 5,182 invalid pensioners. We shall see below (p. 115), that the early American welfare state was largely made up of Civil War veterans. Germany, France and the UK lost a total of 3.75 million soldiers in the 1914–18 war (*Official Year Book of the Commonwealth of Australia*, 1923; McEvedy and Jones, 1978, p. 34).

and Wiseman, 1961, pp. 52–61). Thirdly, it necessitated new forms of governmental control and administration which were again not to be abandoned in the post-war epoch (Middlemas, 1979, p. 19).

The late 1920s and early 1930s also saw what might be described as the first 'fiscal crisis of the welfare state'.[12] The depth of the economic recession of the early 1930s occasioned the earliest major cuts in social welfare provision and demonstrated (1) that it was impossible to sustain actuarially sound social insurance under circumstances of profound economic recession, (2) that demand for social expenditure (especially unemployment compensation) was inversely related to the capacity of the economy to fund it and (3) that to respond to this problem by cutting social expenditure would simply intensify rather than alleviate these economic problems. The scale of the difficulties of the 1930s also probably dealt the final death blow to the belief among the governing classes that the provision of social welfare or even the relief of destitution could be satisfactorily met from voluntary or charitable sources.

New Deal and Historic Compromise

The 1930s was also a decisive period in the development of two of the most widely differing and frequently contrasted welfare state regimes, those of Sweden and the USA. In comparative typifications of welfare state development, these two examples are often recorded as the most developed (Sweden) and the least developed (USA) welfare states and, given the centrality of this opposition, it is worth developing this contrast in some detail.

Ironically, in much contemporary scholarship, the *origins* of the modern American and Swedish welfare states, as a response to the consequences of the Great Depression, are seen to be remarkably similar. Thus, Weir and Skocpol contrast the shared response of the US ('commercial Keynesianism') and Sweden ('social Keynesianism') to the traditionally deflationary policy of the British government (Weir and Skocpol, 1985). Gosta Esping-Andersen has argued that 'at least in its early formulation, the New Deal was as social democratic as was contemporary Scandinavian social democracy' (Esping-Andersen, 1990, p. 28). In both countries, this period of welfare state enhancement also saw profound political realignment and the installation of the Democrats and the Social Democrats, respectively, as 'the

---

[12] In the UK, the 1931 May Committee Report 'compounded of prejudice, ignorance and panic' recommended a cut in public expenditure of £120 m., including a 20 per cent cut in unemployment benefit. In Australia, old age, invalid and some war pensions were reduced under the terms of the Financial Emergency Act, 1931. (Taylor, 1965, p. 287ff; *Official Year Book of the Commonwealth of Australia*, 1932, p. 30).

natural party of government'. Yet the contexts in which these 'similar' institutions were to be developed (and indeed the intentions of those who initiated and developed them) were profoundly different.

It is one of the many myths of the American welfare state that there was little or no public provision of welfare before the 1930s. In fact, 'American welfare practice has a very old history', but it is a practice that 'has always been mediated by the complex structure of American federalism'. Similarly, 'public welfare always has supported more dependent people than private relief'. Yet, in the 'protean mix' of public and private provision which characterizes every welfare state, the private and especially the corporate provision of welfare has always had an unusually prominent role (Katz, 1986, pp. xiii, x, 291).

At the turn of the twentieth century, such limited public relief as there was within the USA was largely locally administered according to local poor law customs (Quadagno, 1984, p. 635; Axinn and Levin, 1975; Katz, 1986). At the local level, public welfare rolls fluctuated wildly in response to changing social and political regimes (Katz, 1986, pp. 3–109). Federal provision was substantially confined to pensions for (Northern) veterans of the Civil War. However, by 1900 these federal veterans' pensions had come to constitute an extremely extensive system of surrogate social welfare. At this time, 'at least one of every two elderly, native-born, white Northern men and many of their widows received a pension from the federal government' and 'pensions were the largest expense in the federal budget after the national debt' (Katz, 1986, p. 200). In 1913, I. M. Rubinow, 'one of the nation's leading social insurance advocates', calculated that American pensions were costing three times as much as the supposedly advanced British system of old age pensions and covering 'several hundred thousand' more people (cited in Skocpol and Ikenberry, 1983, p. 97; Katz, 1986, p. 163). It is little wonder that Skocpol concludes that 'in terms of the proportional effort devoted to public pensions, the American federal government was hardly a "welfare laggard"; it was a precocious social-spending state' (Orloff and Skocpol, 1984, pp. 728–9; Skocpol, 1992). However, as the number of veteran claimants and their dependants declined in the early years of the twentieth century, and despite the mobilization of pensions advocates such as Rubinow, Seager and the American Association for Labor Legislation, there was no attempt to replace the veterans' programmes with a more universal system of old age pensions (see Orloff and Skocpol, 1984, p. 735; Skocpol and Ikenberry, 1983, pp. 95–100; Katz, 1986, p. 128).

There was some advance in other areas of welfare provision by the individual states in the years immediately prior to the First World War. Between 1909 and 1920, forty-three states enacted legislation on workmen's compensation and within two years of Illinois's 'Funds to Parents Act' of 1911, twenty states had provided similar cash relief programmes for widows and dependent children. Indeed, Skocpol argues that with the lapse of the veterans' pension programme, 'the United States looked briefly as if it would fashion an internationally distinctive maternalist welfare state' and we now have an extensive historical record of the major part played by professional women in forging a distinctive welfare regime for mothers and children in the 1920s and into the 1930s (Skocpol, 1992, p. 526; Gordon, 1994). Yet the financial impact of these measures was severely limited and although there was some programme enhancement in the 1920s, the prevalent welfare trend in the post-war New Era was away from the European model of social insurance towards a reliance on occupational welfare (employee representation, workers' shares, company welfare and pensions) under the rubric of welfare capitalism. However, this welfare capitalism was always largely confined to the 'progressive' corporate sector of American capital (to large companies such as Procter and Gamble, Eastman Kodak and General Electric). It was more important as a legitimating ideology than as an effective social practice and certainly wholly unable to respond to the scale of social need generated by the Great Depression (Axinn and Levin, 1975, pp. 130–4; Brody, 1980; Skocpol and Ikenberry, 1983).

Opinions as to which social, economic and political forces shaped and were served by the expanded social policy of the New Deal are vigorously divided. So are judgements as to whether it was the 'social' or the 'economic' side of the New Deal that had the most lastingly influential impact. However, there is near universal agreement that the 'social' side of the New Deal, embodied in the 1935 Social Security Act 'declared the birth of the [American] welfare state and established a basis for its growth and development' (Axinn and Levin, 1975, p. 195). It is also widely argued that this 'charter legislation for American social insurance and public assistance programs' set the parameters for virtually all further developments in America's 'Semi-Welfare State' (Skocpol, 1987, p. 35; Katz, 1986, pp. ix–xiv; Quadagno, 1988).

The 1935 Act legislated for:

1   a federal–state unemployment insurance programme
2   federal grants-in-aid to the states for assistance to:
      (a) needy dependent children
      (b) the blind
      (c) the elderly
3   matching federal funds for state spending on:
      (a) vocational rehabilitation
      (b) infant and maternal health
      (c) aid to crippled children
4   a federal old age insurance programme.

(Berkowitz and McQuaid, 1980, p. 103)

Although the 1935 Act brought the USA in some measure into alignment with the welfare states of Western Europe, it was still a quite limited initiative. The provision of welfare was largely devolved to the individual states, funded from (regressive) payroll taxation rather than from general tax revenue, and allowed for very considerable state 'discretion' and for very substantial 'exceptions'. (Initially, one half of the employed workforce, notably black southern farm workers, was excluded from participation in old age insurance). There was an emphasis upon actuarially sound insurance principles and 'earned benefits', the rhetoric of which long outlived its early compromise in practice. Generally, where entitlement was not earned through insurance payments, benefits were means tested and the 1935 legislation institutionalized the time-served distinction between social security entitlement and residual claims to 'welfare'. Traditional relief of destitution (among the able-bodied poor) remained a local responsibility. The legislation made no provision for either health insurance or a family allowance.

The 1930s was also a decade of major change in the Swedish welfare state and of a still more profound political realignment, the nature of which is no less fiercely debated than that surrounding the New Deal. In fact, the background of national public welfare was already more extensive in Sweden than in its North American counterpart. Sweden had a more developed national bureaucracy and a centralized state tradition dating back over several centuries. Schooling had been compulsory since 1842, state support of sickness and occupational injury insurance had been legislated around the turn of the twentieth century and Sweden had been the first state to introduce universal and compulsory (if minimal) old age pensions in 1913. At the start of the 1930s, Sweden's social expenditure as a proportion of GDP stood at 7 per cent, compared with 4.2 per cent in the USA (Olsson, 1986, p. 5). However, Swedish provision compared with that of its near neighbour Denmark, for example, was very modest. As Esping-Andersen notes:

> the long era of conservative and liberal rule [prior to 1932] had produced remarkably few social reforms. There was no unemployment insurance, except for financially weak union funds, and insurance coverage for sickness was marginal. . . . old age pension . . . benefits were meager at best. In addition, no system of public job creation was in effect when the economic depression led to explosive unemployment. (Esping-Andersen, 1985, p. 153)

It was under these circumstances, with unemployment rising rapidly, that the first Scandinavian Social Democratic government was elected in 1932. In fact, the Social Democrats, with 42 per cent of the popular vote, were reliant upon the coalition support of the peasant-based Agrarian Party, and were consequently obliged to compromise the interests of their own core working class constituency (in welfare reform and full employment) with policies for agricultural price support (in the interests of the rural peasantry). While 'social reform was a top priority [and] the party actually developed a long-range strategy for full social and industrial citizenship . . . by and large, political energies were concentrated on the immediate problems of crisis management and economic relief' (Esping-Andersen and Korpi, 1987, pp. 46–7).[13]

A still more important accommodation was that struck by the newly empowered Social Democrats and organized capital. Rather than pursuing the traditional (maximalist) socialist policy of pressing for immediate socialization of the ownership of capital, the Social Democrats, recognizing the stalemate between organized labour and organized capital that their election occasioned, pressed for a formalization of the division of economic and political control and a division of the spoils of continued and agreed capitalist growth. This celebrated 'historic compromise' ensured that capital would maintain intact its managerial prerogatives within the workplace, subject only to guarantees on rights to unionization, and capitalist economic growth would be encouraged. At the same time, the Social Democratic government would pursue Keynesian economic policies to sustain full employment and use progressive taxation to reduce economic inequality and promote provision for collective needs, such as education, health, and housing. When in the post-Second World War period the defence of welfare institutions and full employment threatened inflation and the loss of international competitiveness, the compromise was complemented by the adoption of the 'Rehn' model, which entailed (1) an 'active manpower policy', facilitating the redistribution and reallocation of labour and capital from less to more efficient enterprises, and (2) a 'solidaristic' wage policy, which would allow for the centralized negotiation of wages and the reduction of wage differentials, through a principle of equal pay for equal work, irrespective of a given company's capacity to pay. In this way, it was hoped that welfare provision and a rising standard of living for the working population could be reconciled with continuing non-inflationary economic growth.

Thus in the 1930s and beyond, the Swedish welfare state was secured as much by *economic* policy – the support of an active labour market policy, public works, solidaristic wage bargaining, deficit budgeting – as by social policy. Indeed, the Swedish social democrats have always shown an awareness of the intimate relationship between economic and social policy upon which the institutional or social democratic welfare state is

---

[13] This 'labourist' reading of Scandinavian experience has been extensively criticized by Peter Baldwin in *The Politics of Social Solidarity*. He insists that 'decisions in favour of a solidaristic solution to social insurance were, in fact, taken at a time before the left had much say in the matter and often against its will' (Baldwin, 1990, p. 93).

dependent and which is recognized in the twin-termed Keynesian Welfare State (KWS).[14] Thus, job creation or full employment may be seen as a more desirable alternative to the payment of unemployment compensation. It may also be the indispensable basis of funding a 'generous' welfare system.

In Sweden in the 1930s, it was then probably Keynesian *economic* policies, rather than innovations in *social* policy, that were the most important component in the nascent welfare state. Nonetheless, there were significant and complementary social policy initiatives. Perhaps the most important of these was the 1934 legislation that increased the state's involvement in what had previously been exclusively a union-managed system of unemployment insurance (Esping-Andersen and Korpi, 1987). In addition, between 1933 and 1938, the Social Democratic government also legislated:

- new employment creation programmes
- a housing programme for families with many children including subsidies and interest-subsidized construction loans
- the indexation of pensions to regional differences in the cost of living
- maternity benefits to around 90 per cent of all mothers
- free maternity and childbirth services
- state loans to newly married couples
- the introduction of two weeks' holiday for all private and public employees.

(Olsson, 1986, p. 5)

A number of other states saw major developments in their welfare states between the wars. Denmark's 'Great Social Reform' of 1933, if less radical than its advocates have claimed, 'nevertheless, remained the fundamental administrative framework of the Danish welfare state for a quarter century' (Johansen, 1986, pp. 299–300; Levine, 1983). New Zealand, which had introduced the first comprehensive pensions for the needy old aged in 1898 and been among the first to introduce family allowances in 1926, created, through its 1938 Social Security Act, 'what could be argued to be, in late 1930s terms, the most comprehensive welfare state in the world' (Castles, 1985, p. 26). This unusually comprehensive measure was:

to provide for the payment of superannuation benefits and of other benefits designed to safeguard the people of New Zealand from disabilities arising from age, sickness, widowhood, orphanhood, unemployment, or other ex-

---

[14] Ashford (1986b) stresses the general importance of the interrelationship between social and economic policy. He argues that historically this was recognized in France but not in Britain; this led to the French welfare state being the more effectively entrenched.

ceptional conditions; to provide a system whereby medical and hospital treatment will be made available to persons requiring such treatment; and, further, to provide such other benefits as may be necessary to maintain and promote the health and general welfare of the community. (Cited in Castles, 1985, p. 27)

Elsewhere, there were substantial if less spectacular advances. In Canada, (means-tested) old age pensions were introduced in 1927 and the 1930s saw a succession of federal–provincial unemployment compensation schemes culminating in the 1940 Federal Unemployment Insurance Act (Bellamy and Irving, 1989; Leman, 1977). Britain, whose inter-war social policy was dominated by the spectre of unemployment, saw modest legislation on the social provision of housing and health care, education, contributory old age pensions, provision for widows and orphans and the steady break-up of the Poor Law (Gilbert, 1970; Fraser, 1973; Thane, 1982). Yet, writing of the UK experience, Parry concludes that 'the creative impulse of the welfare state progressed little from the 1910s to the 1940s' (Parry, 1986, p. 159).

Even where initiatives of this period were very modest, some have argued that the *underlying* changes which permitted the flowering of the welfare state after 1945 were secured in the inter-war years. Such a view is sometimes taken in describing the Beveridge Report not as the founding charter of a radically new British welfare state after 1945, but as a rationalization of existing pre-war legislation. Addison, for example, suggests that Beveridge's 'background assumptions' – full employment and a national health service – were much more radical and innovative than his 'fundamentally conservative' proposals on social insurance (Addison, 1977, p. 213). Similarly, Ashford argues that in France, where advances in pensions, health and accident insurance were limited and painfully slow between the wars, this was the period in which the political compromises and coalitions upon which the developed post-war welfare state was built were themselves fought over and secured. Indeed, he suggests that the very slowness and difficulty of achieving welfare advances in France compared with the UK made these victories and the welfare state thus constructed more secure and entrenched than its less contested British counterpart (Ashford, 1986a, 1986b, 1982). As we have seen, what remains the single most important innovation in the US welfare state dates from the 1930s.

Other significant developments of this period included the evolution in Germany and Italy of a pattern of social policy interwoven with the corporatist institutions of fascism. But everywhere, and particularly under the impact of the mass unemployment of the 1930s, the inter-war years were marked by growing welfare expenditures. Indeed, between 1920 and 1940, Flora and Alber's index of social insurance coverage in

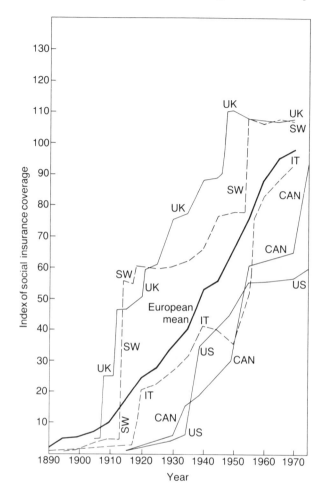

Figure 4.1 The growth of social insurance coverage in Western Europe
UK = United Kingdom, SW = Sweden, IT = Italy, CAN = Canada,
US = United States
Source: Flora and Heidenheimer (1981).

Western Europe more than doubled (Flora and Heidenheimer, 1981, p. 85; see figure 4.1).

1945–1975: 'The Golden Age of the Welfare State'?

Just as the inter-war years have been seen as years of 'consolidation', so has the period after 1945 been widely characterized as ushering in a thirty years' 'Golden Age of the Welfare State'. Upon such an account, the period between 1945 and the mid-1970s is seen as bringing (1) rapid initial reforms to create a much more comprehensive and universal welfare state based on the idea of shared citizenship, (2) a commitment to direct increasing resources towards the rapid expansion of benefits and coverage within this extended system, (3) a very broad-based political consensus in favour of a mixed economy and a system of extended social welfare, and (4) a (successful) commitment to economic growth and full employment.

In fact, this model of the post-war evolution of the welfare state has always been heavily dependent upon the (unique) British experience, and indeed upon a particular, broadly social democratic and 'optimistic' understanding of this experience. Great emphasis is placed upon the consequences of the Second World War – its expansion of the powers and competence of government, the generation of new forms of collective provision and, above all, the broadly shared experience of austerity and mutual mortal danger generating a high degree of citizen solidarity in favour of radical reform. Also stressed is the 'messianic' quality of Beveridge and his proposed reforms, the radical break occasioned by the election of the post-war Labour government and the subsequent development of a broad cross-party consensus ('Butskellism') in favour of compromise of the interests of capital and labour, within which the welfare state was a crucial component.

Recently, this synoptic view of the post-war history of the (British) welfare state has itself come under increasing challenge. First, claims about the impact of the Second World War on the development of social policy have been questioned. It has been argued: (1) that the experience of government planning and state intervention in the war-time period was not an especially promising one, (2) that sympathy for collective provision arose not from the bonds of mutual citizenship but from the perceived threat of a commonly uncertain future and (3) that the pressure for social policy reform came less from a radicalized citizenry than from a trade union movement whose industrial muscle had been much strengthened by war-time full employment. Secondly, it is widely insisted that the social policy reforms proposed by Beveridge (and only partially enacted in the post-war period) represented not a radical charter for a new social order, but a tidying-up and codification of pre-war social legislation. Thirdly, it is argued that the consensus within which the post-war welfare state was said to have developed either never existed or else was much more limited than the traditional social democratic account has allowed (Barnett, 1986; Dryzek and Goodin, 1986; Addison, 1977; Taylor-Gooby, 1985; Deakin, 1987; Smith, 1986; Pimlott, 1988).

There are then serious doubts as to whether this model is fully applic-

able even to the British experience.[15] Yet it retains a significant (if varying) element of truth. In 1948, Article 40 of the newly founded United
Nations' Declaration of Human Rights proclaimed that:

> Everyone has the right to a standard of living adequate for the health and
> well-being of himself and his family, including food, clothing, housing and
> medical care and the necessary social services, and the right to security in
> the event of unemployment, sickness, disability, widowhood, old age or
> other lack of livelihood in circumstances beyond his control. (United Na-
> tions, 1948)

Similarly, Article 38 of the Constitution of newly independent India declared that 'the State shall strive to promote the welfare of the people by
securing and protecting . . . a social order in which justice, social, economic and political shall inform all the institutions of national life' (cited
in Brownlie, 1971, p. 43). Within the developed West, many countries
other than Britain saw major social policy reforms immediately after
1945. In France and Ireland, for example, there was a period of rapid
policy innovation in the late 1940s, and these policy changes had an
immediate effect upon the proportion of GNP devoted to social welfare
(Ashford, 1986a, pp. 255–65; Hage, Hanneman and Gargan, 1989;
Maguire, 1986, pp. 246–7; Kennedy, 1975, p. 11). Indeed, throughout the
developed capitalist world, the post-war period was one of unprecedented
growth and prosperity, and of new and varied forms of government intervention in the economy.

By almost any criteria, these were years of rapid expansion in welfare
state provision. Thus, for example, in Western Europe in the early 1930s,
only about a half of the labour force was protected by accident, sickness,
invalidity and old age insurance. Scarcely a fifth were insured against
unemployment. However, by the mid-1970s, more than 90 per cent of the
labour force enjoyed insurance against income loss due to old age, invalidity and sickness; over 80 per cent were covered by accident insurance
and 60 per cent had coverage against unemployment. The average annual
rate of growth in social security expenditure which stood at around 0.9
per cent in 1950–5 had accelerated to 3.4 per cent in the years 1970–4.
Broadly defined, social expenditure which had in the early 1950s consumed something between 10 and 20 per cent of GNP had grown to
between a quarter and something more than a third of a rapidly enhanced GNP by the mid-1970s (Flora, 1986, vol. 1, p. xxii). A further
indication of this rapid growth after 1960 is given in table 4.5.

---

[15] It has been very properly objected that 'intensive study of the British case' may not be
'the optimal way of starting to grasp the general characteristics of welfare state development' (Flora and Heidenheimer, 1981, p. 21).

Table 4.5   Growth in social expenditure (7 major OECD countries), 1960–1975, as a percentage of GDP (%)

	1960	*1975*
Canada	11.2	20.1
France	14.4	26.3
W. Germany	17.1	27.8
Italy	13.7	20.6
Japan	7.6	13.7
UK	12.4	19.6
USA	9.9	18.7
Weighted average	12.3	21.9

Source: OECD (1988, p. 10).

However we choose to explain this development, the sheer growth in social expenditure throughout this period is one of the more remarkable phenomena of post-war capitalist development.

For many commentators, these developments in social policy may only properly be understood in the much broader context of what in the USA was styled the 'post-World War II capital labor accord' and is more familiarly described in Britain and Western Europe as the 'post-war consensus' (Bowles and Gintis, 1982). In this view, the new social, political and economic order of the post-war world was to be secured around (1) Keynesian economic policies to secure full employment and economic growth domestically within the agreed parameters of an essentially liberal capitalist international market, (2) a more or less 'institutional' welfare state to deal with the dysfunctions arising from this market economy and (3) broad-based agreement between left and right, and between capital and labour, over these basic social institutions (a market economy and a welfare state) and the accommodation of their (legitimately) competing interests through elite-level negotiation (Bowles and Gintis, 1982; Taylor-Gooby, 1985; Kavanagh, 1987; Kavanagh and Morris, 1989). These liberal democratic or social democratic institutions were seen as the best guarantee of avoiding both the economic disasters and the concomitant political polarization of the inter-war years.

This post-war consensus may be thought of in two ways, as a consensus between *classes* or as a consensus between political *parties*. At the *class* level, consensus involved the abandonment by labour of its traditional aspiration for socialization of the economy and of the ideology and practices of 'class war'. For capital, it meant an acceptance of the commitment to full employment, to the public ownership of strategic utilities and support for the welfare state. Both labour and capital were to share in the common objectives (and rewards) of sustained economic growth. This compromise was to be managed by the overarching presence of the government, which would co-ordinate relations between unions and employers, secure the background conditions for economic growth and administer the welfare state. In its *party* form, consensus indicated broad agreement on the constitutional rules of the political game, the marginalization of the extremes of both left and right (both within and outside 'mainstream' parties), a political style of compromise and bargaining, the broad acceptance of predecessors' legislation and the 'mobilization of bias' in favour of certain interests and ideas, including organized capital, organized labour and Keynesian economics (Kavanagh, 1987, pp. 6–7).

In both formulations, there were certain core public policy elements around which the compromise was built. Internationally, there was an endorsement of the open international market and commitment to 'the collective defence of the Western world' (both under American leadership). Domestically, it meant a commitment to (1) the maintenance of a comprehensive welfare state, (2) support of the 'mixed economy' of private and public enterprise and (3) policies of full employment and sustained economic growth.[16]

For many commentators in the 1950s and 1960s, the coming of the post-war era of consensus politics seemed to herald 'an irreversible change'. Within the sphere of the welfare state, Tom Marshall argued in 1965 that there was now 'little difference of opinion as to the services that must be provided, and it is generally agreed that, whoever provides them, the overall responsibility for the welfare of the citizens must remain with the state' (Marshall, 1975, p. 97). Still more confidently, Charles Schottland proclaimed that 'whatever its beginnings, the welfare state is here to stay. Even its opponents argue only about its extension' (Schottland, 1969, p. 14). Much more recently, Mishra comments that 'state commitment to maintaining full employment, providing a range of basic services for all citizens, and preventing or relieving poverty seemed so integral to post-war society as to be almost irreversible' (Mishra, 1984, p. 1). We have already noted that recent scholarship has cast doubt upon the reality of the post-war consensus. Most sceptically, Ben Pimlott has written of 'the myth of consensus', while Deakin insists of the British experience that while 'real convergences in policy between the major political parties and individuals within them certainly took place . . . there was far less homogeneity than is usually believed' (Deakin, 1987; Pimlott, 1988; Taylor-Gooby, 1985). In Sweden, once identified by right-wing social democrats

---

[16] On consensus, see Kavanagh and Morris (1989) and Deakin (1987); for a sceptical view see Pimlott (1988).

as the definitive terrain of the consensual 'middle way', there has been an attempt to redefine the historic accommodation of organized capital and organized labour as a temporary and strategic compromise of irreconcilable differences of interest which are now becoming increasingly manifest (Childs, 1961; Crosland, 1964; Tingsten, 1973; Tomasson, 1969, 1970; Scase, 1977a, 1977b; Korpi, 1979, 1983; Stephens, 1979; Himmelstrand et al., 1981; Pierson, 1986, 1991).

Yet even for its most enthusiastic supporters, the politics of consensus was always recognized to be a *positive-sum* game. Agreement rested upon the capacity to generate a growing economic surplus with which to satisfy simultaneously a multiplicity of disparate claims. In this way, it was reliant upon the fourth element we have identified in the post-war period, that is, the commitment to economic growth and full employment.

Economic growth was seemingly the irreplaceable foundation of the traditional welfare state. It was the basis of Keynesian policies to induce capital investment, the stimulus to support economic activity at levels securing full employment and the fount of resources for increased expenditure on health, education, welfare and social services. It was economic growth that made a reconciliation of the opposing interests of capital and labour viable and sustainable. Fittingly, what has been described as 'the Golden Age of the welfare state' was also a period of unprecedented and unparalleled growth in the international capitalist economy.

Table 4.6 gives some general indication of this growth. In the seven major OECD countries (which at the start of the 1950s accounted for 90 per cent of OECD output) annual growth in GNP stood at 4.4 per cent in the 1950s rising to 5.5 per cent in the years between 1960 and 1973. There

Table 4.6 Annual growth in GNP (7 major OECD countries), 1950–1981, Annual average percentage rates of increase (%)

	1950–60	*1960–73*	*1973–81*
Canada	4.0	5.6	2.8
France	4.5	5.6	2.6
W. Germany	7.8	4.5	2.0
Italy	5.8	5.2	2.4
Japan	10.9	10.4	3.6
UK	2.3	3.1	0.5
USA	3.3	4.2	2.3
Weighted average	4.4	5.5	2.3

Sources: OECD (1966, p. 20); Bruno and Sachs (1985, p. 155).

Table 4.7   Unemployment rates (6 major OECD countries), 1933–1983, Percentage of total labour force (%)

	1933	1959–67	1975	1983
France	–	0.7	4.1	8.0
W. Germany	14.8	1.2	3.6	8.0
Italy	5.9	6.2	5.8	9.7
Japan	–	1.4	1.9	2.6
UK	13.9	1.8	4.7	13.1
USA	20.5	5.3	8.3	9.5
Weighted average	13.0	2.8	4.7	8.5

Source: Godfrey (1986, p. 2).

was substantial international variation in rates of growth. The UK struggled to achieve growth above 3 per cent even in the years of most rapid expansion, while Japan's remarkable growth exceeded 10 per cent per annum throughout the period. In the years after 1960, a number of previously 'underdeveloped' economies (for example, in Spain, Portugal, Greece and Turkey) achieved levels of growth in excess of 6 per cent per annum. Throughout the 1950s and 1960s average annual growth rates within the OECD economies as a whole stood close to 5 per cent while inflation, though rising slowly, stayed below 4 per cent until the late 1960s. This contrasts sharply with experience after 1973 when the average rate of economic growth was more than halved (falling as low as 0.5 per cent in the UK). At the same time, inflation became a persistent problem, peaking at 14 per cent in 1974.

Table 4.7 reveals a parallel pattern in terms of employment. The years of sustained, low inflationary economic growth were also years of particularly low levels of unemployment. The period between 1950 and 1967 in which the average levels of unemployment in six major OECD countries stood at 2.8 per cent contrasts markedly with the experience in 1933 at the height of the depression, when unemployment reached 13 per cent. In fact, the figure for the 1960s is distorted by the persistently high levels of unemployment in Italy and the USA, all the other countries showing averages significantly below 2 per cent. These figures from the 1960s also contrast sharply with the experience after 1970. Unemployment rose throughout the 1970s, peaking at about 8.5 per cent in 1983. This period also saw a particularly steep increase in youth unemployment and in long-term unemployment. In Britain, for example, youth unemployment reached 23.4 per cent in 1983, the proportion of those unemployed for more than a year rose above 40 per cent in 1986, while overall unemployment rates in the early 1980s came close to the worst levels of the 1930s.

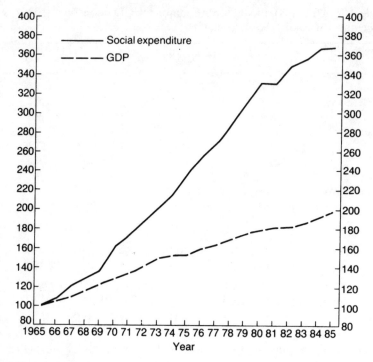

Figure 4.2   Real social expenditure and real GDP, 1965–1985 (1965 = 100).
Source: OECD (1988), p. 13.

Thus the 1950s and 1960s defined a period of sustained economic growth and full employment which contrasted not only with the pre-war years but also with experience after 1973.

Figure 4.2 illustrates the way in which this pattern of sustained economic growth was co-ordinated with an increase in the proportion of national product directed towards social expenditure.

'The Middle Class Welfare State'

Two further social and political consequences of this rapid growth of the welfare state in the post-war period are worthy of particular attention. First, expansion of the social budget brought with it some 'universalization' of the constituency of the welfare state. Tomasson has written of three characteristic phases in the development of the welfare state:

Social welfare before the First World War was a concern of the political Right for the poor. Between the World Wars social welfare was adopted as an issue by the political Left, still for the poor. After the Second World War social welfare became a concern of both right and left but . . . 'not for the poor alone'. (Tommason, 1983, p. ix)

Rarely has the post-war welfare state served simply the interests of society's poorest and most distressed. Almost everywhere, 'the non-poor play a crucial role of (variously) creating, expanding, sustaining, reforming and dismantling the welfare state' (Goodin and Le Grand, 1987, p. 3). Consequently, the nature of *middle class* involvement has been one of the most important (if sometimes neglected) aspects of later welfare state evolution. In fact, the expansion of the welfare state in the post-war period has tended to benefit members of the middle class both (1) as *consumers*, giving rights of access to facilities in health care, education, housing, transport and so on which 'actually benefited the middle classes . . . in many cases more than the poor' and (2) as *providers*, increasing professional employment opportunities within the public sector (Goodin and Le Grand, 1987, p. 91). As Goodin and Le Grand's work on the British welfare state suggests (table 4.8), perhaps counter-intuitively, it is often middle class elements that have been the principal beneficiaries of such redistribution as the broad welfare state allows.

Table 4.8 The distribution of public expenditure on the British social services

Service	Ratio of expenditure per person in top fifth to that per person in bottom fifth
Pro-poor	
Council housing	0.3
Equal	
Primary education	0.9
Secondary education	0.9
Pro-rich	
National Health Service	1.4
Secondary education (16+)	1.8
Non-university higher education	3.5
Bus subsidies	3.7
Universities	5.4
Tax subsidies to owner-occupiers	6.8
Rail subsidies	9.8

Source: Goodin and Le Grand (1987, p. 92).

The Growth of Welfare State Employment

A second general consequence of the rapid expansion of the welfare state in the post-war period is to be found in the radical changes in the composition of the workforce that it has effected. The state, and more especially the welfare state, is now a major employer in all advanced societies. In the 1980s, the British National Health Service was the single largest employer in Western Europe with an annual wages bill in excess of £13 billion (Department of Health, 1989). Within the more general shift in employment from manufacturing to the service sector, state welfare has had a peculiarly prominent role. Studying changes in employment patterns in Germany, Sweden, the USA and the UK, Martin Rein concludes that between the early 1960s and the 1980s, social welfare and 'services to business' have been the only two areas of the service sector of the economy to experience real growth. By the latter period, the 'social welfare industry' accounted for between 11 per cent (Germany) and 26 per cent (Sweden) of overall employment, and social welfare jobs accounted for 20–40 per cent of all employment in the service sector (Rein, 1985, pp. 39–40).

OECD figures suggest that in Denmark by the mid-1980s, government employment (about two-thirds of which is in the social welfare sector) *exceeded* employment in manufacturing. In other countries (for example, Norway and Sweden) the two sectors were close to parity, while in *every* country reviewed, the gap between employment in manufacturing and government services had significantly narrowed since the early 1970s (OECD, 1989, pp. 120–2). Rein noted that the consequences of expanded welfare state employment were particularly pronounced for women, and especially for those women who had passed through higher education. In 1981, between 65 and 75 per cent of college-educated women in Germany, Sweden and the USA were employed in the 'social welfare industries'. The growth of the welfare state has clearly been a major area of growth in female labour force participation, especially for the growing number of professionally qualified women (Rein, 1985, pp. 43–5).

A number of profound (political) consequences have been seen to follow from this pattern of middle class involvement and expanded employment within the welfare state. Therborn, for example, takes it as evidence of the 'creeping universalism' of the welfare state, which has rendered New Right attempts to dismantle it electorally impossible. For the New Right itself, the growth of a highly unionized, middle class public sector workforce was a major source of economic and political crisis in the 1970s. Others have identified new lines of electoral cleavage developing around the welfare state (reliance on the public sector v. reliance upon the private sector), displacing traditional cleavages along the lines of social class (Therborn, 1987; Dunleavy, 1980). Claus Offe has argued that the secure employment and comparative affluence which first attached the middle classes to the 'welfare state project' are now increasingly threatening their defection to neo-liberalism and a consequent residualization of state welfare. These themes are further developed in chapter 6. For now, we return to a more detailed assessment of social policy changes in the post-war period.

1945–1950: Reconstruction

Within the very broad parameters of 'the Golden Age' or more soberly the era of welfare state expansion between 1945 and 1975, it is both possible and useful to offer some further periodization. Thus we may think of the immediate post-war period down to 1950 as defining a period of reconstruction following the debacle of the Second World War. In this period, a number of countries created that broad and systematic platform upon which the developed welfare state was based. In the UK, even before the end of the war, the coalition government had passed legislation to reform secondary education and to introduce family allowances. In the immediate post-war period, the Labour government (partially) implemented Beveridge's reform proposals with the setting up of the National Health Service, the final abolition of the Poor Law and the reconstruction of national insurance and national assistance. The essentials of the post-war British welfare state were in place by 1948.

In France, where social policy enhancement between the wars had been modest, there was a 'major commitment to social security in 1945 and 1946' (Ashford and Kelley, 1986, p. 257). This included a law providing sickness and disability insurance, pension legislation and a law providing for the aged poor. There was also an enhancement of the 1932 family allowances legislation, providing pre-natal payments, additional payments for the third child and a rising scale of benefits as families grew larger (Ashford, 1986a, pp. 183–4). In Finland, where pre-war provision had been still more limited, the years between 1945 and 1950 saw a spectacular average growth rate in social expenditure of 22.2 per cent. Social expenditure as a proportion of central government spending rose from 3 to 13 per cent in the same period. Most of this increased effort was directed towards children and families, health care, the organization of social services, benefits for war victims and state-supported housing construction (Alestalo and Uusitalo, 1986, pp. 202–3, 246). Similarly in Ireland, 'the period from 1945 to the early 1950s was a time of heightened interest and activity in the area of social policy'. During these years, the share of social expenditure in GDP rose by almost six percentage points. The reforms included the enhancement of public health provision, the expansion of social insurance coverage and improved state aid for housing in both the public and private sectors (Maguire, 1986, pp. 246–8, 252; Kennedy, 1975, p. 5).

Not every developed capitalist country participated in this rapid enhancement of social legislation after 1945. In Italy, for example, proposals for a systematic reform of social insurance were rejected following the election of a Christian Democrat-dominated coalition government in 1948, which opted instead to restore the pre-war institutional framework (Ferrera, 1986, p. 390, 1989, p. 124). In New Zealand, the major period of welfare state expansion had *preceded* the Second World War, while it has been said that 'by the end of the Labour administration in 1949 Australia hardly possessed a welfare state' (M. A. Jones, 1980, p. 36). However, the single most (strategic) nation in this period of international welfare state expansion was probably the 'laggardly' USA. While Bowles and Gintis (1982) identify the emergence of a 'capital labor accord' in a number of legislative initiatives in the immediate post-war years, additions to America's own 'semi-welfare state' were quite limited. It was, however, American military and economic power which underwrote the post-war reconstruction of Europe and the new political and economic order of which the welfare state was an essential feature. America was the guarantor and sponsor of Western Europe's 'embedded liberalism' (economic liberalism in a context of state intervention), and thus 'ironically, it was American hegemony that provided the basis for the development and expansion of the European welfare states' (Keohane, 1984, pp. 16–17).

1950–1960: Relative Stagnation

By contrast with the burst of legislative and executive action in the immediate post-war years, which for many commentators heralds the *real* coming of the welfare state, the 1950s was a decade of relative stagnation. In what was generally a period of sustained economic growth, the proportion of resources directed to social expenditure rose very slowly compared with both the years before 1950 and those after 1960. In Western Europe, the average growth in central government social expenditure as a percentage of GDP was something under 1 per cent for the whole decade (Flora, 1987b, vol. 1, pp. 345–449). Strong economic growth means that such figures often mask sustained growth in real social expenditure. Jens Alber writes of the period 1951–8 as the 'take-off' phase of the West German welfare state, but while average real growth in welfare expenditure rose over 10 per cent, its share in a rapidly growing GDP rose by just three percentage points in the same period. Social expenditure commanded a very similar proportion of national wealth at the end of the decade as it had at its beginning (Alber, 1988b; Alber 1986, pp. 15–16; Maguire, 1986, pp. 321–30). However, there were some countries in which the proportion of social expenditure actually fell during the 1950s. In Ireland, for example, central government social expenditure as a proportion of GDP fell by 3.6 percentage points between 1951 and 1960. The share of social expenditure in GDP did not recover its 1951 level until 1964. In the period between 1952 and 1966, public social security expenditure in Australia rose by two percentage points, but this was from 6.1 per cent of GNP to a still modest 8.2 per cent. In New Zealand, growth in the same period was less than 1 per cent (Kaim-Caudle, 1973, p. 53). Of course, these figures for proportionate social expenditure do not give an exhaustive description of welfare state developments. Political disputes over welfare policy – the Swedish pension reforms of 1957 or the introduction of health charges by the British Labour government in 1951, for example – are not captured by these statistics (Esping-Andersen, 1985; Sked and Cook, 1984, p. 96). Nonetheless, the contrast with the 1940s and the 1960s is quite clear.

A number of reasons have been advanced to explain this comparative decline in social expenditure growth. Some have suggested that need was adequately met by the levels of expenditure established in the late 1940s. Others point to the increased private affluence and low unemployment achieved in the sustained economic growth of the 1950s. For some, the element of mutual risk and austerity which war-time conditions generated had evaporated by the 1950s. Tom Marshall wrote that 'the welfare state reigned unchallenged while linked with the Austerity Society and was attacked from all sides as soon as it became associated with the Affluent Society' (Marshall, 1963, p. 282). Others argued that the succession of defeats of left-wing governments marked a political realignment towards the right and the end of the zeal for reform which had characterized the immediate post-war years.

1960–1975: Major Expansion

From about 1960 onwards, we enter a third phase in the post-war development of the welfare state, one that lasts some fifteen years and which is best characterized as an era of major expansion. In terms of the resources devoted to social expenditure, this is perhaps the most remarkable period in the whole evolution of the international welfare states. Thus, the proportion of GDP devoted to social expenditure rose from 12.3 per cent in 1960 to 21.9 per cent in 1975. Both absolute levels and rates of growth varied. By 1975, six countries – France, Germany, Belgium, Denmark, the Netherlands and Sweden – were devoting in excess of 25 per cent of their GDP to social expenditure. Amongst the seven major OECD economies, only Japan (13.7 per cent), the USA (18.7 per cent) and the UK (19.6 per cent) now devoted less than a fifth of GDP to social expendi-

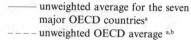

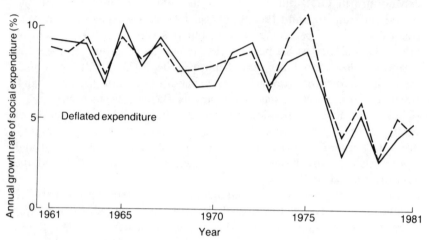

Figure 4.3   The growth of social expenditure in the OECD area, 1960–1981

[a] Prior to 1975 there are no figures for expenditure on education in France. Therefore, only the growth rates for the years after 1975 reflect the growth in expenditure on education in France. The pattern of growth rates over these later years is unaffected by their inclusion.

[b] Average for 17 countries (excluding Denmark and Switzerland except for 1981, when Belgium and Greece are also excluded).

Source: OECD (1985a, p. 19).

ture. In the 1960–75 period, average annual growth in deflated social expenditure was in excess of 8 per cent in Australia, Denmark, Japan and Norway. It fell below 4 per cent only in the UK and Austria. The overall average for the OECD countries throughout this period was 6.5 per cent per annum (OECD, 1988, p. 11).

As figure 4.3 illustrates, the annual growth rate of deflated social expenditure ranged between 7 and 10 per cent throughout the period 1960–75. It experienced a sharp rise in the period immediately after 1973 but fell sharply after 1975. The average growth rate for the years 1975–81 is little more than half of what it had been in the period prior to 1975.

Again, while there was some international variation, three areas – education, health and pensions – commanded some four-fifths of resources throughout this period. There was some change in the distribution of effort between these three areas as expenditure on education first rose and then declined, while expenditure on health and pensions increased steadily. Of the three, pensions appeared to be least vulnerable to retrenchment following the economic reverses of the mid-1970s. Even with the rapidly rising levels of joblessness in the late 1970s, unemployment compensation remained a minor programme, commanding on average less than 5 per cent of social expenditure (OECD, 1985a).

A number of reasons have been advanced to explain this remarkable growth. In part, these are demographic, reflecting not just the growing numbers of old age pensioners but also the rise in the ratio of elderly (who are also disproportionate users of health services) to the economically active. Some point to the central role of the growth of prosperity in this period as generating the necessary resources for the expansion of social programmes (Alber, 1988b). Others offer more political explanations of the growth of social spending stressing, for example, the mobilization of labour movements, socialist parties and others (including the civil rights movement in the USA) in favour of enhanced welfare; the essential role of social spending as a part of the 'capital-labour' accommodation of the post-war consensus; the growing density and capacity of interest groups to mobilize in favour of sectional interests within the welfare state; the increase in urbanization and educational provision leading to greater social and political mobilization.

Many commentators link these explanations of the rapid growth of the welfare state down to 1975 with its problems or 'crisis' thereafter. Indeed, in more or less apocalyptic terms, 1975 is often seen to mark the endpoint of nearly one hundred years of welfare state growth and to bring the threat or promise of its imminent dismemberment. It is to the distinctive theories and experiences of this most recent period that we turn in chapter 5.

5
After the 'Golden Age'
From 'Crisis' Through 'Containment' to 'Structural Adjustment'

Most commentators on the historical evolution of the welfare state have been agreed in identifying a break with a long-standing pattern of growth and development in international social policy from the early or middle years of the 1970s. Some have done no more than draw attention to the slackening pace of welfare state growth in this period (Flora, 1986; Alber, 1988a). Others, particularly those writing from the perspective of the 1970s, drew a much more alarming picture of 'crisis' and 'contradiction' in the welfare state, an unstable condition which challenged either the continuation of the welfare state or even the integrity of the democratic capitalist order itself. It was in this period of the early and mid-1970s that social democratic confidence in the competence of the mixed economy and the welfare state to deliver continuing economic growth allied to greater social equity came under increasing challenge. It was also, as we have seen, the period of the flowering of New Right and neo-Marxist accounts of the welfare state, both of which concentrated on the ubiquity of crisis arising from the inherently unstable and contradictory elements within the post-war welfare capitalist consensus. Twenty-five years later, these more apocalyptic visions of the 'end of the welfare state' seem misplaced. Yet contemporary social policy regimes do seem quite different from those that prevailed in the period down to the 1970s. In this chapter, we seek to make sense of this rather puzzling recent trajectory of the welfare state.

Even in the 1970s, the belief that welfare capitalism was beset by contradictions and vulnerable to crisis was not all that new. It is a view rooted in the work of the great classical political economists and it had continued to be voiced by a minority on both left and right throughout the post-war 'Golden Age' of welfare. What was new in the 1970s was not so much the arguments themselves as their remarkable authority. It seemed as if, in an instant, 'complacency about the momentum of the welfare state gave way to doom-mongering by many in the intellectual elite' (Heclo, 1981, p. 399). With astonishing speed, the warnings of a looming crisis (particularly those of the New Right) seemed to replace the benign assumptions of social democracy as a privileged discourse among governing and 'opinion-forming' elites.

Yet precisely what was intended by the newly authoritative discourse of 'crisis' and 'contradiction' is not entirely clear. Alec Pemberton complains that the meaning of 'contradiction' in Marxist analyses of the welfare state has always been 'notoriously imprecise'. He identifies two main variants: (1) contradiction as '*paradox*' (as in the claim that 'the working class struggles for welfare rights but this inadvertently strengthens the position of capital'), and (2) contradiction as '*opposite effect*' (as in the argument that 'the welfare state is introduced to assist the needy and deprived but, in practice, it worsens their position'). The principal difficulty identified in both usages is that it is unclear in what sense the relationships specified are truly 'contradictory'. The outcomes described may be perverse or even establish 'real oppositions', but they do not entail a contradiction which, properly speaking, is a description of the relationship between two logically inconsistent statements (of the kind, 'This is the final crisis of capitalism/This is not the final crisis of capitalism') (Pemberton, 1983, pp. 289–308; Benton, 1977; Offe, 1984, pp. 130–46). Although Pemberton's strictures are addressed to the neo-Marxist literature, the New Right employ the idea of contradiction in much the same way and the criticism may be applied with similar effect to their usage.

Similar difficulties surround the still more widespread usage, by both right and left, of the idea of a *crisis* of the welfare state. We can identify four distinct senses in which 'crisis' is regularly employed in contemporary discussions. The first (deriving from its medical and dramaturgical origins) sees crisis as a decisive phase in a process in which a long-standing or deep-seated struggle must be resolved one way or another. By analogy, this has been extended to describe any particularly strategic or decisive episode in the historical or social process (Rader, 1979, p. 187). A second usage understands crisis as 'a catastrophe caused by an external blow' (Moran, 1988, p. 397). Offe describes this as a *sporadic crisis concept*, in which the crisis is confined to one event or brief series of events. Offe himself prefers a third contemporary notion, that of 'a *processual* concept of crisis'. Here, crises are 'developmental tendencies that can be confronted with "*counteracting tendencies*" making it possible to relate the crisis-prone developmental tendencies of a system to the characteristics of the system'. On this reading, crises 'need not be seen as catastrophic events having a contingent origin', rather they relate directly to ƈ Offe's (neo-Marxist) sense of contradiction as 'the tendency inherent within a specific mode of production to destroy those very preconditions on which its survival depends' (Offe, 1984, pp. 36–7). These contradictions, when seen within the capitalist mode of production, may call forth 'counteracting tendencies' (this is, indeed, very largely what the welfare state is) but the structural and systemic limitations upon such counteracting tendencies reveal a chronic likelihood 'that contradictions will finally result in a *crisis* of the capitalist mode of production' (Offe, 1984, p. 133). At the same time, all of these more or less technical uses of the term are overlain by the ubiquitous and devalued modern currency of 'crisis' used to describe any (and every) large-scale contemporary problem.

For all its advocates, the idea of a 'crisis of the welfare state' may thus have a wide range of meanings. We may isolate the most important of these as:

- crisis as *turning point*
- crisis as *external shock*
- crisis as *'long-standing contradiction'*
- crisis as *any large-scale or long-standing problem.*

The Crisis of the Post-war Welfare State

The idea of a crisis or of contradictions surrounding the welfare state is then neither entirely new, nor unproblematically clear. We can, however, isolate the early 1970s as the period in which (particularly in the Anglo-American context) the idea of a crisis of the welfare state achieved an unparalleled prominence. The late 1960s had seen the emergence of a growing discontent among both left and right libertarians about the enervating bureaucratic and statist aspects of social welfare (Illich, 1973, 1978; Lasch, 1978, p. 224). It had also been a period of growing political mobilization and renewed industrial action, notably within the public sector trade unions that had themselves been a by-product of welfare state expansion (Jackson, 1987; Hyman, 1989b; Giddens, 1981). All of these contributed to a climate in which social conflict was of renewed interest. But it was above all the end to uninterrupted post-war economic growth that undermined the incremental confidence of the social democrats and set the stage for 'the new pessimism' (Heclo, 1981, p. 398).

The nature of 'the Golden Age' of post-war capitalism is now itself much debated. There has been some tendency to redraw (and shorten) the parameters of the period of sustained economic growth and comparative social peace – on which both the 'end of ideology' and the perspective of open-ended economic expansion were premised – to cover little more than the fifteen years between 1950 and the mid-1960s.[1] But, wherever one places 'the beginning of the end' of this era, by the early 1970s the signs of economic difficulty were unmistakable and the five-fold increase in oil prices which OPEC was able to impose in 1973 precipitated (rather than caused) a severe slump throughout the western industrialized world.

A few figures will illustrate the scale of this economic 'crisis'. Between 1965 and 1973, the economies of the OECD countries showed an annual average growth rate of about 5 per cent. In 1974, this annual growth rate fell to 2 per cent and in 1975, nine OECD economies 'shrank', bringing the annual average growth rate below zero. Although there was some recovery from this low point, there was to be a second oil-price 'shock' in 1979, and for the decade 1974 to 1984, annual average growth was little over 2 per cent (Alber, 1988a, p. 187). Nor were these economic difficulties confined to sluggish growth. By 1975, unemployment in the OECD area had risen to an unprecedented 15 million, a figure that had doubled within a decade (OECD, 1989b). At the same time, inflation accelerated and there was a growing balance of trade deficit throughout the OECD. The 'misery index' (the rate of inflation plus the rate of unemployment) which, for the seven major OECD countries, had averaged 5.5 per cent through the 1960s had risen to 17 per cent by 1974/5. At the same time, levels of investment and levels of profitability fell, while the value of disposable incomes stagnated. Governments throughout the developed West were simultaneously failing to achieve the four major economic policy objectives – growth, low inflation, full employment and balance of trade – on which the post-war order had been based (Gough, 1979, p. 132; Goldthorpe, 1984, p. 2).

One of the clearest manifestations of this economic crisis was growing public indebtedness. As the economic recession deepened, so demands upon public, and especially social, expenditure grew, in part through the inertia of incrementalism, but also through costs that rose directly from economic decline (the costs of enlarged unemployment and social benefits claims). At the same time as demand grew, with the slump in tax-generating growth, revenue declined. This manifested itself in a 'yawning gap between expenditure and revenues' and a rapid growth in the public sector borrowing requirement (PSBR). Most acutely in the period 1973–5, as economic growth (and the capacity to fund state expenditure) declined, public expenditure increased (Gough, 1979, p. 132). About half of the 10 per cent growth in the share of GDP devoted to public expenditure in the OECD countries between 1960 and 1975 occurred in 1974 and

---

[1] The earliest version of O'Connor's fiscal crisis theory appeared in 1970. On the post-war period, see Deakin (1987); Kavanagh and Morris (1989).

1975 (OECD, 1985a, p. 14). In the same period, specifically social spending (on education, health, income maintenance and other welfare services) had taken an increasing share of this enhanced public expenditure, rising from 47.5 per cent in 1960 to 58.5 per cent by 1981 (OECD, 1985a, p. 21). Consequently, concern about state indebtedness and public expenditure was above all concern about the costs of the welfare state.

Different governments responded to this challenge in differing ways and there was not only the customary discrepancy between what these governments *said* and what they *did* but also a divide between what these governments *did* and what people *widely believed them to have done.* But we now have sufficient evidence to place in context the 'crisis' theories of the early and mid-1970s, theories which were themselves a response to these profound economic difficulties and to the short-term reaction of government agencies.

Welfare Capitalism: from 'Contingent Crisis' to 'Systemic Contradiction'?

Perhaps the earliest response to the economic crisis of the early 1970s was to understand it, in Offe's terms, as a 'sporadic crisis'. Upon this view, the essentially sound and well-ordered international capitalist system had been subjected to an 'external shock' or series of shocks which had temporarily thrown it out of equilibrium. Most prominent among these shocks was the oil price increase of 1973 which had precipitated the deep recession of 1974 and 1975. Other candidates for disruption were the consequences of the longstanding US involvement in Vietnam, the rapid rise of (non-oil) basic commodity costs (notably of basic foods) and the breakdown of international monetary exchange relations. What was crucial about all these 'shocks' was that they were essentially *exogenous* (from outside the system) and if not non-replicable (after all OPEC could, and did, impose a second oil price hike) then certainly *contingent.* Paul McKracken's 1977 Report prepared for the OECD, probably the most celebrated statement of this position, concluded that the recession of the early 1970s arose from 'an unusual bunching of unfortunate disturbances unlikely to be repeated on the same scale, the impact of which was compounded by some considerable errors in economic policy' (OECD, 1977). Upon such an account, crisis was *external* to the welfare state in two senses. First, the source of (temporary) economic problems lay outside the prevailing international market order and second, insofar as there was a knock-on problem of funding for the welfare state, this was one which was wholly attributable to the shortfall in economic product and not to the (damaging) interrelationship between social welfare and economic performance.

However, this essentially optimistic view – of a 'hiccup' in economic growth leading to a temporary pause in welfare state growth – was increasingly overtaken in the welfare state area by studies which stressed the contradictions *within the mixed economy* (or liberal representative democracy or welfare capitalism) as the *real* source of crisis. The five-fold increase in crude oil prices was simply the dramatic precipitating event which disclosed the deep-seated *structural* weaknesses of the post-war political economy which had been in the making for twenty-five years, and was manifest to the discerning eye since at least the late 1960s. At the heart of this account was the claim that the end of the period of post-war economic growth was not externally caused but *inherent* in the social, political and economic order of the post-war consensus and especially in its ameliorating institutions for the management of economically based political conflict.

It will be recalled from chapter 2 that this was precisely the position adopted by both New Right and neo-Marxist commentators in response to the events of the early 1970s. For both schools, this crisis could not be understood as 'simply' economic. Rather it was a crisis of the social and political order established after 1945 under the rubric of the Keynesian Welfare State. For both, the problems of the early 1970s expressed the economic and political contradictions inherent in a democratic capitalist society. Such an analysis embraced two further senses of crisis. First, for all of these commentators the post-war order was threatened by the consequences of deep-seated and *'long-standing contradiction'*. Also, typically in its earliest, boldest and most apocalyptic formulations, this perspective raised the spectre of a historical *turning point*. That is, the contradictions of the post-war order were now so acute that a *radical* change was no longer simply desirable, it had become unavoidable. Whatever the radical alternatives, the status quo was not an option.

The neo-Marxist variant of this view was first stated with some force at the turn of the 1970s in O'Connor's *Fiscal Crisis of the State*. O'Connor's study centred upon the claim that 'the capitalistic state must try to fulfil two basic and often mutually contradictory functions – *accumulation* and *legitimization*'. On the one hand, the state must try to maintain or create the conditions under which profitable capital accumulation is possible; on the other, it must also try to maintain or create the conditions for 'social harmony'. He expands the contradiction thus:

A capitalist state that openly uses its coercive forces to help one class accumulate capital at the expense of other classes loses its legitimacy and hence undermines the basis of its loyalty and support. But a state that ignores the necessity of assisting the process of capital accumulation risks drying up the source of its own power, the economy's surplus production capacity and the taxes drawn from this surplus. (O'Connor, 1973, p. 6)

In essence, these imperatives of accumulation and legitimation are *contradictory*. Expenditure to secure legitimization is essential, to defray the otherwise potentially explosive social and political costs of capitalist development, yet these costs must themselves be met via state revenues derived from the profits of capital accumulation. In this way the costs of legitimization, which are to secure circumstances for successful capital accumulation, themselves tend to undermine the very process of profitable accumulation. Correspondingly,

> The socialization of costs and the private appropriation of profits creates a fiscal crisis, or 'structural gap', between state expenditures and state revenues. The result is a tendency for state expenditures to increase more rapidly than the means of financing them. (O'Connor, 1973, p. 9)

This fiscal crisis is intensified by the pluralistic structure and accessibility of liberal democratic politics, which privileges the servicing of organized interests, furnishing 'a great deal of waste, duplication and overlapping of state projects and services'. Thus, 'the accumulation of social capital and social expenses is a highly irrational process from the standpoint of administrative coherence, fiscal stability and potentially profitable capital accumulation' (O'Connor, 1973, p. 9). By the early 1970s in the USA (which was the focus of O'Connor's study) these problems had become intense. Growing tax resistance, intensified hostility to the authority of government, growing mobilization by new social movements among welfare recipients, heightened politicization among a growingly unionized state workforce all intensified those pressures upon government, which generated fiscal crisis. O'Connor insisted that 'by the late 1960s, the local fiscal crisis was almost completely out of hand' and federal attempts to cope with this simply intensified the difficulties at national level (O'Connor, 1973, p. 212). O'Connor doubted that the crisis could be resolved within the parameters of the existing order. For him, 'the only lasting solution to the crisis is socialism' (O'Connor, 1973, p. 221).[2]

The New Right and the Crisis of Liberal Representative Democracy

Even more influential and dramatic as an account of the crisis of the welfare state in this period were the writings of the New Right. From the turn of the 1970s, the technical arguments of Hayek and the public choice

---

[2] It is worth recalling that there were other important neo-Marxist accounts of this process which were less functionalist in character and placed a greater stress upon welfare politics as an aspect of class struggle (see, for example, Piven and Cloward, 1971; Navarro, 1978).

theorists (discussed in chapter 2) were given an enhanced prominence by critics who insisted that the general contradictions underlying social democracy were now beginning to manifest themselves in an immediate and profound crisis of the existing political order. In a 1975 *Report on the Governability of Democracies*, Michael Crozier argued that within Western Europe

> the operations of the democratic process . . . appear to have generated a breakdown of traditional means of social control, a delegitimation of political and other forms of authority, and an overload of demands on government, exceeding its capacity to respond. (Crozier, Huntington and Watanuki, 1975, p. 8)

For the neo-conservatives, the core of this 'democratic distemper' lay in the decline in respect for traditional sources of authority and in the break with traditional constraints upon individual aspirations. At the same time as democratic publics made greatly increased demands of their governments, they were becoming less willing to accept the decisions taken by these public authorities. Indeed, the decline in respect for executive authority and the decline in support for mainstream political parties suggested a general decline in attachment to the traditional forms of representative democratic life. There was a growing mobilization of sectional demands with no recognition of a greater public interest, whether or not represented by the existing government. At the same time, sustained post-war economic growth, the institutionalization of the welfare state and the 'bidding-up' process of adversarial democratic politics had generated a 'revolution of rising expectations' among democratic publics. They were increasingly disposed to claim as non-negotiable 'rights', goods and services to which they had no sound claim. Decline of authority and mutual responsibility within the family meant that social welfare functions traditionally met within the private and family sector generated new claims upon the state – and a population increasingly dependent upon state beneficence.

If for the neo-conservatives, the major problem was one of declining social control and public authority, for the neo-liberals, following the public choice theorists, the major difficulties lay in the relationship between representative liberal democracy and the market economy. Thus, Samuel Brittan wrote in 1975 of the danger of the (self-)destruction of liberal representative democracy being precipitated by 'two endemic threats':

- the generation of excessive expectations and
- the disruptive effects of the pursuit of group self-interest in the market place.

In essence, the 'growth of expectations imposes demands for different kinds of public spending and intervention which are incompatible both with each other and with the tax burden that people are willing to bear' (Brittan, 1975, pp. 129–31). Marrying Schumpeter's account of democracy as the process of elite competition for votes to the insights of the public choice theorists, Brittan argued that liberal representative democracy is imperilled by two underlying weaknesses.[3] First, the process of political competition generates unrealistic and excessive expectations about the possibilities afforded by government action among a largely (and rationally) uninformed voting public. Parties and politicians are systematically disposed to promise 'more for less'. A party which reminds the electorate of the necessary relationship between income and expenditure is likely to prove unelectable. Secondly, the growth of well-organized sectional interests (most especially trade unions) and especially their willingness to use this power to achieve sectional ends intensifies the difficulties of reconciling liberal and democratic government with national economic solvency. In the short term, this contradiction is likely to manifest itself in rising inflation, but 'in the last analysis the authorities have to choose between accepting an indefinite increase in the rate of inflation and abandoning full employment to the extent necessary to break the collective wage-push power of the unions'. However, such governments may be forced 'to choose between very high rates of unemployment and very high rates of inflation, neither of which can be sustained in a liberal democracy' (Brittan, 1975, p. 143). Consequently, Brittan judged that 'on present indications', liberal representative democracy 'is likely to pass away within the lifetime of people now adult' (Brittan, 1975, p. 129).

There were other elements in these accounts of the 1970s. Some argued that the growth in resources and personnel directed towards the public sector as a consequence of the rise of the post-war welfare state had 'crowded out' the private sector investment upon which continued economic growth was dependent. Bacon and Eltis argued of the British experience that there was 'a strong case' for maintaining that 'the great increase in public-sector employment that occurred in Britain in 1961–75 [largely within the welfare state sector] played a significant role in the deterioration of Britain's economic performance' (Bacon and Eltis, 1978, p. 16). Some stressed the growing difficulties of government macro-management in a more open world economy. Others highlighted the particularly entrenched position of public sector trade unions (itself a by-product of expanded welfare state employment), whose wages were politically rather than market-determined (Rose and Peters, 1978, p. 23; Brittan, 1975).

---

[3] On Schumpeter's account of democracy as elite competition, see Schumpeter (1976); Held (1987, pp. 164–85).

For many of these commentators, government overload was intimately related to the spectre of growing *ungovernability*. Rose and Peters, for example, argued that a number of Western governments faced the imminent prospect of 'political bankruptcy' should they fail to show 'the political will to limit growth' of public expenditure in times of declining economic growth and falling take-home pay. While such 'political bankruptcy' would not mean anarchy and fighting in the streets, it would lead to an increase in citizen hostility to the conventional political process, accelerate the process of citizen indifference to the conduct of government and, perhaps most seriously, aggravate the tendency towards tax resistance, with an accompanying growth in the black economy (Rose and Peters, 1978, pp. 31–7). Most apocalyptically, Peter Jay insisted that 'the very survival of democracy hangs by a gossamer thread' and that 'democracy has itself by the tail and is eating itself up fast' (Jay, 1977).

Not all these commentators were so iconoclastic (nor can they all be identified unproblematically with the New Right). Rose and Peters, for example, insisted that any 'attempt to dismantle the policies of the contemporary welfare state would be a response out of all proportion to the cause of the problem' (Rose and Peters, 1978, pp. 38, 232). Yet all were convinced that the continuation of the welfare state status quo was not an option.

Crisis? What Crisis?

By the end of the 1970s, it seemed clear that expectations of a system-threatening crisis – whether a legitimation crisis of welfare capitalism or a crisis of governability of liberal representative democracy – were ungrounded. Nowhere in the advanced capitalist world had the system of representative democracy broken down and certainly no-one could argue that the crisis of welfare capitalism had been resolved by a rapid transition to socialism! Certainly, there had been considerable resistance to retrenchment of public expenditure and rising levels of unemployment. There was some (extremely approximate) evidence of growth in the black economy (a 1986 OECD report placed it at between 2 and 8 per cent of total hours worked in the developed economies) and limited evidence of tax resistance, notably in the meteoric rise of the anti-tax Progress Party in Denmark in 1973 and in the passage of Proposition 13 statutorily restricting state taxation in California (OECD, 1986b). Yet none of this represented a real challenge to the prevailing order which had seemingly been endorsed by the electoral success of right-wing parties in the late 1970s and early 1980s. How then, with hindsight, should we evaluate the 'crisis' theories of the 1970s?

Welfare State Crisis as 'External Shock'

With the rise to prominence of the more dramatic accounts of the New Right and the neo-Marxists, it became commonplace to dismiss the idea of a 'one-off' crisis arising from the quintupling of oil prices as a naive hankering for the 'good old days' of social peace and economic growth of the 1950s and 1960s. Certainly, it was a view with very real weaknesses. First, its confidence in the early re-establishment of the political and economic *status quo ante* was misplaced. Secondly, it lacked a sense of the inter-relatedness of the political and economic problems of the advanced capitalist societies. Finally, it showed little awareness of the very real changes in the balance of economic and political forces that had been the consequence of twenty-five years of post-war economic growth. Yet it is an approach which, with the benefit of still more hindsight, can be seen to have had some substantial strengths. Certainly, the crisis presented itself to many contemporaries as a problem of inadequate economic resources (trying to pay for more welfare with a stagnating national product) and there is indeed good reason to think that the crisis of the early 1970s was, in some senses, much more 'purely economic' than later critics were to allow. Thus, much of the perceived 'spiralling' of welfare costs was due not to 'democratic distemper' but to the logic of demographic pressure and statutory entitlement under circumstances of recession. Further, as the more spectacular predictions of neo-Marxists and New Right analysts failed to materialize, it seems that the difficulties of the welfare state are indeed more substantially about the shortfall of resources available to fund further growth. Such a belief is buttressed by evidence that the best indicator of the capacity of national welfare states to weather the difficulties of the 1970s was not so much a reflection of their *political* complexion (the intensity of their democratic contradictions) as of a given nation's *economic* strength before the 1970s and of its capacity to absorb the oil shock of 1973 (Schmidt, 1983, pp. 1–26).

Even if we concentrate solely upon economic developments, however, it is clear that the changes observed in the early 1970s were both more profound and longer-lasting than the idea of a one-off 'shock to the system' suggests. This new economic context is not adequately defined by one or two hikes in the price of basic commodities but rather by a whole series of changes in the international political economy which cumulatively shattered the stability of the post-war economic order. Such changes include the decline in stable exchange rates, the loss of the hegemonic role of the USA, changing international terms of trade, the rise of newly industrialized countries, changing financial institutions and the sustained impact of new technologies.

The Welfare State and the Crisis of Liberal Democratic Capitalism

The theoretical poverty of the perspective of 'external shock' has often been contrasted with New Right or neo-Marxist critics who are seen to have penetrated the 'depth structure' of contradictions in the welfare state. Certainly, there are considerable strengths in the shared features of these accounts of crisis. They were among the first to develop a modern 'political economy' approach, indicating that while the *symptoms* of the difficulties of the 1970s were economic, their *causes* lay in the inter-relation of social, political and economic forces. They were also among the first to see that the recession of 1973–4 was not simply a 'blip' in the continuing process of unfettered post-war economic growth. They demonstrated that inflation had not just a political *consequence* but also, in part, a political *cause*. They drew out the political consequences of the growing complexity and complicity of government, of greater bureaucratic and organizational density and of the rise of organized and sectional interests, under circumstances of representative democracy and full employment.

The glaring weakness in this analysis, however, was that its claims about a challenge to advanced capitalism and/or liberal representative democracy went largely unfulfilled. In the UK, where the prognoses were often the most gloomy, there has been little real threat to the political process. There is evidence of growing electoral volatility (sometimes masked by the plurality voting system), of declining public deference to government, of the intensified prosecution of sectional interests and of a break with elements of consensus government. During the 1980s, there was an erosion of local government democracy, the circumscription of some civil liberties, the curtailment of trade union rights and quite substantial changes to the welfare state itself. All of these met with more or less fierce resistance. But there has been no real threat of a breakdown of liberal democratic government and, until the election of the Blair government, limited interest in major constitutional reform. In the same period, a right-wing government was returned to office four times, while welfare spending in the major areas (pensions, health and education) remained largely intact (Hills, 1997).

Why were analysts on both left and right so mistaken about the *consequences* of the welfare state structures they helped to reveal? First, there is an element of misunderstanding the nature of the welfare state. For the New Right, the welfare state was seen largely as an unproductive deadweight on the economy, imposed through the dynamics of irresponsible (social) democracy. In the prevalent Marxist account, the welfare state was the necessary legitimating trade-off for (the unacceptable social costs of) capital accumulation. For both, the inevitable outcome was fiscal crisis. But such a view is difficult to reconcile with the historical development of the welfare state outlined in chapter 4. The welfare state was *not* generally an imposition of organized labour through the pressure of electoral politics. It was as much (if not more) the product of conservative or liberal regimes. It was as frequently (if not more often) status-preserving or market-supporting as it was decommodifying. In fact, evidence that, as both New Right and neo-Marxists seem to assume, the welfare state dampens capitalist economic growth is limited at both 'micro' and 'macro' levels (Pfaller, Gough and Therborn, 1991). Similarly, the claims that public spending displaces private investment or that social benefits represent a real disincentive to labour are thinly grounded. Certainly, under some circumstances and as part of a broader constellation of forces, social spending might be complicit in poor economic performance. But this is something very different from the claim that social spending *causes* poor economic performance (Pen, 1987, pp. 346–7). Indeed, Nicholas Barr argues that the welfare state has a 'major efficiency role' and that, in a context of market failures, 'we need a welfare state for efficiency reasons, and would continue to do so even if all distributional problems had been solved' (Barr, 1987, p. 421; Blake and Ormerod, 1980; Block, 1987).

The British case is peculiarly instructive in this context. Britain was often portrayed in the literature of the 1970s as the country with the most pronounced problems of overload, ungovernability and welfare state malaise, so much so that this complex was often identified as 'the English disease' (see, for example, Jay, 1977). Yet we have seen that the UK was not an especially large welfare spender, nor were the terms of her social benefits either very generous or particularly 'decommodifying'. There were consistently more extensive and generous welfare states with a far better economic record. The size and disposition of the UK public sector and welfare state might contribute to Britain's economic difficulties, but only in a context of much longer established problems of economic growth and capital formation (Gamble, 1981). Conversely, as Mishra points out, New Right critics at least tended to neglect those welfare states with a good economic record (Austria, Sweden) or to attribute their success to fortunate and extraneous circumstances (Mishra, 1984, p. 56). In general, this 'Anglocentric' bias (which has long been observed by continental analysts of the welfare state) is also a clue to the weakness of the more apocalyptic theses of contradiction and ungovernability (Flora and Heidenheimer, 1981a, p. 21). Thus Anthony Birch maintains that the New Right thesis is only sustainable for Britain at a very particular historical moment. Seeking to extrapolate from these very particular circumstances, a general theory of the prospects for representative liberal democracy is quite unwarranted (Birch, 1984, pp. 158–9).

A number of more specific problems can also be identified in these accounts. New Right critics in particular have tended to overstate the powers of trade unions. Even at the height of their ascendancy in the early 1970s, unions were essentially the reactive and defensive organizations of labour (Clarke and Clements, 1977; Hyman, 1989a). All governments, and not only those who saw it as potentially therapeutic, have found it difficult to control unemployment. This, in concert with growing international competition and greater capital mobility, has radically curtailed even this limited power of trades unions. Similarly, the last fifteen years have seen no inexorable rise of social democratic parties, irresponsibly promising 'more for less'. Indeed, the British Labour Party consummated its electoral rehabilitation by insisting on every possible occasion that it had ditched the commitment to 'tax and spend'. Despite the ubiquitous talk of governments 'buying' electoral victories through irresponsible manipulation of the economy, such empirical evidence as there is, suggests that the impact of the 'political business cycle' has been greatly exaggerated (Alt and Chrystal, 1983).

Finally, it is worth drawing attention to the inadequacies of the accounts of legitimacy that underpin many of these accounts of crisis. Both left and right suggest that the difficulties surrounding the welfare state are likely finally to express themselves as a crisis of legitimacy of the democratic capitalist order (Habermas, 1976; Wolfe, 1979). But it seems clear that this is to operate with a conception of legitimacy which belongs to constitutional theory rather than to political sociology. The principle of legitimacy as the acknowledged right to rule is not one that has a prominent place in the day-to-day thinking of the democratic citizen. As Rose and Peters indicated, even 'political bankruptcy' does not mean fighting on the streets (Rose and Peters, 1978). Michael Mann has given definitive expression to the view that the 'social cohesion of liberal democracy' rests primarily upon an *absence* of considerations of legitimacy, upon the fact that the average citizen does not have a comprehensive view of the legitimate claims and limitations of governmental authority. It is a mistake to look to a legitimation crisis where legitimacy is not constituted in the way that analysts of its anticipated crisis suppose (Habermas, 1973; Wolfe, 1979; Mann, 1970).

Restructuring and Retrenchment: The Crisis Contained

As the crisis tendencies of the 1970s failed to precipitate sudden and dramatic change, attention gradually shifted towards an assessment of the ways in which the end of the post-war growth society had been 'managed' from within the parameters of existing economic and political institutions. At the end of the 1970s, Ian Gough raised the perspective of crisis as a process of *restructuring*, in which new circumstances could be established for the renewed accumulation of capital. Gough argued that such a restoration of long-term profitability was only possible through a systematic weakening of the power of working-class organizations and a *retrenchment* of the political and social rights that had been institutionalized in the post-war advanced capitalist world (Gough, 1979, pp. 151–2).

This perspective came to set the agenda for a second and distinctive species of theories that dominated discussion in the 1980s. Following Taylor-Gooby (1985, p. 14), we may think of these as *'crisis containment'* theories. In such accounts, it is argued that the challenge which seemed in the 1970s to be addressed to democratic advanced capitalism itself has, in practice, been displaced upon the social and economic policies that constituted the post-war welfare state. In practice, interventions in areas of social and economic policy have been successful in the limited though decisive sense that they have managed to contain and control, if not actually to resolve, those tendencies which earlier theorists had thought would imperil the very continuation of liberal democracy. If it was any longer appropriate to speak of a crisis, this was now a crisis *within* the institutions of the welfare state itself.

Three sets of claims are characteristic of this 'crisis containment' theory. First, it is suggested that throughout the advanced capitalist world there has been a break with the political consensus for a managed economy and state welfare that characterized the post-war period. Secondly, this change has been made possible by a 'sea change' in public opinion, which has moved from support for collective solutions to problems of social need to a preference for market provision to satisfy individual welfare demands. Thirdly, and most importantly, these changes have in their turn opened the way for cuts in welfare entitlements and a 'restructuring' of public welfare provision. This indicates a move away from the model of a universalist, rights-based welfare state towards a more residualist, needs-governed system of public relief. We should consider each of these claims in a little more detail.

The End of the Consensus

'Crisis containment' theorists argue that while critics were right to observe a severe challenge to the post-war consensus in the heightened social and political struggles of the early 1970s, they were wrong to identify this with an unmanageable threat to the prevailing democratic capitalist order. The perceived 'contradictions' of welfare capitalism have been, if not definitively resolved, then at least effectively managed. This has been achieved through a radical reconstruction of the social and political order of the advanced capitalist societies, a reconstruction in the interests of capital and parties of the right, achieved through an abandonment of the post-war consensus.

Although this process has taken different forms in differing countries, according to specifically local conditions, its definitive and most articulate expression was seen to be the rise of 'Thatcherism', both in the UK and, by extension, elsewhere. Despite its self-ascribed single-mindedness and conviction, the precise meaning of 'Thatcherism' remains unclear (see Jessop et al., 1988, pp. 3–56). For some, perhaps for Mrs Thatcher herself, it signifies, above all else, a rejection of the politics of consensus. According to Gamble, it represents 'a coherent hegemonic project', summarily constructed around the twin themes of 'the free economy and the strong state' (Gamble, 1988, p. 23). It is sometimes given a wider and international resonance, indicating a more generalized policy response to the perceived economic and social problems of the 1970s. Thus, Dennis Kavanagh writes that:

> economic recession and slow economic growth undermined popular support for the welfare consensus in a number of . . . states. The Thatcher governments' policies of tax cuts, privatization, 'prudent' finance, squeezing state expenditure and cutting loss-making activities has had echoes in other western states. (Kavanagh, 1987, p. 9)

It is not perhaps surprising that 'the Thatcher agenda' should have had an appeal for right-wing incumbents in the UK, the USA and perhaps West Germany in the early 1980s. What was seen as still more decisive for the proponents of 'crisis containment' was the extent to which avowedly socialist or social democratic governments were forced to adopt 'austerity' measures which mimicked the policies of right-wing governments. This might be taken to describe the experience of the Labour government in the UK in the late 1970s. To an extent, it even spread into the heartland of the welfare state in Scandinavia (particularly in Denmark). But perhaps most instructive was the experience of the Socialists in France, who, though elected on a radical socialist manifesto in 1981, were abruptly forced to 'U-turn' and embrace the politics of austerity. What seemed to divide this 'Thatcherism with a human face' from the real thing was a lack of enthusiasm for the policies adopted.

The 'Sea Change' in Popular Opinion

This *political* abandonment of consensus could not have been effected, it is argued, had there not been a wholesale erosion of popular support for existing welfare state arrangements. There are some who argue that the working class never had a strong attachment to the idea of welfare rights and social citizenship, and who trace 'the long hostility of working people to what is perceived as dependency on public provision' (Selbourne, 1985, p. 117). Certainly, most commentators concede that public attitudes to welfare have always been ambivalent and that even where support for the welfare state has appeared to be strong, such strength has often been 'brittle'. On this basis, the economic downturn of the early 1970s afforded an opportunity for 'a full-scale assault on the welfare consensus', a consensus which 'has never taken deep root, and [which] was therefore relatively easy to dislodge by the return of an incisive neo-liberal rhetoric in the wake of the significant material shifts in working-class experience in the mid-1970s' (Golding and Middleton, 1982, pp. 229, 205). According to John Alt, people's support for the welfare state was seen to be basically 'altruistic . . . supporting a benefit which will largely go to others'. In economic 'good times', when people's earnings are rising, they may be willing to afford such 'altruistic policies'. But times of 'economic stress', such as the 1970s, tend to be associated with 'less generosity' and a preference for 'spending cuts over taxation' (Alt, 1979, p. 258).

Perhaps the single clearest (and most widely challenged) statement of the case for a decline in public support for state welfare came from the Institute of Economic Affairs. In a survey of British public opinion on welfare, Harris and Seldon claimed to have isolated 'a large, latent but suppressed desire for change in British education and medical care among high proportions of people of both sexes, all ages and incomes, whether officially at work or not, and of all political sympathies' (Harris and Seldon, 1987, p. 51; see also Harris and Seldon, 1979, p. 201).

Further evidence of this decline in popular support for the welfare state was premised on the growing electoral difficulties of social democratic parties and the renaissance of the political right. Social democrats have long been identified as 'the party of the welfare state'. Their rise in the 1960s was often associated with the incorporation of the welfare state in advanced capitalist societies. Correspondingly, the decline in their popularity in the 1970s was seen as evidence of a decline in support for the welfare state itself.

Here again, the most familiar examples are those of the UK, the USA and West Germany. But perhaps more important were the examples of a shift to the right in the heartland of the welfare state. Of these, the most important examples were Denmark and, of course, Sweden where the return of a 'bourgeois' coalition in 1976 brought to an end 44 years of continuous social democratic government. But evidence of the decline in support for socialist parties was Europe-wide. The proportion of votes going to all left parties (social democratic, socialist and communist) fell from 41.3 per cent in the 1960s to 40.1 per cent in the 1970s. In the same period, support for conservative parties crept up from 24.6 to 24.9 per cent. In the early 1980s, the proportion of the conservative vote advanced to 25.3 per cent. Between 1977 and 1982, incumbent socialists were defeated in Britain, West Germany, Belgium, Holland, Norway, Luxembourg and Denmark. In 1975, there were more than twice as many socialist as conservative cabinet ministers in European governments (54.1% contrasted with 25.1%). By 1982, the Conservative parties had established a one percentage point lead over the socialists (37.6% conservative; 36.4% socialist). Lane and Ersson concluded that the socialist parties' position 'was reinforced during the 1950s and the 1960s; in the 1970s and early 1980s, however, a decline to a lower level set in'. For the parties of the right, by contrast, the data 'confirm the hypothesis of a conservative revival in the 1970s and early 1980s' (*Economist*, 1982a, pp. 35–6; Lane and Ersson, 1987, pp. 112–15).

'The Cuts'

The third, and possibly the most important element in the 'crisis containment' perspective was the spectre of cuts and 'restructuring' in social expenditure. On the basis of a change in popular and electoral opinion, and given the successes of parties of the right and the breakdown of the politics of consensus, it seemed that the 1980s must be a decade of welfare retrenchment. Many commentators, both advocates and opponents, anticipated a retreat from a universal welfare state based on citizenship towards a more modest policy of the relief of destitution upon the basis of demonstrated need in a context of declining resources for welfare.

The first public expenditure White Paper of the newly elected UK Conservative government in 1979 maintained that 'public expenditure is at the heart of Britain's present economic difficulties' and, as we have seen, the single largest (and fastest-growing) aspect of this public spending was social expenditure (HM Treasury, 1979). Accordingly, the welfare state looked particularly vulnerable to retrenchment and within a year of Thatcher's election, Ian Gough was arguing that:

> Britain is experiencing the most far-reaching experiment in 'new right' politics in the Western world. [A number of] policy shifts . . . contribute to this aim: legal sanctions against unions, mass unemployment by means of tight monetary controls, the cutting of social benefits for the families of strikers, a reduction in the social wage on several fronts, and a shift to more authoritarian practices in the welfare field. It represents one coherent strategy for managing the British crisis, a strategy aimed at the heart of the post-war Keynesian-welfare state settlement. (Gough, 1983, pp. 162–3)

Much the same process was identified in the USA. Here it was said in 1986 that 'the Reagan administration and its big business allies have declared a new class war' against the working class and those reliant on social assistance (Piven and Cloward, 1986, p. 47). Writing in the same year, Michael Katz insisted that:

> In the last several years, city governments have slashed services; state legis-
> latures have attacked general assistance (outdoor relief to persons ineligible
> for benefits from other programs); and the Reagan administration has
> launched an offensive against social welfare and used tax policy to widen
> the income gap between rich and poor. (Katz, 1986, p. 274)

Perhaps even more telling were the prospects for retrenchment in the
continental European welfare state. In September 1982, the *Economist*
argued that 'during the 1980s, all rich countries' governments ... are
likely to make ... big cuts in social spending'. Within a month, it was
reporting 'the withering of Europe's welfare states'. In Germany, there
were to be delays in pension increases, the collection of sickness insurance contributions from pensioners and an end to student grants. Holland faced 'a savage cutback', while the one-time leading welfare state,
Denmark, was to seek a 7 per cent cut in public spending through reducing levels of unemployment compensation and introducing new charges
for children's day care. Most saliently, the newly elected socialist government in France was introducing new charges to meet non-medical hospital costs and increasing social security contributions in a quest to curb
spending by $12 billion in a full year. Only the perverse Swedes were 'the
exception that proved the rule', re-electing a socialist government on an
anti-cuts programme (*Economist*, 1982b, pp. 67–8).

Crisis Contained?

'Crisis containment' offered a clear account of the breakdown of the
post-war consensus, of a popular political shift to the right and of an
unpicking of the fabric of the welfare state. It suggested that this change
had successfully addressed the threat of systemic crisis that had been
identified in the mid-1970s and displaced it upon a more modest and
piecemeal, if squalid, crisis for those in society who were most reliant
upon the support of public services. How convincing is this second school
of crisis thinking?

The End of Consensus?

We have seen that it is possible to define consensus as either inter-party
or inter-class but that, in whichever form, it could be isolated in policy
terms around (1) the maintenance of a comprehensive welfare state, (2)
support of the 'mixed economy' and (3) policies of full employment and
sustained economic growth. There were always those opposed to consensus, and though we are now inclined to think of the breach with consensus as an intervention from the right, it is worth recalling that some of the

earliest mobilization against the social democratic consensus came from the left in the late 1960s and early 1970s. Similarly, while we think of the break being consummated towards the end of the 1970s, 'the beginning of the end of consensus' might be as convincingly retraced to the late 1960s. Even if we identify the demise of consensus with this later date, it is worth recalling that some on the left welcomed this as an opportunity to radicalize politics around the failure of the social democratic 'management of capitalism'.

One of the lessons of empirical research on the welfare state in the 1980s and 1990s has been to trace the *diversity* of developments in the last twenty years. Faced with similar difficulties, though under nationally variable circumstances, there has been a variety of responses within the Western welfare states. As the nature of the consensus varied among countries, so too has the process of its 'deconstruction' been far from uniform. Thus the consequences of the election of parties of the right committed to reform in Sweden (1976), the UK (1979) and Germany (1982) were widely different given the variation in national backgrounds. So, too, was the experience of reforming parties of the left, as the contrasting examples of the Labor administrations returned in Australia (1983) and New Zealand (1984) show (Castles, Gerritsen and Vowles, 1996).

The UK: The Definitive End of Consensus?

The most abrupt and conclusive 'end to consensus' is often ascribed to the UK, in which a quarter of a century of 'Butskellite' agreement between Conservative and Labour parties was seen to yield in 1979 to the radically anti-consensus politics of Thatcherism. Here is potentially the most fruitful ground for finding the 'end of consensus'. Certainly, the polemical hostility to consensus was clear. In 1981, Margaret Thatcher dismissed consensus as 'the process of abandoning all beliefs, principles, values and policies' (cited in Kavanagh and Morris, 1989, p. 119). In the 1979 election campaign, the Conservatives presented themselves as a party breaking with the exhausted legacy of post-war politics. This break extended to each of the major policy elements of consensus. In terms of the 'mixed economy', there was a commitment to return publicly owned industries to the private sector and to limit government interventions in the day-to-day management of relations between employers and employees. There was a commitment to sustained or enhanced economic growth, but this was to be achieved by an *abandonment* of Keynesian economics and the commitment to full employment in favour of monetarism and supply-side reforms. On the welfare state, there was to be a drive to cut costs by concentrating resources upon those in greatest need, to restrain the bureaucratic interventions of the 'nanny state' in the day-to-day life of citizens, a greater role for voluntary welfare institutions and the encouragement of individuals to make provision for their individual welfare through the private sector (encouraging private pensions, private health care and private education).

Certainly, the 1979 general election in the UK may be described as a 'watershed'. Labour had been in office for eleven of the previous fifteen years. This election brought to power a Conservative government that remained in office for eighteen years and won four consecutive elections. The 1979 election also saw a major defection of skilled working class voters from Labour to Conservative. Yet in judging the breach with consensus that it represented, one must be a little circumspect.

First, the break-up of consensus pre-dates the election of the Conservatives in 1979. The first two years of the Heath government (1970–2) had been committed to the sort of neo-liberalism that the 1979 Thatcher government promised. It was the Labour government of 1974–9 that presided over the earliest retrenchment in welfare spending and a (then) unprecedented rise in post-war unemployment. In so far as there was a kind of Keynesianism to be abandoned in Britain, the symbolic moment of change is often identified with Jim Callaghan's speech to the 1976 Labour Party Conference. With the shift in Labour policy after 1976 (and the imposition of cash limits), sentiment drifted away from the egalitarian revisionism of the post-war period (in which the welfare services were to be part of a gradualist strategy of equality) towards the more residualist aspiration of 'protecting the weakest in hard times'. In the great public services (such as health and education) the watchword was affordability; in terms of income maintenance and cash transfers, the ideology, at least, was to concentrate resources where they were most needed.

Turning to the record of the Thatcher government after 1979, political practice did not always match the radical party rhetoric. Certainly, unemployment was allowed to reach unheard of levels (officially in excess of three million), a string of major public corporations and utilities were returned to the private sector (notably British Telecom, British Gas, British Airways and water supply and sewerage services). There was a major (and popular) drive to sell off public housing and limited cuts in expenditure on education. Yet in the period of the first Thatcher administration total social expenditure showed a significant growth of about 10 per cent, rising as a proportion of GDP from 21.7 to 23.6 per cent. Much of this increase was the consequence of extremely high levels of unemployment and low economic growth (Taylor-Gooby, 1985, p. 72). In 1985–6, social expenditure stood at £36 billion, a third higher than its 1979 level (Kavanagh, 1987, p. 217).

It was only under the third Thatcher administration (after 1987) that major reform of the welfare state (beyond the transformation of public housing) was attempted. The period between 1988 and 1990 has been described as initiating 'the most decisive break in British social policy since the period between 1944 and 1948', the years in which the modern British welfare state was created (Glennerster, Power and Travers, 1991). As well as the implementation of the government's Social Security Act 1986, these years witnessed the passage of the Education Reform Act 1988, the Housing Act 1988, the National Health Service and Community Care Act 1990 and the wholesale reform of the NHS following the publication of the White Paper *Working for Patients* in January 1989.

These changes were certainly hugely consequential and, at the time of their introduction, were vigorously contested both by the opposition parties and by organized interests within the public sector as an assault upon the welfare state. Yet we should be clear that what was transformed by this flurry of legislation was, above all, the accepted *modes of delivery* of public services. There was certainly an aspiration to control costs, above all by improving the 'efficiency' of the public sector, and this was often presented in terms of the capacity of the market to extract a much-enhanced output from a more-or-less static input (or, rather less glamorously, to increase workloads and squeeze the pay of public sector workers). But this was not the classical New Right response to inefficiency and illiberalism in state welfare (which is to transfer the provision of welfare services from public administration to private markets). Although there has been a significant privatization of welfare effort over the past twenty years, this has more commonly been transferred to women in families rather than to markets and (again with the partial exception of housing) there has been no wholesale transfer of state welfare provision into the private sector.

At the most generic level, the strategy of reform in the public services since 1987 – sometimes referred to as the *new public management* – has been to introduce private sector management, organization and labour market practices into the public sector in the expectation that the sector can thus be made to deliver the sorts of service and efficiency that it is supposed the private sector (and its competitive environment) has already realized. More specifically, and most clearly in the areas of health and education, there has been an aspiration to introduce 'internal markets' within the domain of public provision. In these reforms, public funding has been retained but steps have been taken to divide the *purchasers* from the *providers* of services. The intention is that individual units (schools, colleges or health care trusts) should compete for consumers of their services. The purchaser of these services (parents, patients or their surrogates) should be able to move their custom between providers with relative ease. Greater information (examination results, waiting list times, proportion of successful procedures, prices) should make it possible for consumers to make effective choices. With resources broadly following consumer choices, competition should encourage efficiency and reward the most successful producers.

Although the techniques of new public management have also been applied within the Department of Social Security (by far the single largest area of government administration), the idea of the 'internal market' has rather less purchase in the field of income maintenance. Here, the policy changes of the last decade have been less innovative and more incremental. Although the government has sought 'value for money', its overwhelming concern has been to constrain absolute levels of spending. This is unsurprising. The social security budget constitutes the single largest item of social expenditure: at around £100 billion nearly one-third of all public spending. An increasingly important secondary theme has been the impact of benefit levels and entitlements upon the (changing) labour market. Conservative governments were committed to greater labour market flexibility, not least by making it more attractive to be in low-paid work than in receipt of unemployment benefit or income support (a rather ancient principle of 'less eligibility' which can be retraced at least to the Poor Law Amendment Act of 1834). The carrot has been some form of income supplement for families with a low-waged breadwinner, while the sticks have been a repeated tightening of entitlement to state support and constraint upon the level of improvement of benefit rates. Most recently this tightening of terms and conditions has included the replacement of unemployment benefits and income support by a more stringently administered Job Seeker's Allowance and closer medical supervision of entitlement to Incapacity Benefit.

Our overall judgement on the end of consensus needs to be nuanced. First, there is reason to think that the post-war consensus was much more short-lived and provisional than some accounts of its 'Golden Age' would suggest. It was unravelling long before the arrival of Mrs Thatcher. The erosion of the policy elements of consensus is quite uneven and some of the welfare components of consensus (public education and the NHS) have survived better than, for example, the commitment to full employment or the governing apparatus of 'corporatism'. At the same time, and after a period of more or less real contestation, we can see the emergence of a rather differing consensus amongst 'governing opinion', well represented by the policy stance of Blair's New Labour on 'welfare to work'. In so far as there is an emergent 'new consensus', it is certainly more 'market-driven' and 'to the right' of the post-war regime. Yet it is not really built around the New Right agenda which informed so much Thatcherite rhetoric, but rather around the social policy elements of what has been called the 'Washington Consensus' (see Williamson, 1994). We can take the Washington Consensus to refer to the views of those very senior policy makers in international organizations such as the IMF, the World Bank and the OECD who 'advise' governments throughout the world on the best (or as it may seem only) means of securing the great desideratum of long-term economic growth. Of especial importance for social policy are the following key priorities:

- *Fiscal discipline*   government budget deficits should be small or preferably non-existent
- *Tax reform*   tax regimes should be broadened and redesigned to reduce marginal rates and spur economic participation
- *Public expenditure*   government spending should be concentrated on those areas which are economically productive (giving priority to 'investment' in health and education rather than 'redistribution' through social transfers)
- *Deregulation*   governments should reduce regulation to promote economic activity (including the deregulation of labour markets and a reduction of social costs for employers).

It is worth observing that, whilst the 'post-war consensus' applied in differing ways to a range of affluent and democratic liberal democracies, the 'Washington Consensus' is seen to apply to a much wider constituency – anyone who wishes to see their nation prosper in an increasingly global economy and society.

Changes in Public Opinion

A second element in the 'crisis containment' thesis was the claim that, in contrast to the period in which the post-war consensus was constructed and sustained, popular opinion has now shifted away from support for equity and citizenship through the welfare state. Crudely put, public welfare was something which people would support in economic 'good times', when both public and private consumption could rise, but to which they were much less sympathetic in times of economic stagnation. A strictly temporary and provisional support for the welfare state had been dissipated through an appeal to traditional and much more deep-seated hostility to the poor and indolent.

The fullest review of international public opinion on the welfare state is still Coughlin's *Ideology, Public Opinion and Welfare Policy*. Across a sample of eight rich nations he found that:

> public attitudes toward the principles of social policy have developed along similar lines both of acceptance and rejection. The idea of collective responsibility for assuring minimum standards of employment, health care, income, and other conditions of social and economic well-being has everywhere gained a foothold in popular values and beliefs. And yet the survey evidence suggests a simultaneous tendency supporting individual achieve-

ment, mobility, and responsibility for one's own lot, and rejecting the elimination of aspects of economic life associated with capitalism. (Coughlin,
1980, p. 31)

Levels of support varied between 'big spenders', such as Sweden and
France, and 'low spenders', such as the USA and Australia but broadly
similar patterns emerged. The same areas – pensions, public health insurance, family/child allowances – were most popular (and expensive), and
the same sort of provision – unemployment compensation and public
assistance – the least popular. Not only between nations, but between
social classes and across political sympathies, it seemed that everyone
likes pensions and no-one likes 'scroungers' (Coughlin, 1980, p. 52).

Taylor-Gooby's (1989) review of the international evidence from six
developed countries a decade later revealed lower absolute *levels* of popular support, but a similar *ranking* of both countries and programmes. The
survey material recorded majorities everywhere for increased state spending on health care (88% in the UK and 81% in Italy), and a clear
(unweighted) majority for increases in old age pensions (with support
highest again in the UK and Italy, with positive responses of 75% and
76% respectively) (Taylor-Gooby, 1989, p. 41). Overall, Taylor-Gooby
concluded that:

> the attitudes of the citizens of the six nations correspond more closely to
> the traditional post-war settlement than they reveal any enthusiasm for
> change, although within this framework there are substantial national vari-
> ations . . . Social welfare that provides for mass needs is warmly endorsed,
> but provision for minorities, whose interests challenge the work ethic, re-
> ceives meagre approval. Direct social engineering to advance equality of
> outcomes is not endorsed. (Taylor-Gooby, 1989, pp. 41, 49)

Tang's later (1997) review of public attitudes to the welfare state in
Britain and the USA across three decades shows continuing popular support for social programmes continuing within both jurisdictions. Most
remarkably, a Eurobarometer survey (1993, p. 82) of opinion in the European Union found huge majorities in favour of quite radical welfare
rights: 'By 96% to 3%, everyone must have the right to suitable accommodation at reasonable cost . . . By 87% to 9%, the right to work should
be guaranteed . . . By 94% to 4%, everyone must be able to be cared for,
without the costs of care preventing it'.

Overall, the pattern of popular attitudes to state welfare is complex but
stable. There is public hostility to certain areas of state provision, probably some repressed demand masked by state compulsion, hostility to
certain categories of beneficiary and some support for private/market
provision of welfare services. These views are not new, however, and they

coexist with widespread popular endorsement of the most expensive and extensive elements of state provision. There is little evidence here of large-scale popular backlash against the welfare state.

The Decline of the 'Welfare State Party'

We have seen that, however doubtful is the *historical* basis of such a claim, the welfare state has come to be strongly identified with socialist and particularly social democratic parties. Another source of evidence of decline in popular support for the welfare state is thus to be found in the decline of these parties of the welfare state. Evidence of such a decline was considered above. It included (1) a series of defeats of social democratic governments in Europe and North America between 1977 and 1982, (2) a long-term decline in left voting after 1960 and (3) a fall of more than a third in socialist participation in government between 1975 and 1982. It is clear that there was a movement (perhaps more properly a counter-movement) against the left in this period. However, obituaries for 'the strange death of social democracy' are surely premature (Kavanagh, 1987, pp. 4–5). The combined electoral strength of the left in Western Europe which had stood at 40.1 per cent through the 1970s advanced to 42.5 per cent in the period 1980–3. In the 1980s, while the right captured or re-tained power in the UK, the USA and West Germany, the left retained or reclaimed office in Sweden, Norway, France, Spain, Portugal, Greece, New Zealand and Australia (Mackie and Rose, 1991; *Electoral Studies*, 1989).

In the 1990s, the record continued to be a mixed one. The French Socialist Party rode a roller-coaster with its catastrophic defeat in the National Assembly elections of 1993, actually being outstripped by the Canadian Conservatives, whose vote tumbled from 43 per cent in 1988 to just 16 per cent in 1993 (and from 154 MPs to just 2). In 1992 and 1996, the Republicans lost the US Presidential elections, whilst in 1997 the British Conservative Party after eighteen years in office went down to its worst defeat of the twentieth century. Meanwhile, in Australia, New Zealand and Spain, which had spent much of the 1980s under Labor or Socialist rule, electoral ascendancy passed to the right. Lane, McKay and Newton's long-term survey (1997) showed surprisingly little movement in overall levels of support for parties of the left (and the right) between the 1960s and the 1990s. The view, sometimes expressed in the 1980s, that parties which called themselves Labour or Socialist or Social Democrat could never get elected has proven to be quite unfounded (though parties have generally given up on the attempt to win office under the label 'Communist'). Much more salient is the issue of whether such parties can still pursue distinctively social democratic policy objectives and whether it is still appropriate to style them 'welfare state parties'. This is an issue to which we return in chapter 6.

'The Cuts'

We have already reviewed the general evidence of cuts in welfare state provision since the early 1970s. A fuller survey of the evidence reveals important changes underlying a seemingly rather stable pattern of expenditure. Certainly the very dramatic patterns anticipated by the proponents of fiscal crisis in the 1980s have not emerged. Over the past fifteen years, social spending in most countries has continued to grow faster than GDP. Certainly, there has been a major restraint in the levels of *growth* of social expenditure. Between 1960 and 1975, real growth in social expenditure stood at about 8 per cent a year. Between 1975 and 1981, this rate of real growth was halved to just over 4 per cent (OECD, 1984). During the 1980s, the proportion of GDP devoted to social expenditure rose on average across the OECD by about 2 per cent, although most of this growth had been achieved by 1983 (OECD, 1994, p. 69). Only three countries (Ireland, Belgium and West Germany) saw reduced social expenditure ratios in the 1980s, while these ratios continued to increase substantially in nine countries (Canada, Greece, France, Norway, Denmark, New Zealand, Spain, Italy and Finland). Overall, the pattern was similar to that experienced in the European Union:

> Between 1980 and 1983 social protection expenditure as a percentage of GDP continued the upward trend of the 1970s. The efforts of governments to reduce the burden of social protection were fairly successful between 1983 and 1989. After 1989, under the combined effect of increased demand on the social protection system and the economic recession, social protection expenditure as a percentage of GDP again began to grow rapidly. (Eurostat, 1996b, p. 133)

In the severe recession of the early 1990s, average expenditure on social protection throughout the European Union rose from 23.7 per cent of GDP to 26.5 per cent (Eurostat, 1996c, p. 168).

Yet this gross pattern of marginal long-term increases in social expenditure overlain by cyclical fluctuations relating to the state of the economy gives us a very partial picture of what is happening. For we have to relate this incremental growth in social spending to a changing pattern of demand for social protection. The welfare state is quintessentially a form of provision for the elderly. Even in the depth of recession in the early 1990s, unemployment (and related job-creation measures) accounted for less than 10 per cent of social expenditure throughout the European Union. Expenditure on the elderly and health care (which is disproportionately concentrated upon older people) accounted for four-fifths of social spending. The world's population is ageing and with it comes a growing demand for effective forms of income maintenance (and health care and housing provision) for those who are no longer economically active. At the same time, other social changes – the growth in single-parent families, the increase in part-time and 'non-standard' employment, long-term mass unemployment and so on – place increasing pressure upon social budgets.

There are also important changes in the distribution of the *costs* of this welfare provision. Whilst governments' capacity to raise taxes has not collapsed (indeed the average across the OECD has risen from 34 per cent in 1980 to 37.4 per cent in 1996), there has been a change in the incidence of the tax burden (*Economist*, 1997). In general, governments have decreased their dependence upon (progressive) income tax and taxes on corporations in favour of a greater reliance on indirect (sales) taxes and user charges. There is a widespread belief in governing opinion that we have reached the limits of what democratic publics are willing to pay in direct taxes (although these levels vary quite widely between states) and that, for example, more of the costs of employment-related benefits must be met by employees' social security contributions rather than by employers or general taxation. Similarly, across a range of jurisdictions, there have been moves to transfer part of the costs of the residential care of the infirm elderly towards these elderly people themselves or their families and there is, as we shall see in chapter 6, an almost desperate search to find alternative forms of pension provision which will relieve the state of part of its present burden.

As Paul Pierson's (1994) work has shown, even the most committed neo-liberal governments (under Reagan and Thatcher in the 1980s) found it extraordinarily difficult to 'roll back' welfare state expenditures. There have been real cuts. The first Bolger administration in New Zealand implemented benefit cuts of unprecedented severity in its 1991 budget (Kelsey, 1995, p. 276). Still, it was forced to back down on its plans to curtail (comparatively generous and expensive) state superannuation for the elderly, and social expenditure actually *rose* between 1989 and 1993 from 20.2 to 23.9 per cent of GDP. This reflects a more general pattern. There have been real cuts in some forms of welfare provision (reduction in levels of benefit or the elimination of public services). More generally, the value of benefits has been allowed to fall (through a failure to upgrade in line with general inflation), access to services or benefits has been made more difficult (more means testing and tighter eligibility criteria) and recipients have had to pay for more of the services they receive (reducing government subsidies to service providers, more asset testing, a greater reliance on co-contributions). This pattern of retrenchment is reflected in table 5.1.

Table 5.1   Retrenchment of benefits in OECD countries

Type of benefit	Change	Examples
Old age pensions	Raising retirement age	UK, New Zealand, Italy, Japan
	Increase in qualifying period for a full pension	France, Portugal, Ireland, Finland
	Lowered basis for upgrading of benefits in line with inflation	UK, France, Spain
	Income testing of pension	Austria, Denmark, Australia
Disability	Stricter test of incapacity	UK, USA, Netherlands, Norway
	New time limits, reduced benefits	UK, USA, Netherlands
Unemployment	Reduction in duration of benefits	Belgium, UK, Denmark, USA
	Reduction in level of benefits	Germany, Ireland, New Zealand, Switzerland
	Reduced eligibility	Netherlands, UK, Belgium
Family allowances	Declining real value or decreasing eligibility	UK, Spain, Netherlands

Source: Ploug (1995, pp. 65–7), *International Social Security Review*, 2 (1996, pp. 20–5).

Conclusion

Talk of a 'crisis' in the welfare state shows no sign of abating. Yet evidence of crisis in any of the principal senses in which it has been addressed in this chapter is extremely thin. Claims about the destabilization of liberal democracy, the decimation of social expenditure, the withdrawal of public support for major welfare programmes have been poorly vindicated. By contrast, the experience of the past twenty years and, in particular, the governing response of the past decade, is perhaps best seen in terms of the process of *structural adjustment* (see, for example, OECD, 1987b). Although often thought of as a process of retrenchment recommended by First World bankers to Third World governments, structural adjustment actually describes a much broader repertoire of strategies which have been pressed upon governments across the globe. In the face of profound changes in the national and international economic environment, governments are seen to have 'adjusted' their social policy regimes. Echoing the arguments about post-Fordism, governments have sought to adapt their national economic regimes to a changed climate for investment and to promote movement in the direction of greater 'flexibility' and enhanced 'competitiveness'. In general, this has meant promoting micro-economic reform (more flexible labour markets, privatization, flatter tax regimes, greater openness to foreign investors), bearing down on public expenditure (by reducing the level and incidence of public services and introducing 'efficiency gains' in the public sector) and trying to move from a 'passive' (social transfers) to an 'active' (retraining and work placement) welfare state. Although the policy agenda is seen increasingly to be set by (global) markets, this is not quite the response that those on the New Right anticipated (and would have welcomed). For while the state may increasingly act through *regulating* rather than actually *delivering* services, at the same time it may actually become more active and intervene more intensively (and intrusively) in the day-to-day life of (at least its dependent) citizens. There has certainly been no straightforward 'withdrawal' of the state in favour of markets.

Yet the consequences of structural adjustment are still likely to be profound. Exposing national economies and national corporatist arrangements to a largely unregulated world economy has transformed the circumstances under which any government might seek, for example, to pursue a policy of full employment or to redistribute wealth through a progressive taxation system. Secondly, changes in the economy nationally and internationally (and the social policy reforms that follow from this) may transform the configuration of individuals' interests and the political articulation of those interests. The character of a welfare state cannot be adequately measured by levels of aggregate spending. Long-term high levels of unemployment amidst societies of generally rising affluence, increasingly segmented labour markets and new patterns of consumption may change the disposition of social expenditure. Rising levels of social spending and continuing public endorsement of the popular elements of the welfare state may well be consistent with an internal transformation from a solidary, universalistic, citizenship-based welfare state towards a system based on the more generous provision of insurance-style entitlement and a further deterioration in the position of the poor and stigmatized (Alber, 1988a, pp. 187–9; see also Parry, 1986, pp. 155–240). This is reflected in the concerns of those who have written of the emergence of a '40–30–30 society' in which the opportunities and circumstances of those in the bottom third of society increasingly diverge from those of the most affluent 40 per cent (Hutton, 1995).

Finally, what may remain in the face of all our evidence is an *intellectual* crisis of the welfare state. That is, the social democratic vision of the welfare state as the mechanism for taming capitalism through redistributive social policy is losing its authority. Its core elements, the commitment to economic growth, the enabling capacity of the state bureaucracy, the attempt to exercise indirect control over capital, are increasingly under challenge. The 'welfare state malaise' of which Therborn writes, is identified not only by the New Right or neo-Marxist left but also by 'supply-side socialists' and ecologists (Therborn, 1986). Can, or indeed should, social democrats still strive to be 'the party of the welfare state'? It is to such questions about the future of the welfare state that we turn in the final chapter.

6
Beyond the Welfare State?

In this final chapter, I return explicitly to the issue of whether and in what sense we are moving towards social and political arrangements that are 'beyond the welfare state', and particularly to the challenge that such changes pose for traditional social democracy. Some of the most important grounds for anticipating such a transformation in welfare arrangements were contained in propositional form towards the end of the Introduction. Summarily, these suggested that existing welfare state arrangements were unlikely to survive because of (1) the long-term incompatibility of the welfare state with a market economy, (2) changes in the international political economy leading to an erosion of class compromise between organized labour and organized capital, (3) changes in class structure and patterns of consumption leading to an erosion of the alliance for public welfare between middle and working classes, (4) changes in class structure and patterns of consumption leading to an erosion of class solidary action within the 'broad' working class itself and (5) the incompatibility of a growth-based welfare state with the securing of genuine individual and social well-being. In this final chapter, I assess these claims in the light of the evidence considered in earlier chapters. We shall see that at least some of the problems raised in the Introduction, and more fully elaborated in the following theoretical chapters, arise from a serious misunderstanding of the nature and history of the international welfare states, but also that a very serious challenge remains, particularly for social democrats.

Markets v. the Welfare State

This element of misunderstanding is particularly clear in some of the more apocalyptic claims made about the incompatibility of the welfare state and the market economy. In chapter 5, we saw that claims of crisis and contradiction in the welfare state were largely misplaced, and the more dramatic forebodings of the mid-1970s much exaggerated. In 1997, the World Bank, long seen to be in the vanguard of calls for 'more market', issued a report calling for a focus upon improving states' effectiveness, insisting that 'an effective state is vital to the provision of the goods and the services – and the rules and institutions – that allow markets to flourish and people to lead healthier, happier lives. Without it, sustainable development, both economic and social, is impossible' (World Bank, 1997, p. 1). In part, misunderstanding of the state–market relationship arose from imprecision in the use of the core terms 'crisis' and 'contradiction'; in part, it built upon misreadings of the political forces behind the rise of the welfare state, of the nature of its interaction with the economy and indeed of the extent to which welfare states have always been (varyingly) subordinate to the logic of the market. It was also informed by some improbable claims about the ways in which varying interests within the welfare state could find effective political expression and mobilize real political power.

Of course, as we saw in chapter 5, there has been some transfer of allocative effort from bureaucracies to markets. The delivery of social services through semi-autonomous agencies (such as the Benefits Agency and the Child Support Agency), the introduction of compulsory competitive tendering, the extensive use of performance indicators, league tables and quasi-markets are all examples of the greater use of market-like processes within the welfare sector. But it is important to see that this is not really delivering on the reform agenda which the New Right first set out in the 1970s. The original and 'authentic' aspiration of the New Right was to *replace* states with markets. Ideally, neo-liberals wish to see the state's role confined to the legal regulation of privately provided welfare services and (perhaps) the sponsorship of those unable to fend for themselves. For the most part, this is not what has happened. Much more typically, governments have introduced market-like structures *within* the public sector and, despite the fairly ubiquitous talk of empowering clients, it is clear that the principal motivation has been to discipline producers and contain costs. For a variety of reasons, running welfare states has become increasingly difficult over the past twenty-five years. But the claim that we have now to choose to have *either* a market economy *or* a welfare state, or indeed the belief that we can choose to have a market economy *without* some form of state provision of welfare, is no more compelling now than it was twenty or even a hundred years ago.

However, it might be argued that, while historically we have avoided this choice between state and market, such an accommodation will no longer be available to us in the twenty-first century. Students of the welfare states' 'growth to limits' have argued that the failure to constrain future growth in the welfare budget (at least as a proportion of national wealth) will tend in the long run to undermine popular support for welfare state institutions (as public expenditure increasingly squeezes out the choices of private consumers). Could it be that the pressures arising from *demographic change* in the twenty-first century will so overburden the public welfare system as rather belatedly to trigger an institutional crisis of the welfare state?

A Demographic Crisis of the Welfare State?

Clearly the demographic challenge of an ageing population is a real one and has been a pressing concern of social policy makers for more than a decade. At its simplest (and most extreme), the argument is that the ageing profile of the world's national populations means that at some point in the new century existing welfare state systems (and their patterns of income transfers) will become unsustainable. The mature welfare states were created in societies where pensions were small and the years spent in retirement comparatively few. We now have much more generous pension provision (and much more extensive public health care, another good which is disproportionately consumed by the elderly) and periods in retirement which may stretch into decades. The view is that, as the aged dependency ratio rises into the next century, the tax demand upon a smaller working age population will become so excessive that the implicit 'inter-generational' pact upon which welfare state funding depends will collapse.

A version of this story has been pressed by a number of major international economic organizations, including the OECD (1988) and perhaps, above all, the World Bank, whose report *Averting the Old Age Crisis* has been extraordinarily influential. This account begins from the premise that existing social security 'programs are beset by escalating costs that require high tax rates and deter private sector growth – while failing to protect the old'. These programmes are said to have 'spun out of control' (World Bank, 1994, p. 1). Global ageing, especially in less developed countries, means that the situation can only get worse unless new welfare regimes are developed. The World Bank's solution favours a 'multi-pillar' approach with the state confined to providing a minimum (probably means-tested) pension to alleviate poverty. Pension provision above this minimum should be wholly secured within the private sector and divided between compulsory savings mandated (but not controlled) by government and a third and entirely voluntary pillar for those who wish to raise their retirement income still further. The major transfer of activity and investment into the private sector should, in line with the World Bank's other major ambition, promote economic growth, thus ensuring a bigger pie out of which future pensions will have to be paid. The World Bank's favoured model is not, then, one of the sclerotic European welfare states but the lean and largely privatized Chilean.

In practice, as the World Bank report recognizes, the demographic impact of an ageing population is likely to vary quite substantially between different countries. Within the OECD, 'between 1986 and 2040, increases in the number of elderly people over 75 are likely to vary between 30 per cent (Sweden, Denmark) to nearly 400 per cent (Australia, Canada, Turkey)', (OECD, 1988, p. 10). Overall, it has been estimated that 'the effect of demographic changes could be to raise pension expenditure by about 5 per cent of national income by the year 2020' (OECD, 1987b, p. 170). Clearly, there is a fear that as dependency ratios rise, so the rising demands placed upon current workers to fund services for the growing numbers of pensioners may lead to a breakdown of the 'inter-generational contract' upon which pension provision in a Pay-As-You-Go system depends. Inasmuch as the welfare state is a system of provision for the elderly, which substantially it is, it clearly faces a formidable challenge in the early to middle years of the next century.

However, this will not necessarily precipitate a crisis for the welfare state. Long-term projections about population change may be reliable but similar anticipations about dependency ratios and their financial consequences are acutely sensitive to quite minor (but cumulatively substantial) changes in workforce participation rates, levels of unemployment, levels of economic growth and changes in retirement ages. The interaction of these several variables makes forecasting for the middle years of the twenty-first century extremely hazardous. A fairly minor upward revision of the retirement age, for example, may make a quite substantial difference to projections of dependency ratios in thirty or forty years' time. The reform of pensions provision is clearly a very long-term business and, for both states and individuals, it pays to think a long way ahead. It is not at all clear, however, that governments would be justified in making precipitate policy changes now, on the basis of extremely tentative predictions and questionable assumptions about the elderly population in 2040 (Thane, 1987; Taylor-Gooby, 1988). It is also worth noting that even quite sluggish economic growth may have a significant cumulative effect upon the capacity of the developed economies to support a growing dependent population. In one of the few assessments of its kind, made amidst the doom-mongering of the mid-1980s, Davies and Piachaud

(1985) indicated that in the UK, at least in the brief period between 1984 and 1989, very modest economic growth (of between 1 and 2%) would allow some upgrading of benefits without a growth in the proportional 'take' of welfare from the national economy. As John Hills's excellent (1997) survey points out, if pensioners' benefits in the UK were to be updated in line with the increase in earnings over the next fifty years (a strategy which both major UK parties have abandoned as too generous) it would add roughly 4 per cent to GDP, the same increase as was experienced in the welfare budget in three years of recession in the early 1990s (Hills, 1997, p. 12). There are also a number of problems with the World Bank's preferred strategy of relying very heavily upon the private sector. These include the problems of regulation, sufficiency of income maintenance for the low paid and the peculiar character of pensions as a consumer purchase. Even in a heavily regulated environment, ten years of personal pension promotion in the UK has been replete with (ongoing) scandal (see Waine, 1995). There is a danger that the move towards a means-tested minimum state pension with most of the work of income maintenance done by private pension entitlement is likely to reproduce in retirement the growing disparity of incomes which has been a feature of economic development over the past twenty years (see Beattie and McGillivray, 1995).

Finally, it is worth noting that insofar as there is a 'demographic problem' of an ageing population in the twenty-first century, this is a challenge not just for the welfare state but for the developed societies and their economies much more generally. In whatever way, the costs of supporting an ageing dependent population will have to be met from current economic output. Some alternative mix of public and private provision *may* ease the burden on the public sector and this *may* be more economically efficient. But no juggling of the labels 'private' and 'public' can dissolve the core requirement to support a growing dependent population out of current economic production. Overall, it may be that the real limits to the welfare state lie not so much in the faltering capacity of the economy as in (changing) patterns of political will and political support. We return to this issue, and particularly its consequences for social democracy, below.

Welfare State Regimes

There are then rather limited grounds for supposing that either now or in the envisageable future the welfare state will collapse because of its incompatibility with a market-based economy or because of the unsustainable burden of an ageing population. In fact, amidst the seemingly ubiquitous talk of widespread cuts and a generalized crisis over the last ten to fifteen years, even those governments most powerfully committed to a reduction of the welfare state have found it to be stubbornly evasive of financial constraint (Pierson, 1994). In the UK, the Conservative government enjoyed uninterrupted tenure of office for eighteen years and evinced a strong ideological commitment to lessening the role of the state in welfare and reducing the 'burden' of public expenditure. Yet, at the end of the Conservative's period of office, welfare state expenditure was little different from what it had been in 1979 (Hills, 1994). In the USA, David Stockman, the disgruntled ex-Director of the Budget in the Reagan Administration, asked why the Republicans had failed to 'tame' the welfare state.

> In the answer lies the modern dirty little secret of the Republican Party: the conservative opposition helped build the American welfare state brick by brick during the three decades prior to 1980. The Reagan Revolution failed because the Republican Party decided to stick with its own historic handiwork. (Stockman, 1986, p. 437)

That these most committed and entrenched New Right governments failed to transform existing welfare state expenditures does *not* mean that nothing has changed. Of statutory provision for the unemployed in the UK, for example, Atkinson and Micklewright argued that changes in the 1980s 'made the system less generous and have weakened the role of unemployment *insurance* as opposed to unemployment *assistance*' (Atkinson and Micklewright, 1989, p. 125). In the 1990s, unemployment benefit was abolished and replaced with the much more conditional (and further time-limited) Job Seekers' Allowance (see M. Jones, 1996). In the USA, Katz argues that the first Reagan administration had considerable success in cutting income maintenance and social service programmes (such as AFDC, food stamps and child nutrition) (Katz, 1986, pp. 286–9). In 1995, Bill Clinton began to deliver on his commitment to 'end welfare as we have known it', by abandoning the federal commitment to AFDC (Edelman, 1997). But, as we saw in chapter 5, while 'unpopular' areas of welfare state expenditure have been subject to considerable constraint, the most popular (and expensive) areas have proved to be much more difficult to control (Pierson, 1994). In the USA, for example, Katz argues that while the Reagan administration enjoyed successes in its 'offensive against social welfare . . . social insurance . . . has proved nearly impregnable' (Katz, 1986, p. 274). In the UK, the budget of the NHS rose throughout the 1980s, while repeatedly popular complaints were of *under-* rather than of *over-*spending (Bosanquet, 1988).

It now seems highly improbable that the welfare state in any advanced industrial society will simply 'wither away'. What is much more likely is that welfare states will be varyingly 'reconstructed' so as to reflect a new pattern of rights and interests. In chapter 5, we saw that such a process of 'reconstruction' is already under way. It is a process which cannot be adequately measured by simply plotting changes in aggregate social expenditures. 'The crucial issue', as Esping-Andersen (1990, p. 118) observes, is 'not aggregate expenditures, but welfare state structuration'. Thus, what may be most important in assessing these likely futures for the welfare state is not so much sheer survival, nor even the level of expenditure, but the *type of welfare state regime*. It is this last feature that may be changing most rapidly and profoundly.

A Typology of Welfare State Regimes

We can begin to think about these differing types of welfare state regime by considering some of the following criteria:

Scope: Universal/Selective
Range: Expansive/Delimited
Quality: Optimal/Minimal
Instruments: Public consumption/Social transfers
Financing: Tax-based/Contributory
Benefit type: Earnings-related/Flat-rate
Redistribution: Progressive/Regressive

(Alber, 1988b, p. 452)

In fact, in themselves these criteria are insufficient to define even a simple 'left–right' division in welfare state regimes. While it is hard to imagine a 'left' welfare state being (intentionally) regressive in its redistribution, the support of earnings-related benefits may have a place in both a 'right' welfare state (preserving existing status/income differentiation) and a 'left' welfare state (ensuring broad support for the welfare state beyond the poorest and militating against 'residualism'). Similarly, means testing is often seen as a policy favoured by the right as a way of minimizing welfare costs. However, it is sometimes seen, when combined with funding from progressive general tax revenue, as, for example, in the Australian welfare state, as a strategy for effective redistribution of resources towards the poor (see Shaver, 1988). Finally, a number of commentators have remarked upon the seeming similarity of the calls from both left and right for reforms to integrate the taxation and benefit systems and in the left's schemes for a basic guaranteed income and the New Right's call for a negative income tax (Hill, 1990, pp. 157–67). Even the call for vouchers, long seen as an exclusively right-wing proposal, has its left-of-centre advocates (see Le Grand and Estrin, 1990, pp. 198–204).

Thus, these general criteria must themselves be placed in some overall *strategic* context. One of the most influential and earliest attempts to offer such a further classification is to be found in Richard Titmuss's three models of social policy. Titmuss isolated:

1 The *residual welfare model*, which is 'based on the premise that there are two "natural" (or socially given) channels through which an individual's needs are properly met; the private market and the family. Only when these break down should social welfare institutions come into play and then only temporarily'.
2 The *industrial achievement-performance model*, which 'incorporates a significant role for social welfare institutions as adjuncts of the economy. It holds that social needs should be met on the basis of merit, work performance and productivity'.
3 The *institutional redistributive model*, which 'sees social welfare as a major integrated institution in society, providing universalist services outside the market on the principle of need'.

(Titmuss, 1974, pp. 30–1)

Titmuss's classification remains a useful one but, as a typology for welfare states, it has been criticized both because most actual welfare states embrace elements of all three models and because (in practice) it has been used to underpin *evolutionary* accounts of the development of the welfare state from a residual through an industrial achievement-performance towards an institutional basis.

Certainly the most influential attempt to bring this classification up to date is to be found in the work of Gosta Esping-Andersen (1990), organized around the idea of welfare state *'regime clusters'*. In Esping-Andersen's view, if it is appropriate to think of all the states of developed capitalism as welfare states, then these are clearly welfare states of rather differing kinds. Such differences are not, however, linearly distributed between low spenders and high spenders or between residual and institutional models. Indeed *level* of social expenditure may not be a reliable indicator of the character of any given welfare state. More important is the extent to which welfare state measures are either market-supporting or market-usurping (*decommodifying*). The differing welfare states are seen to cluster around three ideal typical regime types:

1 The *liberal welfare state* is dominated by the logic of the market. Benefits are modest, often means tested and stigmatizing. The principle of 'less eligibility' requires that welfare should not undermine the propensity to work. The state encourages the private provision of market forms of welfare (private insurance/occupational welfare).
   Typical examples: USA, UK, Canada, Australia, New Zealand
2 In the *conservative/'corporatist' welfare state*, 'the liberal obsession

with market efficiency and commodification was never pre-eminent' and correspondingly the granting of social rights was never so contested. Private insurance and occupational welfare are 'minimal'. However, the emphasis of social rights is upon upholding existing class and status differentials and its redistributive effects are 'negligible'. Such welfare states often have their origins in pre-democratic or authoritarian regimes which sought to use social policy as a means of defusing the threat of working class mobilization (Bismarck in Germany, Taafe in Austria). In many cases, corporatist regimes are shaped by the church, and this tends to determine their conservative attitude to the family (gender differential benefits to support the traditional form of the male-dominated family), and their support of the principle of *subsidiarity* (in which the state should support and deliver only those forms of welfare which other intermediary institutions, and notably the church, are unable to provide).

Typical examples: Austria, France, Germany, Italy

3 The *social democratic welfare state* is characterized by universalism and the usurpation of the market. It is envisaged as 'a welfare state that would promote an equality of the highest standards, rather than an equality of minimal needs'. Benefits are graduated in accordance with earnings, but this is a way of securing universal support for, and participation in, a universal insurance system. Unlike the other regimes, the state is not seen as a second or last resort, but as the principal means of realizing the social rights of all its citizens. It is, of necessity, committed to the principle of full employment, since 'the enormous costs of maintaining a solidaristic, universalistic and decommodifying welfare state' can be best and perhaps only achieved 'with most people working, and the fewest possible living off social transfers'.

Typical examples: Sweden and Norway

(Esping-Andersen, 1990, pp. 26–33; see also Rein,
Esping-Andersen and Rainwater, 1987)

The Regimes Debate

Much of the burgeoning comparative welfare state literature of the 1990s can be seen as a 'settling of accounts' with Esping-Andersen. Two of these developments have been of especial interest. First, there has been an attempt to identify additional or alternative 'regime types'. Secondly, there has been an insistence that Esping-Andersen's focus upon decommodification (and thus, by implication, the world of waged work) needs supplementing with other classificatory criteria.

In the first category is Castles and Mitchell's (1992) reinterpretation of Esping-Andersen's original classification. Castles and Mitchell insist that there is a fourth and 'radical' regime type lurking in Esping-Andersen's evidence. These states (Australia, New Zealand and the UK) appear as 'liberal' in Esping-Andersen's classification, but Castles and Mitchell insist that their distinctive combination of low expenditure *plus* high levels of redistribution merit consideration as a distinctive *radical* regime-type. Of course, this 'radicalism' may now be a part of history, since taxation regimes in all these states (especially New Zealand and the UK) are much less progressive now than when the relevant data was collected (in the 1980s). But their analysis contains a more general and extremely salient point, which is especially well illustrated by the Australian experience. It is that quite conventional welfare state goals may be delivered through quite unconventional (and sometimes consequently unreported) channels. Thus, a quite central aspect of 'decommodification' in the Australian context is the 'award' system of judicial wage setting which dates back to the 1920s and which is still a crucial component in the operation of labour markets. Similarly, (internationally quite variable) levels of home ownership may have a decisive impact upon the (in)equality of welfare outcomes which standard redistributive indices do not fully capture. Even means testing has a quite different resonance in Australia from that which European commentators might anticipate (and perhaps incorporate in their welfare models). Interest in these welfare state alternatives (which their supporters, at least, would classify as broadly social democratic in intent) has intensified as the social democratic welfare state and, above all, 'the Swedish Model' has been seen to be in serious difficulties (Lane, 1995; on Australia, see also pp. 206–7 below).

A second area of particular interest for those seeking to build upon Esping-Andersen's typology has been the emergent welfare states of southern Europe. Stephan Leibfried (1993) has identified a distinctive type of welfare state in what he characterizes as the 'Latin Rim' countries of the European Union (Portugal, Spain, Greece and, in some limited respects, Italy and France). He described these as 'rudimentary welfare states', playing 'catch up' with their more developed northern neighbours. Typically, these welfare states promised much but had quite underdeveloped delivery systems and relied, in practice, on much older systems of social support from the family and the Catholic Church. More recently, Maurizio Ferrera (1996) has outlined a number of distinctive features which serve to define the 'southern' model of welfare. These include a highly fragmented and distorted system of income maintenance (with pensions ranging from the hugely generous to the negligible), a (partially realized) commitment to national health care systems and the delivery of services through a mixture of underdeveloped state institutions and clientelistic party political networks. There is an indication that in some of these states the combination of substantial policy commitments, clientelistic party politics and a weak state capacity (to raise taxation and deliver well-regulated services) may trigger 'fiscal crises' more severe than those so far weathered (with some difficulty) in northern Europe.

So far, the comparative study of welfare states and the attempt to construct sophisticated typologies has tended to be focused upon those countries with the most developed economies. These are the states with the richest statistical bases and in which most of the researchers live! There has, however, been increasing interest in welfare arrangements outside these areas. The political economy of Japan and its employment-related welfare have long been part of the ageing industry of 'explaining' the Japanese 'economic miracle'. In more recent years, this interest has spread into the neighbouring 'Asian tigers' although, thus far, attempts to construct a Japanese or 'Confucian' model of welfare have met with qualified success (Jones, 1993; Goodman and Peng, 1996; Esping-Andersen, 1997). Another area of heightened interest has been the 'transition' welfare states of the former Soviet Union, particularly those in eastern Europe (see Deacon 1992, 1997). Of course, welfare was deeply embedded in the 'full employment' regimes of the old Soviet-style economies. A crucial aspect of processes of marketization and privatization in these states has been the transformation of public welfare provision. There is evidence of substantial variation in post-communist experience, related to both the general state of the economy and the administrative capacity of the new states. Finally, there has been a growing interest in welfare arrangements in Latin America. The object of the greatest attention here has been the Chilean pension system which has been exhaustively surveyed and reviewed ever since the World Bank (1994) recommended it as a model to be followed throughout the Western world and 'the answer' to the problems of ageing societies.

A second set of responses to Esping-Andersen has come from those who insist that the almost exclusive focus upon labour-market indicators to classify welfare states is misplaced. *Decommodification* is an inappropriate measure of welfare entitlement for those whose welfare opportunities are not (or are not predominantly) defined by their relationship to the formal labour market. Critics insist that Esping-Andersen is still too beholden to a traditional social democratic model of what a welfare state should be (a full employment society with extensive universalist rights) and unaware of the limitations of such an account as an ideal of social citizenship. The most important source of these criticisms has been a number of feminist writers. Thus Jane Lewis (1992) constructs an alternative typology comparing a number of European welfare states in terms of their varying correspondence to a 'male-breadwinner model' in which social policy is built around the gendered division of 'breadwinning for men and caring/homemaking for women'. Within this typification, Lewis identifies Britain as a 'strong male-breadwinner' state which, despite the removal of many explicit forms of discrimination against women, still underwrites a gendered welfare state (through, for example, its failure to make adequate child care provision): 'while no effort is now made to stop women working, the assumption is that women will be secondary wage earners and, despite the large numbers of women in paid employment, they tend to be in short part-time, low status work' (Lewis, 1992, p. 165). In Lewis's classification, France is characterized as a 'modified' male-breadwinner state (with much of the modification being routed through family policy) with Sweden as the weakest male-breadwinner state. In a similar contribution, Orloff (1993) seeks to reconcile mainstream and feminist accounts in proffering an account of regimes which is much more sensitive to the gendered impact of existing social policy provision (and omissions). She draws attention to family as a dimension of welfare delivery, to the gendered impact of the state's treatment of paid and unpaid labour and to the gender blindness of prevailing conceptions of welfare citizenship and decommodification. She adds two further elements to regime classification: differential access to paid work and 'the capacity to form and maintain an autonomous household' (Orloff, 1993, pp. 318–20).

Finally, in this context, there has been a growing concern that Esping-Andersen's classification applies best to more traditional 'employment societies', that is to societies which, even if they did not support full employment, built their welfare apparatus around lifelong (male) involvement in waged work. Increasingly, developed economies have deviated from this model. Apart from the obvious rise in unemployment, there has been a transformation in the gender composition of the workforce, in the balance between full-time and part-time employment, in (perceived) levels of job security and so on. Increasing numbers of people enter the workforce late or leave it early or participate on an intermittent basis. Low wages, short hours and activity in the informal economy mean that a declining proportion of the adult population of working age are developing an entitlement to 'earned' or contributory benefits (see, for example, Commission on Social Justice, 1994).

Globalization: Regime Convergence 'at the bottom'?

Through the work of Esping-Andersen and his critics, we now have a much greater sense of the full diversity of international welfare states' experience. Welfare states vary not just in their size, but also in terms of the bases of their funding, their patterns of entitlement, their forms of delivery and their redistributive capacity. The extent to which welfare regimes treat *all* their citizens equally, as the feminists have amply shown, varies significantly from state to state. There is then some irony that, just as the tools for comparative analysis of welfare state diversity are becoming more sophisticated, we are faced with a process, *globalization*, which at least some of its advocates suggest is inexorably driving all social policy regimes in the same direction (often, in a precipitate 'race to the bottom'). This position was discussed in some detail in chapter 2. At its simplest, the argument is that processes of globalization (above all, the integration of global financial and labour markets) are stripping national governments of discretion over domestic economic policy. States under these circumstances are thought to be concerned, above all, with fostering national *competitiveness*, which in turn is said to mean lowering taxes on capital (by reducing social costs) and increasing the attractiveness of labour (by constraining wages and raising skills). For many commentators, it is above all else this process of globalization which is moving us towards social and economic circumstances that are 'beyond the welfare state'. How sound is this judgement?

Although some critics prefer to describe the changes that have taken place in the world economy as 'internationalization' rather than 'globalization', there can be little doubt that very significant changes have taken place. In the OECD, international trade grew by some 50 per cent between 1960 and 1989. The world stock of foreign direct investment nearly quadrupled between 1980 and 1990. Most dramatic of all has been the rate of growth in international financial movements. Turnover in world currency markets increased from $150 billion per day in 1986 to $900 billion in 1992 (Busch, 1997, p. 23). Of course, these apparently dramatic figures can mislead. Much of the new foreign direct investment, for example, is *between* the more developed states of Europe, North America and Japan, rather than, as the globalization story might suggest, into the low-cost, newly industrialised economies and some have suggested that the 'new' international openness, in fact, marks a *return* to the sorts of levels that prevailed in the period before 1914 (Hirst and Thompson, 1996). Unusually, Garrett and Mitchell (1995) argue that in respect of income transfers and for the period down to 1990, globalization actually *increased* OECD governments' welfare effort. But whatever weight one attributes to these qualifications, it is clear that there have been some very real changes. The deregulation of international markets and of financial institutions has weakened the capacities of the interventionist state, rendered all economies more 'open' and made national capital and more especially national labour movements much more subject to the terms and conditions of international competition. Inasmuch as the postwar welfare state truly was a *Keynesian* Welfare State, those changes in the international economy which have precipitated a decline in Keynesianism can be seen to have had a very material effect on welfare state regimes. The prospects for sustaining long-term, corporatist arrangements within particular nation states (including the institutionalization of a 'social wage') look much less promising in a deregulated international economy.[1] If talk of a 'race to the bottom' in terms of social protection is exaggerated, there is nevertheless significant evidence of 'competitive deregulation' and 'regulatory arbitrage' as states seek to attract internationally mobile capital and 'price' the unskilled and semi-skilled back into work (Cerny, 1995, 1997).

Yet we need to be cautious in drawing any straightforward predictions about the future 'demise' of the welfare state from this evidence. Many commentators insist that under the new international economic order, the state will still be very active. Indeed, states may actually increase their interventions in, for example, training and retraining and in the transition from education to work (Offe, 1987). Certainly, a number of recent reforms under the general rubric of 'welfare to work' have seen a much more 'active' state involvement in the management of unemployment and the unemployed, and insofar as welfare state interventions have an *efficiency* effect – improving the nation's stock of 'social capital' – we might expect such interventions to *increase* under more internationally competitive circumstances (see Barr, 1987, above, p. 148). At the same time, the rise of supra-national institutions in the new economic order may enhance welfare state interventions. As we shall see, the harmonization of social policy throughout the European Community, the adjudications of the European Court and the enactment of the European Social Charter may force certain member states to *increase* their welfare provision (Cram, 1997). We also need to exercise a little caution in attributing every episode of welfare state 'downsizing' to the forces of globalization. In an era of welfare state retrenchment, as Paul Pierson points out (1994), the politics of welfare is about the avoidance of blame and bowing to the irresistible pressure of anonymous global economic forces may sometimes serve as a convenient excuse for hard-pressed politicians. Untangling the 'pull' and 'push' in particular policy episodes is never easy, but it is worth remembering that politicians may have good cause to attribute unpleasant changes to globalization.

We should be cautious, as well, about assuming that the pressures of globalization will impact in just the same way upon all welfare states or indeed that there will necessarily be real convergence around a single model of 'the welfare state after globalization'. Some welfare states are more exposed to international pressures than others. A number of commentators in the USA, for example, argue that, whatever its impact else-

---

[1] On the much-contested relationship between corporatism, organized capitalism and the welfare state, see Middlemas (1979); Cawson (1986); Panitch (1986); Pierson (1991).

where, globalization has comparatively little to do with the reform of US welfare institutions (see Martin, 1997). In the West European context, Rhodes argues that whilst the pressures of globalization may be common, they call forth differing sorts of responses in the several regime types that Esping-Andersen and others have identified (Rhodes, 1996). Britain, for example, has gone much further than its continental neighbours in deregulating labour markets, leaving it with a pattern (of lower unemployment but higher income inequality) that is rather more like that of the USA. Similarly, both Australia and New Zealand 'opened' their economies to international forces during the 1980s but the pattern of deregulation which followed was qualitatively different in both countries (Castles, Gerritsen and Vowles, 1996).

In fact, quite as important as the 'direct' impact of globalizing forces upon domestic welfare regimes has been the 'indirect' influence it has had upon the restructuring of domestic political interests and capacities. Developments here would include the further prioritizing of the interests of financial over manufacturing capital and the diminishing influence and capacity of organized labour. At the same time, economic interests amongst the working population have been reordered, with greater income dispersion, differences of interest between those in the 'sheltered' and internationally exposed sections of the economy and a decline in opportunities for those with few marketable skills, which has made the problem for those at the lower end of the social scale not so much poverty as *social exclusion*. In the global economy, class may be experienced 'less and less as collective fate' and much more as an aspect of 'an individual's "biography"' (Giddens, 1994, p. 143). The costs of retrenchment do not, then, fall evenly across the population but rather tend to reflect the new balance of political forces. Thus, despite the talk of targeting, the reconstruction of the British welfare state has tended to see a squeeze upon the standard of provision for those poorest and most dependent on the state and at least a partial protection of the mainstream and popular areas of the mass welfare state (education, health and pensions) as well as a transfer of public spending effort from public to private sector housing (Taylor-Gooby, 1985, 1988).

The Welfare State: A Victim of its own Success?

Finally, we should consider the claim that, in fact, it is the previous *successes* of the welfare state which imperil its continued well-being. This claim takes a number of forms. First, it is argued that a changing division of labour and changing taxation regimes under the welfare state generate a new social and electoral division between those primarily dependent upon the welfare state (for income and/or employment) and those whose welfare is more immediately dependent upon the private sector. This is seen to undermine that alliance between working and middle classes or that commonality of interest within the broad working class upon which the post-war welfare state was constructed. Sectoral differences (of public v. private) override more traditionally defined class differences (of manual v. non-manual workers). In electoral terms, the welfare state now attracts a broad but minority coalition of interests (within both middle and working classes). But this is characteristically outweighed by a majority based upon the nurturing of the private sector, a majority which now embraces a significant section of the skilled, regularly employed and often home-owning working class (see, *inter alia*, Dunleavy, 1980; Dunleavy and Husbands, 1985; Heath and Evans, 1988).

Secondly, it is argued that the very security and affluence which the welfare state has guaranteed (above all to the securely employed middle classes within the welfare state sector) generate a growing incentive for these same social actors to *defect* from reliance upon state-provided welfare. The defection of sections of the middle class (and increasingly of the more affluent and securely employed sections of the working class) from support of public provision, encourages a transformation from a mass-based universal welfare state towards a system of much more residual provision for the poor and dependent. This process is encouraged by a general rise in affluence and 'consumer sovereignty' in the developed industrial countries. As the population becomes increasingly used to exercising its enhanced purchasing power to acquire non-standardized goods and services within an increasingly diverse marketplace, so, it is argued, do consumers wish to exercise increasing choice and discretion over such vital commodities as health care and educational provision. All these changes will not lead to the disappearance of the welfare state, it is suggested, but they will move it ever more clearly from a 'universal' towards a 'residual' regime (OECD, 1988; Offe, 1987).

The UK, in which the process of change is seen to have been most pronounced, is a useful testing ground for these claims. Evidence of a change in patterns of electoral support is keenly contested and other cleavages (for example, those based upon geographical or functional region) are sometimes given greater weight than the public sector/private sector divide (Johnson, Pattie and Allsopp, 1988). Nonetheless, considerable evidence has been marshalled to suggest that the public/private divide was an important component of the remarkable electoral successes of the Conservative governments of the 1980s, particularly in explaining the limited shift of middle class votes towards the Labour Party and of skilled working class votes towards the Conservatives (Dunleavy, 1980; Dunleavy and Husbands, 1985; Heath and Evans, 1988). Changes in government spending and tax allowances have encouraged a continuation of the long-term post-war trend of growth in owner-occupation of housing and in private pension schemes. Private health insurance has increased rapidly (from a very low base) and there has been some expansion of private education. While there is continuing popular support for mainstream areas of the welfare state, there is also some evidence that this support may be becoming increasingly fragile and that it 'coexists with concern at standards in the state sector' (Taylor-Gooby, 1988, p. 14).

However, these changes do not straightforwardly evidence a transfer of support from public to private welfare premised on the self-defeating successes of the welfare state. First, as we have seen, the welfare state has never been straightforwardly a barometer of popular sympathy for collective provision. Just as there were sources other than public opinion at the origins and in the development of the welfare state, so we should anticipate that other policy sources and objectives will influence its 're-structuring'. Secondly, the privatization of welfare builds upon already well-established forms of the non-state allocation of goods. Thus, for example, the growth of owner occupation and of occupational pensions was as much a feature of the 'Golden Age' of the welfare state as it has been of the years of retrenchment and 'restructuring'. Thirdly, 'private' welfare does not always correspond to individual consumers making welfare choices within an unregulated welfare market. For many of the beneficiaries of private health insurance, these benefits are provided by their employers and are properly a part of the system of occupational welfare. Similarly, it is state interventions, especially in the form of tax expenditures, that make particular forms of private welfare – be it schooling or housing or pensions – sufficiently attractive to trigger 'defections' or 'opting out' of the state system. As Taylor-Gooby notes, the choice of private rather than public provision is influenced by 'the capacity to pay, the structure of subsidies and the availability and quality of alternatives' (Taylor-Gooby, 1988, p. 9; see also Taylor-Gooby and Papadakis, 1987). While there is a long-standing belief that for workers 'affluence equals privatism', at least in the field of welfare, the picture is more complex (see, *inter alia*, Sombart, 1976, Goldthorpe et al., 1968). Greater affluence (the capacity to pay) may make private provision a possibility. However, the take up of this opportunity is likely to be further influenced by (1) the ways in which state or employers *subsidize* particular types of welfare choices, (2) the extent to which the state offers an attractive alternative and (3) the extent to which 'anti-defection' incentives are built into the public system.

To accept that greater affluence and the expression of greater consumer choice must *necessarily* lead to a defection from welfare state provision is to concede too much to the New Right position, before their claims have been properly tested. However, at the same time, it should be recognized that there is no unshiftable alliance in favour of a citizenship, mass-based and universal welfare state. Whatever sort of welfare state we have is likely to be shaped by political choices and state structures. Under present circumstances, that political alliance which will support mass welfare state provision must be seen to be potentially fragile and the welfare state correspondingly vulnerable to a process of deep-seated 'restructuring'.

Growth to Limits or Limits to Growth?

One final proposition about the transformation of the welfare state raised in the Introduction needs to be considered here. It is of a rather distinct character from the other claims. In essence, it is the view that further development of the welfare state should be resisted not because historically it has been anti-progressive, but because the welfare state is irrevocably tied to a strategy of economic growth and the imperatives of this economic growth are no longer consonant with the meeting of real human needs and the sustainable securing of human welfare. We have seen that this is the core claim of the Green critique of the welfare state.

It is certainly true that, while the welfare state has frequently been held responsible for depressing economic growth, the expansion of the welfare state has itself been premised upon the remarkable growth of the Western industrialized economies after 1945. Most advocates of the welfare states' growth have seen the generation of a greater economic product as the necessary basis for enhanced (re)distribution. Recent years have seen the rising popularity of a series of arguments which insist that present patterns of economic growth – and particularly the exhaustion of finite resources and the generation of waste which it is beyond the capacity of the ecosystem to absorb – are inconsistent with the long-term sustainability of the human species. In this most fundamental sense, the growth-based welfare state is inconsistent with the securing of general human welfare. It is also argued that the human and social costs of economic growth – stress-related illness, the diseases of affluence, unsatisfying labour and the direct economic costs of these social ills – make the 'economy of the welfare state' self-defeating. Inasmuch as the welfare state is irretrievably tied into an unsustainable pattern of economic development, it is antithetical to the realization of real long-term welfare.

These are powerful arguments. While the precise parameters of sustainability remain contested, and estimations of the required changes in our economic practice fluctuate wildly, there is little doubt that existing patterns of economic exploitation and economic growth cannot be supported indefinitely (Pearce, Markandya and Barbier, 1989; Dobson, 1995; Jacobs, 1996). As is now widely recognized, however, the issue is not necessarily one of arresting economic growth. The problem is rather one of ecological equilibrium or sustainability and a sustainable economy may permit of economic growth. It is *unsustainable* growth – growth which overloads the capacity of the ecosystem to process natural waste or which exhausts finite resources without offering substitutes – that is inimical to long-term welfare. There is lively disagreement about how precisely sustainability should be defined and how it can be achieved, whether through a more regulated market and tax incentives, through a more interventionist state or through the decentralization of economic and decision making to the most local level (Jacobs, 1989; Pearce, Markandya and Barbier, 1989; Dobson, 1995).

Whatever the economic parameters of this problem, it is clear that it presents a very specific and intractable social and political challenge. Amidst the many general difficulties, we can identify at least three specific challenges which immediately confront the welfare state. First, it seems impossible any longer to proceed as if the welfare state could be solely concerned with the *redistribution* of an exogenous economic product. Some sort of positive-sum welfare state economy *may* still be possible, but the belief that economic growth can be allowed to proceed untrammelled and its dysfunctions compensated for by the welfare state, is no longer tenable when the character of growth and its consequences for social welfare is so problematic. Secondly, if we take the global nature of the problem of economic growth and its welfare consequences seriously, we cannot continue to understand the securing of welfare as a purely national issue, as an issue for conventional national welfare states. It is now widely recognized that the neighbourhood effects/external costs of economic growth fall upon an international or even upon a global community. Thirdly, changing parameters of economic growth and a global economy mean raising not only the issue of intergenerational welfare, but also the more immediate question of intra-national or inter-regional equity. Sustainable development may allow of some economic growth, but given the sorts of constraints which sustainability may require us to impose, is it possible for the Western welfare state economies to continue to command even their present proportion of economic resources? In this sense, the problem for the future of the welfare state is not primarily an economic one (sustainable growth might make available a modestly growing social product). The real and more daunting challenge is to discover political institutions which are consistent with the dictates of sustainability and the securing of general human welfare, and then to realize them.

The Challenge to Social Democracy

Overall, evidence that we are moving towards circumstances that are 'beyond the welfare state' is rather mixed. Certainly, there is limited reason to believe that we face a simple crisis brought on by the economic, political or demographic contradictions of the welfare state. Some system of public provision of welfare looks set to stay with us into the indefinite future. But the types of welfare state which we will inhabit (and these are already quite different throughout the Western industrialized world) seem liable to change under the impact of a range of economic, social, political and ecological pressures. These pressures, and the changes that may follow from them, present varying problems for many of the accounts of welfare state development which we have reviewed in this book. But for none of these is the challenge as acute as it is for social democracy, both as a political practice and as a political ideology. We have seen that it is mistaken to describe the welfare state as 'the institutional embodiment of social democracy', and while the welfare state has had an important place in social democrats' strategic thinking, it is probably also mistaken to think that they have characteristically seen the welfare state as an 'engine of equality' (see Hindess, 1987). Yet the challenge facing the welfare state is peculiarly severe for social democrats. Changes in the global economy have done much to discredit the traditional political economy and generally reformist strategy of social democracy. Changes in the class basis of the welfare state and the imperilling of the sorts of social and electoral alliances upon which this was built are above all threats to the social base of social democratic forces. Finally, the critique of a policy based on the extraction of a social levy upon a growing market economy seems above all to confront the rationale of post-war social democracy and the 'costless' social change which the Keynesian welfare state seemed to promise.

The challenge of a 'restructured' welfare state is above all then a challenge for social democracy, and with the return to power of a number of centre-left governments in the mid-1990s, this became an 'active' issue in a way which, for much of the 1980s, it had not been. In the closing pages of this chapter, I consider a number of alternative responses to this impasse. Broadly described, these respond to the difficulties of the social democratic welfare state by advocating (1) an *'updating' of the traditional institutions of 'social justice'* to bring these in line with the economic and social circumstances of the 1990s, (2) the replacement of the existing complex (and outdated) apparatus of social democratic welfare states with a maximum *basic income* for all citizens and (3) an abandonment of the traditional aspirations of the welfare state in favour of a commitment to *the generative politics of positive welfare*. In assessing these alternatives, I draw some general conclusions about the nature of the state and of democratization under any revised form of social democracy.

Reinstating Social Justice: The Case of the Borrie Commission

In December 1992, the late John Smith, leader of the British Labour Party, established a Commission on Social Justice under the auspices of the Institute for Public Policy Research (IPPR) and the chairmanship of Sir Gordon Borrie. It was the task of the Commission to consider how the aspiration to social justice within the welfare state (broadly conceived) might be reconciled with the imperatives of a modern social and economic order. In some sense, the task of the Commission was to generate a reform agenda for the welfare state which would reconcile traditional social democratic ambitions (brought broadly under the rubric of 'social justice') with a transformed social and economic environment.

When the Commission's final report appeared in the autumn of 1994 (Commission on Social Justice, 1994, p. 18), it rendered social justice in terms of 'a hierarchy of four ideas':

1   That the foundation of a free society is the equal worth of all its citizens, expressed most basically in political and civil liberties, equal rights before the law and so on;
2   That everyone is entitled, as a right of citizenship, to be able to meet their basic needs for income, shelter and other necessities . . . the ability to meet basic needs is the foundation of a substantive commitment to the equal worth of all citizens;
3   That self-respect and equal citizenship demand . . . opportunities and life chances ['That is why we are concerned with the primary distribution of opportunity, as well as its redistribution'];
4   *To achieve the first three conditions of social justice*, we must recognize that although not all inequalities are unjust . . . unjust inequalities should be reduced and where possible eliminated.

The Commission concluded that a series of 'revolutionary' changes (globalization of the economy, a transformation of the status and working lives of women and a drastic shift in the relationship between state and citizen) had made the old social democratic routes to social justice impassable. The old agenda, using taxation and social expenditure to protect the vulnerable and to redistribute wealth, would no longer work. This strategy of 'the levellers' had to give way to an 'investor's strategy' based upon 'a new combination of active welfare state, reformed labour market, and strong community' (p. 96):

Investors believe we can combine the ethics of community with the dynamics of a market economy. [They believe] that the extension of economic opportunity is not only the source of economic prosperity but also the basis of social justice. The competitive requirement for constant innovation and higher quality demands opportunities for every individual ... to contribute to national economic renewal; this in turn demands strong social institutions, strong families and strong communities, which enable people and companies to grow, adapt and succeed. (Commission on Social Justice, pp. 95, 4)

Happily, for the Commission, 'the extension of economic opportunity is not only the source of economic prosperity but also the basis of social justice'. The call for a virtuous marriage between efficient production and just distribution (of both wealth and opportunities) is developed in the central policy chapters of the Commission's Report. This aspiration is especially clear in the priority given to education: 'Lifelong learning is at the heart of our vision of a better country' (p. 120). The primary emphasis is upon the production of wealth through developing a highly skilled and adaptable workforce. Maximizing the skills and earning capacity of individuals optimizes both individual *and* social welfare. Work 'is the heart of wealth and welfare' and 'paid work remains the best pathway out of poverty, as well as the only way which most people can hope to achieve a decent standard of living' (p. 151). Consequently, the Commission insisted that 'Government must accept its responsibility to secure full employment' and it identified three strategies for maximizing employment:

Increasing the demand for labour.   Above all through internationally co-ordinated macro-economic action to stimulate economic growth.
A fair and efficient distribution of unemployment and employment.   This would involve a jobs, education and training strategy (JET) combining incentives and opportunities for new employees and employers 'to get the long-term unemployed and lone mothers back to work'. It would also involve a reallocation of opportunities and responsibilities between men and women in the performance of paid and unpaid work.
Rewarding employment.   Normally, paid work should guarantee an adequate income. The government should legislate for a minimum wage and minimum legal rights for workers, including the right to trade union representation.

The Social Justice Report was widely seen as a blueprint for the future of the welfare state but it is clear that the Commission's conception of the welfare state is a broad one and its prior concern is with welfare generated through value added in the formal economy. In an increasingly global market economy, the only way to achieve a broadly distributed prosperity is said to be through an economy of high added value, built upon a skilled, adaptable and innovative workforce in circumstances where government intervenes to promote the fullest possible levels of employability. In support of this view, the Commission insisted that 'a higher social security budget is a sign of economic failure, not social success' (p. 104). Nonetheless, the Report does include quite detailed plans for the creation of an 'active' and 'intelligent' welfare state. Overall, the strategy is for a social security system that promotes pathways 'from welfare to work'. In what is becoming a truly global politicians' cliché, the welfare state is to be changed 'from a safety net cushioning economic failure into a trampoline for economic success' (p. 103). In meeting this ambition, however, the Report rejected widespread means testing in favour of a 'new universalism' constructed around 'a modern social insurance system'. Institutional structures would need to reflect the fundamental changes to patterns of employment and family formation that have taken place since the inauguration of the Beveridge system, including benefits for part-time workers and the self-employed, as well as new provision to reflect parental responsibilities. But the primary motivation for reforming means-tested benefits is to overcome disincentives to taking up paid work and thus to produce the preferred transition from welfare to work.

The 'New' Social Democracy: An Assessment

The Manifesto with which the British Labour Party won a landslide victory at the 1997 General Election spoke of marrying traditional values to new institutions. To what extent does the Social Justice Commission succeed in giving an account of just such a modernization in welfare state institutions? Certainly, the virtuous circle of education, work and welfare and the happy marriage of equality and efficiency which the Report sets out are attractive ideas, not least as a counterpoint to that orthodoxy of the right which insists that the route to economic efficiency lies through ever greater inequality and that the only way to increase employment is to press for ever lower wages. And yet, unhappily, we cannot be so sure that the transition to an economy which marries equality and efficiency is actually so easily achieved. The Report certainly subscribes to an essentially optimistic view of globalization which, far from forcing unskilled labour in the developed economies to compete with the cheapest of Third World workers, will create new employment opportunities for highly skilled, high value-added employees in the West. But can we be confident that this is really what will happen? Already the countries of the Pacific Rim are moving to equip themselves to compete in these value-added labour markets, making more substantial investment in training and education. With the best intentioned of active governments, we cannot be confident that an undermanaged global economy will necessarily secure adequate employment opportunities for all those who want waged work – and certainly not at wages which will support them and their families. It is certainly possible that dual labour markets and the division between core and peripheral workers will prove much more intractable than the confident noises about training and reskilling suggest. Evidence from the Australian Labor Party's labour market reforms of the early 1990s suggests that getting the long-term unemployed back into the workforce is both hard and expensive (Junankar and Kapuscinski, 1997).

If this is the case, what should happen when equality and efficiency do *not* coincide? And what if democratic publics are reluctant to fund the provision to overcome discrimination? Social justice (even upon the Commission's quite modest definition) would seem to require that equality should take priority over efficiency but it is hard to foresee the circumstances in which a government would be willing and able to realize this commitment. These hard questions are largely defined away by the Report's confidence about what is possible. In what we might see as a classically social democratic move, the hard questions about justice – how should limited resources be (re)distributed – are finessed by the expectation that overall economic growth will make such issues irrelevant.

Ranking second in the Commission's four propositions on justice is the belief 'that everyone is entitled, *as a right of citizenship*, to be able to meet their basic needs for income, shelter and other necessities'. This commitment to meeting basic need is closely connected to the first and prior proposition in so far as 'the ability to meet basic needs is the foundation of a *substantive* commitment to the equal worth of all citizens'. The real difficulty is in establishing just what constitutes basic need, how extensive is the domain of social provision according to need (rather than according to some other distributive principle, such as merit and desert) and to what extent such entitlement is a measure of citizenship? When the demands of economic reconstruction conflict with entitlement based upon citizenship, which principle will yield? Similar difficulties surround the Commission's commitment to equality of opportunity which far from being 'a rather weak aspiration, is in fact very radical, if it is taken seriously' (IPPR, 1993, p. 9). In fact, much of the Commission's case for equality of opportunity is really a case against existing forms of discrimination (in education or in the labour and housing markets, for example). For the most part, it stops short of a consideration of those inequalities that arise from the unequal control of investment decisions. Thus, characteristically, it concentrates on unequal *pay* rather than wider inequalities of *wealth*. This is surely, in part, because the Commission does not wish or is not able to address those forms of inequality which are endemic to capitalism. In the end what we have is something like a recommendation for 'citizenship in one class'.

Justifiable Inequalities?

The final principle identified by the Commission is that '*to achieve the first three conditions of social justice*, we must recognize that although not all inequalities are unjust ... unjust inequalities should be reduced and where possible eliminated'. The idea of *justifiable inequalities* is a key component of social democrats' meliorist thinking. It is given its most systematic statement in John Rawls' 'difference principle'. In attempting to establish those general principles which would define a just society, Rawls argues that, with a number of basic civil liberties secured, 'social and economic inequalities are to be arranged so that they are to the greatest benefit of the least disadvantaged'. Potentially, the difference principle is very radical and might require the very substantial redistribution of resources. It is not a principle of economic equality (since wealth differentials may always be justified by their capacity to sponsor improvements in the social well-being of society's least advantaged). However, once 'the difference principle is accepted ... it follows that the minimum is to be set at that point which ... maximizes the expectations of the least advantaged group' (Rawls, 1973, p. 285).

In fact, the Borrie Commission's advocacy of justifiable inequalities is much less radical and more pragmatic than this. It is not clear if they favour inequalities on grounds of justice ('generally people get their due') or utility ('it's not very fair, but it is very productive') or the sheer awfulness of the available alternatives ('command economies are unworkable and authoritarian'). Probably it is a mixture of all three. Whatever Rawls or anyone else may say, it just is the case, so far as the Commission is concerned, that people generally accept that inequalities in the market arising from luck or natural talent or effort are deserved and to this extent the inequalities to which they give rise are (seen to be) just.

In the end this is a fairly traditional social democratic strategy. The instruments of policy may be rather different – there is less emphasis upon the state and redistribution, rather more upon the extension of opportunity and self-provisioning. But the overall ambition remains one of redressing social ills through growth (more work, more tax revenue, more welfare generated in the market economy). In some sense, the Commission's case for social justice rests upon an economic gamble that growth can be delivered. Of course, to some extent, all but the most ascetic conceptions of social justice rest upon generating a social surplus. But the principles outlined here make out a rather weak case for increased justice *if the economy does not grow* or *if it does not grow fast enough*. From this there follows a question about the environmental limits of such a conception of social justice. The Commission rules out of its remit (perhaps with some justification) a consideration of the international and intergenerational elements of social justice. But if we take such claims seriously, the traditional social democratic case – that growth can be a surrogate for redistribution – looks very much weaker. Perhaps we can still be persuaded of their case within what is still an affluent middle-sized Western European state. But can we really accept it for an increasingly global economy and society, in which distribution between rich and poor seems to be becoming still more unequal? If not, we shall need rather different criteria of social justice which can confront 'hard' questions of redistribution.

'The Second Marriage of Justice and Efficiency': The Case for a Basic Income

In essence, the Social Justice Commission's Report can be seen as an attempt to renovate and reinvigorate the institutional framework through which social democratic welfare states have been organized, to bring this in line with important changes in the contemporary economy and society. The approach of advocates of a basic income solution to these problems is rather different and potentially much more radical. For them, securing those enduring core *values* which the best of social democratic welfare states embodied – perhaps, above all, the promotion of social justice – is only possible now through a radical institutional reform which abandons many of social democracy's traditional solutions. At the heart of this reform agenda is the proposal to introduce for all citizens an unconditional basic income (BI).

> A *basic income* . . . is an income paid by the government to each full member of society (1) even if she is not willing to work, (2) irrespective of being rich or poor, (3) whoever she lives with, and (4) no matter which part of the country she lives in. (Van Parijs, 1995, p. 35)

BI might be set at different levels for different categories of persons (with a higher rate for the elderly and disabled and a lower rate for children) but it is unconditional in as much as it is paid to all residents/citizens of a political community as individuals without any test of income or wealth and irrespective of employment status or indication of a 'willingness to work'. The level of BI is an open question. It is not defined in terms of some notional set of 'basic needs'. A BI might fall below subsistence level (and need to be 'topped up' by other sources of income) or it could, as in the account of BI's most sophisticated contemporary advocate, Philippe Van Parijs (1995), be set at the maximum sustainable level (presumed to be much above subsistence). Certainly, most supporters aspire to see the BI reaching a level at which it would 'replace' all existing income maintenance benefits and allow for the abolition of all personal reliefs set against income tax (McKay, 1998).

The advocates of BI devote considerable intellectual energy to showing, perhaps at first sight counter-intuitively, that their scheme has a powerful claim to be both just and efficient. Objections to the claim that BI is just have focused upon the belief that an *unconditional* BI gives the idle 'something for nothing', enabling them to exploit the hard-working members of society whose efforts are taxed to pay for their idleness. This objection is resisted on the basis that a part of economic wealth in any period is the consequence of the accumulated assets and knowledge of earlier generations and the productive capacity of our natural environment, both of which constitute a common stock of resources for the use of which *all* of society's members are entitled to some compensation. In Van Parijs's account (1995), all of those who take up scarce resources (including in his account the scarce resource of jobs) owe a rent to the rest of society and this would be the source of BI. A second claim – that a maximal BI would be economically efficient – is also resisted with some well-worn arguments. Critics insist that a BI set at even a quite modest level would undermine incentives, discouraging the less skilled from entering the labour market and placing a fiscal burden upon capital and more skilled workers which would encourage them to lessen their effort or withdraw from the formal economy. Supporters of a BI are generally sanguine about these objections. At one level, they resist the idea that maximizing GDP and participation in paid employment is so desirable. Critics, like Van Parijs, argue that what we should be seeking to maximize is not income but real freedom for all (allowing individuals to choose as freely as possible what it is they want to do with their lives). They argue, too, that traditional accounts have privileged paid employment over other forms of work (especially the unpaid labour of women within the household) which have often not been seen to count as work at all. But even within a more traditional framework, BI is recommended as efficient – allowing individuals to take on work at very low wages (because of the income support that a BI would provide), allowing workers to retrain without excessive cost, to start new enterprises without undue risk, encouraging greater flexibility in forms of work and easier movement between household and employment. In general, the greater economic flexibility which a BI underwrites is said to 'completely overshadow' concerns about the disincentive effects of the new tax regime upon which it would be based (Van Parijs, 1992, p. 233).

Basic income has been widely commended amongst its supporters as a way out of the impasse of contemporary social democratic welfare policy. The post-war social democratic welfare states were able to forge a workable, if quite imperfect, marriage of justice and efficiency. But typically these regimes were built around progressive taxation, full employment, corporatist industrial relations, massified semi-skilled labour, Fordist labour processes and constrained capital mobility. Although, as we have seen in earlier chapters, it is quite misleading to suggest that all citizens fared equally well under these regimes, it makes some sense to talk of these welfare states as incorporating at least an aspiration to common citizenship. Nearly all of the circumstances that characterized these traditional social democratic welfare states are now imperilled. Even if, as we have also seen already, claims about 'jobless growth', globalization of capital markets and tax resistance are exaggerated, the social policy context is profoundly changed. If the full (male) employment Keynesian welfare state is a thing of the past we may now need new social and economic arrangements to deliver a 'workable' form of justice and efficiency. It is in meeting this specification that BI is most often recommended. Where lifelong employment (and its attendant pension and social insurance rights) are much less certain, where relations between men and women and between both and the world of formal employment are so changed, where marriage is for many a serial experience, the old remedies are becoming increasingly unworkable. Social democrats are exhorted to move from a defence of what remains of the Fordist welfare state towards BI as the underpinning of a 'second marriage of justice and efficiency' (Van Parijs, 1992).

Basic Income: An Assessment

The proponents of an unconditional BI have some very powerful arguments on their side. A part of the promise of post-war social democracy was to check income inequality. Yet the last twenty years have seen a systematic trend towards greater income inequality which has now spread to virtually all the developed welfare states. The provision of a BI promises to reverse this trend. Set at a moderately high level, it would also replace the jungle of existing conditional benefits and entitlements (and various poverty traps) with a clear and unambiguous commitment to adequate baseline incomes. For its proponents, it offers a reform which is radical and egalitarian but without posing an implausible challenge to the institutional apparatus of existing private-ownership market economies. Its breach with traditional social democracy's unrelenting (if sometimes unstated) commitment to economic growth will seem timely to many. But problems remain. Some (quite sympathetic) critics challenge the plausibility of the ethical case for an *unconditional* BI. Stuart White (1997), for example, takes issue with Van Parijs over the latter's insistence that an unconditional BI does not entail the exploitation of those who work by those who choose not to work. Whilst a small unconditional BI might be justified on the basis of equal entitlement to the world's inanimate assets, most economic wealth is the product of co-operative social effort and those who will not contribute in any way to this collective effort are, so White concludes, not entitled to draw an income from the efforts of those who do. Similarly, many remain sceptical about what is in the end an empirical claim that the efficiency-enhancing side-effects of reform (enhanced flexibility) will outweigh the disincentive effects of the increased tax take required to fund a BI.

But perhaps the most profound problem for the BI case is political. BI's two great claims to feasibility are, first, that dysfunctional societies of intensifying environmental degradation allied to growing inequality like ours are in the medium to long term unsustainable and, second, that the reform they promise is radical and egalitarian but consonant with capitalist market economies. Unfortunately, as a wealth of public choice literature shows, the existence of dysfunctionality is not in itself a guarantee that reform – even a reform that disadvantages no-one – will be forthcoming. Certainly, the property regime of a fully implemented BI capitalism would be quite different from anything that operates under that label now – and would not necessarily recommend itself to everyone as an improvement on the present order. At the same time, it is hard to see where the large-scale political support for BI is to be found. In Britain, for example, the Greens are the only party committed to BI. The Liberal Democrats, who were the only major party committed to (a very low level of) BI, have reversed that commitment. The Labour Party is pursuing a 'welfare to work' alternative which *intensifies* the connection between employment and income. The context for reform, which the advocates of a BI do so much to illuminate, is, of course, one in which traditional social democratic solutions have been rendered obsolete at least in part because of a perceived tax reluctance on the part of democratic publics. It is not yet clear that democratic publics in developed welfare states are ready for the cultural revolution which the explicit disconnection of employment and income allied to a significantly increased tax burden (whatever the attendant benefits) would bring. One further issue of feasibility concerns the community within which reform (however gradualist) might be introduced. Can there be BI capitalism in just one country or just one economic community and, if not, through what sort of political mechanism (and what enforcement agency) might it be introduced? None of these objections could be said to weigh exhaustively against the idea of BI. It is about as clear as it can be that the old solutions (of various kinds) do not work. If the advocates of BI are right about the sorts of changes that our societies are undergoing, the time is coming when politicians and public will *have* to take these ideas seriously. But in a context where most people believe that politics is about the serving of powerful interests before it is about the promotion of an ethically optimal community, BI may still struggle to get a fair hearing.

Generative Politics and Positive Welfare

A rather different but still quite radical challenge to traditional social democratic thinking about the welfare state is posed by the recent work of the social theorist Anthony Giddens. Most systematically in *Beyond Left and Right* (1994), Giddens locates the contemporary problems of the social democratic welfare state in the much broader context of the changing character of late modernity and its corresponding political modalities. For much of modernity, so Giddens argues, to be radical was usually to be some sort of a socialist. But at the end of the millennium, in the face of all their political disappointments, socialists seem to have been left with little more than the 'conservative' plea to 'defend the welfare state'. Whilst conservation proves to be an important value for Giddens in a world increasingly threatened by ecological disaster, the transformation of modernity through which we are now living requires that radical politics be radically rethought – and this means a wholesale reorientation of the view that the social democratic left has traditionally taken of welfare.

The broader context which requires this rethink of the welfare state is defined by four major developments. First, there is the intensification of *globalization*, not just as an economic but also a political and cultural force. Second is the extent to which we now live in a *post-traditional social order* in which nothing can be taken for granted and in which every relationship and every aspect of self-identity is provisional and in some sense 'up for grabs'. Third, our societies are characterized by a growth in *social reflexivity* in which our much more provisional and 'chosen' identities and institutions are constantly monitored and permanently vulnerable to redefinition and reformation. Fourth, all these changes take place in a context of increasingly *manufactured uncertainty* and *manufactured risk*. Life has always been risky and our futures uncertain, but increasingly we can see that these uncertainties are the product not of nature but of (quite often intentional) human intervention in the natural world.

Socialism was the radical politics of a 'simpler' modernity, the welfare state an appropriate mechanism for dealing with external (rather than manufactured) uncertainty:

> The 'class compromise' of welfare institutions could remain relatively stable only so long as conditions of simple modernization held good. These were circumstances in which 'industriousness' and paid work remained central to the social system; where class relations were closely linked to communal forms; where the nation-state was strong and even in some respects further developing its sovereign powers; and where risk could still be treated largely as external and to be coped with by quite orthodox programmes of social insurance. None of these conditions holds in the same way in conditions of intensifying globalization and social reflexivity. (Giddens, 1994, p. 149)

New circumstances of reflexive modernity require a much greater emphasis upon the active involvement of citizens (as individuals, families or groups) in making their own welfare arrangements in a process of active engagement with the state. They also offer the opportunity to move from a *productivist* society, driven by an addiction to economic growth (with its attendant twin compulsions to work and to consume), towards a *post-scarcity order*: not a society of abundance, but a society in which the virtues (and vices) of economic growth are given their proper weight rather than unquestioned primacy. In this context, Giddens calls for a new emphasis upon *life politics* – a politics which is about 'how (as individuals and as collective humanity) we should live in a world where what used to be fixed either by nature or tradition is now subject to human decisions' – and *generative politics*, a politics which 'exists in the space that links the state to reflexive mobilization in the society at large . . . a politics which allows individuals and groups to *make things happen*, rather than have things happen to them' (Giddens, 1994, p. 15).

From this follows Giddens's commitment to the idea of *positive welfare*: welfare as the creative, bottom-up, self-activity of citizens and their voluntary associations pursuing greater autonomy and happiness in a 'reflexive engagement with expert systems' (Giddens, 1994, p. 153). Traditional welfare states have treated risks as external (as misfortunes, such as ill health or unemployment, which just happen to people) and its citizens as passive recipients of the state's largesse. They have also operated with a set of assumptions about people's lifestyles (full-time lifelong employment for men, childrearing in stable heterosexual marriages for women) which just do not square with the ways we (choose to) live now. Increasingly, so Giddens argues, we have to recognize that social contingencies, such as ill health, are often the product of individuals' perverse behaviour or neglect (as in the case of smoking or obesity). Remedies lie not just in the hands of the state but in individuals, families and groups exercising 'lifestyle responsibility' (and making themselves happier in the process), often, though not necessarily, in partnership with the state. Given the greater diversity and changeability in individuals' lives (in terms of employment, marital status, household composition and so on) we also need welfare arrangements which foster a *politics of second chances* (Giddens, 1994, p. 172). Giddens insists that existing 'passive' welfare states *can* create demoralizing patterns of welfare dependency and social exclusion, arguing, for example, that retirement at 65 is an arbitrary imposition of inactivity upon a (growing) group of the population which is generally healthy and keen to be economically active (Giddens, 1996, 256–7). What is needed is a welfare regime which is empowering, which provides the opportunities (and sometimes the resources) which will enable individuals to take responsibility for their own well-being.

What would a positive welfare regime look like? Giddens is not prescriptive (since positive welfare is supposed to be permissive rather than obligatory) but he does have a number of indicative suggestions:

> [A system of welfare in a post-scarcity order] would have to escape from reliance on 'precautionary aftercare' as the main means of coping with risk; be integrated with a wider set of life concerns than those of productivism; develop a politics of second chances; create a range of social pacts or settlements, not only between classes but between other groups or categories in the population; and focus on . . . a generative conception of equality. (Giddens, 1994, p. 182)

He envisages a series of social pacts (between rich and poor or between the sexes, for example) in which both sides would trade off something with the other (in terms of employment opportunities or childcare responsibility but not, so Giddens insists, wealth) in order to yield a positive-sum welfare gain for both parties. In substantive terms, he envisages a greater emphasis upon health promotion, a larger role for private pensions and the targeting of benefits and the abolition of statutory retirement (Giddens, 1996). Overall, Giddens's ambitions are quite radical and unambiguous: 'would there still be a welfare state in a post-scarcity society? There would not' (Giddens, 1994, p. 195).

Positive Welfare in a Post-Scarcity Society: An Assessment

How compelling is this account of a radical route to the dissolution of the welfare state? Certainly, Giddens presents a substantial challenge to some very deep-seated assumptions about welfare. His focus upon the problems of the welfare state arising from a changing environment of risk management offers some very distinctive insights into the possibilities of reform and he is surely right to draw attention to the character of the traditional welfare state settlement as gendered and productivist. He is also right to argue that welfare institutions need to respond to changing patterns of employment and family formation, and that citizens of the welfare state are both more capable and more desirous of organizing their own welfare than a paternalistic state has often assumed. It may even be true, as Giddens insists, that being wealthy does not make you happy! And in judging Giddens's account, we should bear in mind that it is written under the rubric of 'utopian realism' – that is, 'it has utopian features, yet is not unrealistic because it corresponds to observable trends' (Giddens, 1994, p. 101).

Yet it is quite unclear that this adds up to a compelling programme of reform for social democrats (or anyone else). In part, this is because Giddens's novel and interesting concern with risk management leads him to downplay other elements in welfare state composition. Social insurance was never 'actuarially sound' and it was there not just to protect against life's contingencies but also to underpin citizenship, to foster 'social solidarity', to meliorate economic inequality and, in some cases to reallocate the social costs of wage labour or maintain income. Giddens's focus upon the preventative elements of health care and the necessity for individuals to take responsibility for their own well-being is well justified. But it is also a part of mainstream public sector healthcare thinking and should not be confused with the claim that individuals are principally responsible for the circumstances that give rise to their ill-health. It is widely accepted that there is an epidemic of childhood asthma in many developed countries. This might reasonably be seen as a side-effect of living in a 'productivist' society, but can hardly be attributed to the patient's self-neglect. Large areas of the welfare state – perhaps, above all, education – do not really fall under the logic of risk management at all. Again, there is clearly some merit in Giddens's endorsement of the claims that welfare states tend to be 'bureaucratic' and 'dependency-creating'. But what is really crucial here are the counter-factuals (that is, the resources with which the welfare-disempowered are imagined to become powerful). However 'clever' (in Giddens's very particular sense) the poor may be, it is hard to see them reflexively working themselves up into full membership of society's mainstream. One of Giddens's most powerful insights is his condemnation of the enforced dependency of 'retirement pensioners'. But (albeit for rather different reasons) states are already moving in the direction that Giddens recommends (towards later retirement, greater formal gender equality and a downgrading of the basic state pension). They are also tangling with (or else avoiding) a whole series of problems to do with inter-generational and intra-generational equity which the moves towards a greater reliance on private pensions and/or other mechanisms of income maintenance implies.

It is clear that Giddens's generative model of welfare in a non-state context relies upon a series of *social pacts* (most grandly that between rich and poor). But it is unclear how these pacts are to be brokered, maintained and policed. To some extent, the welfare state has always been seen as a social pact between rich and poor in which the rich trade off some part of their wealth in return for the poor's quiescence in a regime in which the wealthy retain most of their wealth. The breakdown of this compact may express itself in rising crime against property (though, of course, it remains the poor who are most frequently the victims of such crime). There is now a wealth of public choice literature (classically, see Olson, 1965) to show that the fact that two groups have a mutual interest in some institutional arrangement which will benefit both is no guarantee that such an arrangement will be established and maintained. The generalized interest that both rich and poor have in a clean environment and freedom from the tyranny of a productivist society is rather implausible as the source of a new social compact between them.

Two final reservations might be entered against Giddens's account. First, it could be argued that Giddens allows too much weight to the disempowering of the nation-state. We have already seen that evidence for the coming 'end of the nation-state' is rather patchy. The element of discretion for individual states seems to have receded (indeed this is a large part of the social democratic 'problem') but states have not really shrunk or reduced their tax take over the last twenty years of extended 'crisis'. The idea of a welfare society 'which increasingly forms part of a globalized order, rather than being concentrated within the nation-state' certainly looks to be towards the utopian pole of utopian realism (Giddens, 1994, p. 191). Behind this lies a still more fundamental problem. The *post-scarcity order* lies on 'the "other side" of capitalism' (p. 12). On several occasions Giddens makes clear that we are still dealing with class societies which can be described as capitalist, yet this tends to fall out of his analysis of the ways in which welfare states may be reformed. Critics are bound to feel that the persistence of inequality has at least as much to do with (global) capitalism as the institutions of the welfare state and there is certainly no hint here as to how we are likely to reach that 'other side' of capitalism. The key problem of social democracy is that it seems to have lost the capacity which it was once understood to have to 'tame the excesses of capitalism'. That it should have lost that competence is not the same as saying that this particular problem has gone away.

Conclusion: Defending the Welfare State

At the end of the twentieth century, no-one can write innocently of the benevolent power of the state. If the experience of Stalinism and fascism, to name but two of the most infamous tyrannies of the twentieth century, were not enough, there is also a tradition, perhaps best represented by Foucault, which charts the chronic and petty incursions of the state in the day-to-day life of the modern citizen. If we add to this the rather more mundane 'failures' of social democracy, there can be little surprise that the state in general, and the welfare state in particular, should have become so unfashionable. Yet, in these concluding pages I wish to mount a partial defence of the state's role in welfare, based on the comparative and historical evidence collated in this study.

Perhaps the most basic premise of this defence is the ubiquity of the welfare state. We have seen that welfare states come in a variety of forms and sizes, supported by disparate political and economic forces, seeking to realize differing social outcomes. Certainly, the state may not be needed in all those areas in which it presently intervenes and it may be that such interventions as it does make need not take their present form. Nonetheless, the prospects of any developed society moving towards a 'minimal state' are extremely remote and the idea of marginalizing the welfare state is likely to prove to be both utopian and socially regressive. As we saw in chapter 6, within the envisageable future, the 'real' issue is not going to be whether we have a welfare state (nor even how much it will cost) but what sort of a welfare state regime it will be. The state's allocation of welfare may be changing but nowhere is it disappearing or yielding to a minimal state uninterested in the welfare status of its population. Indeed, the aspiration to move towards a more 'active' welfare state indicates a growing interest on the part of the state in the status and conduct of its welfare clients.

One response to this universality of the welfare state is to insist that, if it has to be maintained as a 'regrettable necessity', we should at least be seeking to minimize its size and the scale of its social interventions. This aspiration to move welfare allocation away from the state takes two especially influential forms. First, there is an initiative, popular in a range of new social movements, to bypass the state by returning welfare to more localized, non-hierarchical and non-bureaucratized forms of communal self-administration. Secondly, there is the neo-conservative strategy of limiting the state's intervention by returning the allocation of welfare to markets (and families). Whatever the practical limitations of these initiatives (and I have attempted to show earlier in the book that these are considerable), they also suffer from a number of weaknesses in principle.

On the first initiative, critics are surely right to point to the difficulties of securing personalized and sensitive social provision through the massified institutions of a legal-administrative state apparatus. But while the development of new forms of welfare self-administration which they recommend is extremely healthy (and ought where appropriate to be supported by the state itself), this is not best understood as an *alternative* to the welfare state. For example, there are circumstances in which anonymity, non-discretionary provision and a professional relationship (which are often seen as characteristic weaknesses of the state sector) may be preferable to a less formal and community-based response. On the ground, the voluntary and not-for-profit sectors are often developing not as an alternative to, but in partnership with, the local state. The state may still be needed to support those who lack the various resources to secure self-help, to benchmark acceptable levels of informal provision and to protect individuals where the interventions of their carers are inappropriate. It is difficult to see how the compulsory revenue-raising power of the state, or many of the services that it funds, could be replaced by some other agency. We may even feel, as Titmuss argued, that there is a special moral quality in meeting the 'needs of strangers' which is best effected through the anonymity of the state. Feminists are surely right to argue that welfare citizenship needs to be rethought and recast – but not abandoned. Strengthening social citizenship and guaranteeing the integrity of the sorts of alternative welfare institutions which new social movements commend may well require a selective strengthening of some of the powers of the interventionist state.

In turning to the neo-conservative response, it is necessary to confront directly the claim that returning welfare functions from the state to the market can be properly considered a process of empowering ordinary citizens. It may certainly enhance the power of certain actors (and sometimes quite 'ordinary' ones) in certain contexts, but consumer sovereignty is not a surrogate for citizen sovereignty. Returning the allocation of (still

more) welfare opportunities to the market is likely to make welfare outcomes still less equitable than under existing welfare state regimes. And,
in the end, claims about the greater efficiency of markets are empirical. If
markets or quasi-markets do not deliver greater efficiency (as at least
some critics have insisted is the case with NHS reform) we have a good
case for seeking an alternative. Furthermore, it is not clear that the intensified individuation of welfare choices is a viable long-term option. In
many ways our current global position requires us to make more, not
fewer, collective choices and necessitates, alongside a possible enhancement of the market in some areas, its stricter regulation in others. In the
end, it is not at all clear that, in the welfare field, the state which governs
least, governs best. To choose a state which intervenes as little as possible
in the social allocation of welfare is to choose a very particular type of
social regime – and not necessarily one we should all be disposed to call
'the best available option'.

Some of these points can be illustrated by returning to the Green agenda
for social and political reform. Green activists are amongst those who
call for a decentralization of welfare provision and for more local, informal and discursive forms of decision taking ('thinking globally whilst
acting locally'). Yet the problems which the Greens have helped to isolate
– of unsustainable growth and maldistribution of global resources – clearly
require enhanced decision making and powers of enforcement at a national and especially a supra-national level. Certain Green welfare initiatives (for example, a guaranteed basic income or a guaranteed right to
sabbatical leave in all forms of employment) actually imply a much larger
role for the state (Dobson, 1995, pp. 112–15). If Green politics are to be
something more than an act of faith, the question of institutional and
constitutional reform in large-scale contexts is unavoidable. The market,
with its seeming decentralization of decision making, is not in itself a
solution. If we think of a position that is sympathetic to both the Green
agenda and to markets (as, for example, in the Pearce report *Blueprint for
a Green Economy*), we see that markets are imagined to give environmen-
tally 'efficient' allocations only within a previously given and politically
chosen framework. Pearce argues that markets can maximize efficiency
and effectiveness at a given level of resource exhaustion or environmental
spoilation, but these framework-setting levels (and crucially decisions about
inter-generational distribution) must be the outcome of political processes and can only be reached through the agency of the state (Pearce,
Markandya and Barbier, 1989). Thus, if we accept even a very weak and
market-sympathetic form of the Green argument that unsustainable economic growth cannot be allowed to continue, then we have a very strong
case for the increased politicization of economic decision making.

Still The Social Democratic Challenge

This leaves a formidable challenge, one which is again most severe for social democracy and its sympathizers. Historically, social democrats 'abandoned' the political agenda of a more traditional socialism on the grounds that the welfare state could deliver an expansive sense of citizenship and increasing social and economic equality within the framework of a (largely) privately owned market economy. Now it seems that, for a whole series of reasons outlined in this book, welfare states are less and less able to guarantee these forms of citizenship and equality but that, often for the very same reasons, alternative routes to 'progressive' outcomes are blocked. For Giddens (1994), this leaves the rather sad spectre of social democrats reduced to defending the ever-diminishing terrain of a form of welfare state which social change has rendered obsolete. Under these circumstances, what, if anything, can be done?

The first point is to resist being swept away by the riptide of globalization. As we have seen, there can be little doubt that processes of globalization have significantly altered the circumstances in which states have to act and that a part of the traditional social democratic policy repertoire is now redundant. In the light of this, it is worth insisting that states have not been comprehensively disempowered and that the much-heralded 'race to the bottom' in terms of social provision has yet to take place. Global (financial) capital markets may be increasingly imaginable (though as yet far from fully consummated), but a global labour market (and with it, a global labour market regime) surely is not. And we have also seen that, in some contexts, a strategy of globalization may be actively *chosen* by political actors, even if they then sell this policy to their constituency as 'unavoidable' and 'externally imposed'. Globalization effects are probably felt most acutely in those areas which are closely related to the governance of labour markets (even if the difficulties in the provision of public goods is more widespread), but even here different options are available. In terms of taxation, globalization has probably had more of an impact upon the distribution of the tax burden (which has generally become less progressive) than upon the capacity of states to raise revenue. As the evidence of Perraton et al. (1997) makes clear, the range of options may have narrowed and the choices to be made may be harder. But there still are choices and what states choose to do still makes a difference. Even in an age of growing income inequality and narrowed policy options, welfare states still moderate income inequalities, generally in favour of women and the elderly (see Hills, 1997). Our survey also shows that different welfare states are differently placed to respond to what may be a near-universal challenge. Whilst recent years have seen a great deal of 'policy transfer' in the welfare arena, they have also seen the persistence of different welfare practices based in quite diverse welfare regimes. In sum, globalization is a process with very real effects, but it is not the death-knell of the welfare state.

Secondly, it is worth considering the new policy instruments which states and the growing number of transnational and inter-governmental agencies (often themselves the product of the pressures of globalization and regionalization) may use. In this context, the European Union presents a particularly interesting example. Despite much talk of the 'social dimension', evidence of an emergent 'European welfare state' is extremely scarce. If, however, we focus not upon positive enactments but upon the extent to which EU institutions have constrained the social policy autonomy of constituent states or the ways in which enactments in other policy fields have had a social policy effect, the role of the European Union will look much more extensive. Thus, 'the last three decades, and especially the most recent one, have witnessed a gradual, incremental expansion of EU-produced regulations and, especially, court decisions that have seriously eroded the sovereignty of national welfare states' (Leibfried and Pierson, 1995, p. 51). European Court of Justice determinations have had a significant policy-making impact in areas such as working hours, equal pay, pension rights and parental leave. Moves to ensure the integrity of a comprehensive single market have involved subjecting national state's social security provision and employment law to community-wide regulation, giving rights to non-citizens and to citizens living beyond the boundaries of their native nation-state. Numerous measures have been taken to limit the opportunities for 'social dumping', 'regime hopping' and various forms of 'regulatory arbitrage'. At the same time, the Community has always pursued social policies under some other name and, in this context, the role of the Structural and Social Funds is dwarfed by the salience of the Community's enduring 'big spender': the Common Agricultural Policy.

Three points emerge from the European experience. First, *regulation* and the enactment of *legal decisions* may be just as important as instruments of social policy as the more traditional forms of service provision. States with legal jurisdiction but depleting resources may look to the experience of the Commission and the European Court of Justice as agencies which influence policy outcomes without the command of significant revenues. Secondly, even the most unshackled of global markets will still require some state-like regulation – if only to protect property rights – and this is a terrain upon which battles over social provision may be engaged. The growth of transnational and inter-governmental institutions (including GATT, the WTO, the World Bank) may not have matched the rapid expansion of global markets, but it is still significant. Thirdly, size does provide some insulation from global trends. Nearly all commentators are agreed that the size of the US domestic market, whilst not isolating it from global pressures, has lessened the immediate impact upon its welfare regime (whose reform is much more widely attributed to domestic sources). We should not assume that there are no forms of transnational or inter-state governance which can guarantee at least minimum international standards of social protection.

A third area of growing interest is provided by a range of non-European welfare states. We have seen that the World Bank has repeatedly drawn policy makers' attention to the Chilean experience, particularly as a model for transition to a largely private and fully funded pensions regime. Of especial interest to social democrats is the recent (and not-so-recent) experience of social provision in Australia. On conventional measures of welfare effort (most simply, the proportion of GDP devoted to social expenditure), Australia has always appeared 'ungenerous'. There is no system of social insurance and virtually all benefits are means-tested. The idea of welfare citizenship is largely absent. In Esping-Andersen's classification (1990), it appears as a small, liberal market-oriented welfare state. But this is rather misleading. Australian welfare arrangements have always been quite different from those with which we are familiar in the most comparable advanced industrialized societies in Europe and North America. In particular, an unusual degree of social protection has been delivered through the occupational structure and much of Australia's 'welfare effort' is not captured by an exclusive focus upon the conventional mechanisms of social security provision. Indeed, what is most distinctive about the Australian experience is that, from early in the century until at least the 1970s, most social protection was secured not through the state's social security apparatus but rather by the regulation of a highly protectionist economy and, above all, through a mandatory and legally stipulated 'fair wages' policy. The combination of a 'fair wage', tight labour markets, protection for domestic industries and high levels of owner occupation made for a social policy context which was quite different from that which prevailed in Europe. In combination with a system that offered flat-rate and means-tested benefits funded out of general taxation, the Australian social security regime tended to be small but quite strongly redistributive.

Between 1983 and 1996, the old 'Australian Settlement' was overhauled by an Australian Labor Party (ALP) government (led by Bob Hawke and Paul Keating) under the rubric of globalization (the 'necessity' of opening up Australia to the world economy). This reform involved the sorts of deregulatory measures which have been seen elsewhere – floating the currency, privatizing state-owned businesses, flattening tax regimes, constraining public expenditure – but sympathetic commentators (Castles, 1994; Whiteford, 1994) have detected a continuing commitment to maintain the essentials of the Australian system of social protection. In so far as this was achieved, it was through a mixture of increased targeting alongside some benefit enhancement. Amongst the most interesting reforms was the staged introduction of a system of compulsory workplace superannuation (see Pierson, 1998). Employers and employees were mandated to make contributions to individual employee pensions funds (held in a highly regulated private sector) with the government making matching contributions for some lower-paid contributors. The principal work of redistribution in old age would still be done by the (means-tested) pension, with most superannuated workers having a retirement income above the entitlement threshold.

The lessons to be drawn from the Australian experience are not straightforward. Critics insist that the Australian system never matched Western European models of welfare citizenship and that the Hawke–Keating reforms were not about 'refurbishment' but the pursuit of a rather more straightforwardly neo-liberal agenda. Whatever one's verdict on the overall experience of these reforms, they do raise a number of interesting and more general issues. First, if we are concerned with resource *outcomes* rather than institutional *procedures* there may be alternatives to the social democratic tradition (though this may entail real costs in term of citizenship, for example). Secondly, there may be ways of targeting resources which do not bear the stigma (and avoid the worst problems of perverse incentives and draconian effective marginal taxation rates) with which they are associated in a European context. Thirdly, they are an interesting experiment in what may (and may not) be possible through state regulation of labour markets and social protection and an illustration of the prospects for change in a comparatively small but highly redistributive welfare state. As Herman Schwartz (1998) has observed, labour in Australia has long faced those circumstances – of state indebtedness and highly mobile capital – which are part of the *new* context for labour movements elsewhere. Under these circumstances, the history of the institutional response of both the political and industrial wings of Australia's labour movement should be of especial interest to social democratic forces elsewhere, though it is quite clear that other 'unique' aspects of the Australian situation mean that any simple attempt at 'policy transfer' is likely to fail.

A final point is worth making here. Esping-Andersen (1985) was right to argue that the welfare state cannot carry all the burden of society's responsibility for social welfare and collective provision, while leaving the economy 'to look after itself'. If the sole focus upon redistribution was a plausible social democratic strategy at some earlier historical stage, it is not so any longer. Paradoxically, the weakening of *indirect* control over investment decisions requires that the question of *direct* control be re-addressed and social democrats need to consider policies and practices which might make for a more equitable distribution of primary (rather than redistributed) income. This may look fanciful in a world of sharpening income inequality and for some even a 'step back' to a set of traditional socialist concerns that have been even more comprehensively outmoded by the changes that have imperilled welfare states. But the situation need not be quite so hopeless. There are a number of policy instruments, some of them quite modest, which might afford the possibility of redistributing economic power. Perversely, some of these (including, for example, reform of pension funds) might be more 'respectable' or 'with the grain of public opinion' than attempts at more redistributive taxation or an increase in social expenditure.

Conclusion

The welfare state is certainly paradoxical. On the one hand, it is extraordinarily mundane, concerned with the minutiae of the pension and benefit rights of millions of citizens. On the other, the sheer scale of its growth is one of the most remarkable features of the post-war capitalist world and it remains one of the dominant, if sometimes unnoticed, institutions of the modern world. In recent years, it has become a major political concern of both the political left and, more especially, the political right. But this new or revived interest is, as we have seen, often based upon a quite mistaken reading of its historical evolution and its political consequences. Recommendations from most political quarters are substantially weakened by these misunderstandings.

In particular, we have seen that the notorious spectre of a 'crisis of the welfare state' is itself a part of this wider misunderstanding. For many, the crisis was real enough, but is now passing. For others, the crisis looms in front of us, brought on by 'irresistible' changes to the global economy or the 'unmanageable' ageing of the population. It is certainly true that many of the most difficult and the most 'political' decisions about welfare lie in the future. Questions about the relationship between economic and social policy, between employment and income, between political decision making and economic decision making, between state and market, between this and subsequent generations, will have to be addressed anew. When they are, it is likely that the welfare state will prove to be not just part of the problem, but part of the solution too.

Bibliography

Addison, P. 1977: *The Road to 1945*, London: Quartet.

Alber, J. 1982: *Von Armenhaus zum Wohlfahrtsstaat*, Frankfurt: Campus.

Alber, J. 1986: Germany. In P. Flora (ed.), *Growth to Limits*, vol. 2. Berlin: De Gruyter, 1–154.

Alber, J. 1988a: Is there a crisis of the welfare state? Cross-national evidence from Europe, North America, and Japan. *European Sociological Review*, 4(3), 181–207.

Alber, J. 1988b: Continuities and changes in the idea of the welfare state. *Politics and Society*, 16(4), 451–68.

Albertsen, N. 1988: Postmodernism, post-Fordism and critical social theory. *Environment and Planning D: Society and Space*, 6, 339–65.

Alestalo, M. and Uusitalo, M. 1986: Finland. In P. Flora (ed.), *Growth to Limits*, vol. 1. Berlin: De Gruyter, 197–292.

Alston, L. J. & Ferrie, J. P. 1985: Labour costs, paternalism and loyalty in Southern agriculture: a constraint on the growth of the welfare state. *Journal of Economic History*, 45 (March), 95–117.

Alt, J. 1979: *The Politics of Economic Decline*. Cambridge: Cambridge University Press.

Alt, J. and Chrystal, K. A. 1983: Political business cycles. In J. Alt and K. A. Chrystal (eds), *Political Economics*. Brighton: Wheatsheaf, 103–25.

Amenta, E. and Carruthers, B. G. 1988: The formative years of U.S. social spending policies; Theories of the welfare state and the American states during the Great Depression. *American Sociological Review*, 53, 661–78.

Amenta, E. and Skocpol, T. 1989: Taking exception: explaining the distinctiveness of American public policies in the last century. In F. Castles (ed.), *The Comparative History of Public Policy*. Cambridge: Polity.

Ashford, D. E. 1982: *British Dogmatism and French Pragmatism: central–local policymaking in the welfare state*. London: Allen and Unwin.

Ashford, D. E. 1986a: *The Emergence of the Welfare States*. Oxford: Blackwell.

Ashford, D. E. 1986b: The British and French social security systems: welfare states by intent and default. In D. E. Ashford and E. W. Kelley (eds), *Nationalizing Social Security in Europe and America.* London: Jai Press, 245–71.

Ashford, D. E. and Kelley, E. W. (eds) 1986:   *Nationalizing Social Security in Europe and America.* London: Jai Press.

Atkinson, A. B. and Micklewright, J. 1989:   Turning the screw: benefits for the unemployed, 1979–1988. In A. B. Atkinson, *Poverty and Social Security.* London: Harvester Wheatsheaf, 125–57.

Axinn, J. and Levin, H. 1975:   *Social Welfare: a history of the American response to need.* New York: Dodd, Mead and Co.

Bacon, R. and Eltis, W. 1978:   *Britain's Economic Problem: too few producers.* London: Macmillan.

Balbo, L. 1987:   Family, women and the state: Notes towards a typology of family roles and public intervention. In C. S. Maier, *Changing Boundaries of the Political.* Cambridge: Cambridge University Press, 201–19.

Baldwin, P. 1990   *The Politics of Social Solidarity: class bases of the European welfare state 1875–1975.* Cambridge: Cambridge University Press.

Bane, M. J. 1988:   Politics and policies of the feminization of poverty. In M. Weir, A. S. Orloff, T. Skocpol (eds), *The Politics of Social Policy in the United States.* Princeton: Princeton University Press, 381–96.

Barbalet, J. M. 1988:   *Citizenship: rights, struggle and class inequality.* Milton Keynes: Open University Press.

Barnett, C. 1986:   *The Audit of War.* London: Macmillan.

Barr, N. 1987:   *The Economics of the Welfare State.* London: Weidenfeld and Nicolson.

Barrett, M. 1980:   *Women's Oppression Today: problems in Marxist feminist analysis.* London: Verso.

Barry, J. 1998:   Social policy and social movements: ecology and social policy. In N. Ellison and C. Pierson, *Developments in British Social Policy.* London: Macmillan, 218–32.

Beattie, R. and McGillivray, W. 1995:   A risky strategy: reflections on the World Bank Report *Averting the Old Age Crisis, International Social Security Review,* 48, 3/4, 5–22.

Beechey, V. and Perkins, T. 1987:   *A Matter of Hours: women, part-time work and the Labour Movement.* Cambridge: Polity.

Bellamy, D. F. and Irving, A. 1989:   Canada. In J. Dixon and R. P. Scheurell, *Social Welfare in Developed Market Countries.* London: Routledge, 47–88.

Bendix, R. 1970:   *Embattled Reason: essays on social knowledge.* New York: Oxford University Press.

Benton, T. 1977:   *Philosophical Foundation of the Three Sociologies.* London: Routledge and Kegan Paul.

Berkowitz, E. and McQuaid, K. 1980:   *Creating the Welfare State: the political economy of twentieth century reform.* New York: Praeger.

Bernstein, E. 1909:   *Evolutionary Socialism.* London: Independent Labour Party.

Beveridge, W. H. 1942:   *Social Insurance and Allied Services.* London: HMSO.

Bhavnani, R. 1994:   *Black Women in the Labour Market.* London: Equal Opportunities Commission.

Birch, A. 1984: Overload, ungovernability and delegitimation. *British Journal of Political Science*, 14(2), 135–60.

Blake, D. and Ormerod, P. 1980: *The Economics of Prosperity: social priorities in the eighties*. London: Grant Macintyre.

Blitz, R. C. 1977: A benefit–cost analysis of foreign workers in West Germany. *Kyklos*, 30, 479–502.

Bloch, A. 1997: Ethnic inequality and social security. In A. and C. Walker (eds), *Britain Divided*. London: CPAG.

Block, F. 1987: Social policy and accumulation: a critique of the new consensus. In M. Rein, G. Esping-Andersen and M. Rainwater (eds), *Stagnation and Renewal in Social Policy: the rise and fall of policy regimes*. New York: Sharpe.

Block, F., Cloward, R. A., Ehrenreich, B. and Piven, F. F. 1987: *The Mean Season: the attack on the welfare state*. New York: Pantheon Books.

Bosanquet, N. 1983: *After the New Right*. London: Heinemann Education.

Bosanquet, N. 1988: An ailing state of national health. In R. Jowell, S. Witherspoon and L. Brook (eds), *British Social Attitudes*, 5th edn. Aldershot: Gower, 93–108.

Bottomore, T. and Goode, P. (eds) 1978: *Austro-Marxism*. Oxford: Oxford University Press.

Bowles, S. and Gintis, H. 1982: The crisis of liberal democratic capitalism. The case of the US. *Politics and Society*, 11(1), 51–93.

Bowley, M. 1967: *Nassau Senior and Classical Economics*. New York: Octagon.

Brenner, J. and Ramas, M. 1984: Rethinking women's oppression. *New Left Review*, 144, 33–71.

Brittan, S. 1975: The economic contradictions of democracy. *British Journal of Political Science*, 5(2), 129–59.

Brody, D. 1980: The rise and decline of welfare capitalism. In D. Brody (ed.), *Workers in Industrial America: essays on the twentieth century struggle*. New York: Oxford University Press, 48–81.

Brown, C. 1984: *Black and White Britain: the third PSI survey*. London: Heinemann.

Brown, M. and Madge, N. 1982: *Despite the Welfare State: a report on the SSRC/DHSS programme of research into transmitted deprivation*. London: Heinemann Educational.

Brownlie, I. (ed.) 1971: *Basic Documents on Human Rights*. London: Oxford University Press.

Brubaker, W. R. (ed.) 1989: *Immigration and the Politics of Citizenship in Europe and North America*. London: University Press of America.

Bruce, M. 1968: *The Coming of the Welfare State*, 4th edn. London: Batsford.

Bruno, M. and Sachs, J. D. 1985: *Economics of Worldwide Stagflation*. Oxford: Blackwell.

Burrows, R. and Loader, B. 1994: *Towards a Post-Fordist Welfare State?* London: Routledge.

Busch, A. 1997: 'Globalisation: some evidence on approaches and data'. Paper presented to Workshop on 'Globalisation and the Advanced Capitalist State', 25th ECPR Joint Sessions, Berne, Switzerland.

Cameron, D. R. 1978: The expansion of the public economy: a comparative analysis. *American Political Science Review*, 72(4), 1243–61.

Carby, H. V. 1982:   White woman listen! Black feminism and the boundaries of sisterhood. In Centre for Contemporary Cultural Studies, *The Empire Strikes Back*. London: Hutchinson, 212–35.

Carens, J. H. 1988:   Immigration and the welfare state. In A. Gutmann (ed.), *Democracy and the Welfare State*. Princeton: Princeton University Press, 207–30.

Cashmore, E. E. and Troyna, B. 1983:   *Introduction to Race Relations*. London: Routledge and Kegan Paul.

Castles, F. G. 1978:   *The Social Democratic Image of Society: a study in the achievements and origins of Scandinavian social democracy in comparative perspective*. London: Routledge and Kegan Paul.

Castles, F. G. 1982:   The impact of parties on public expenditure. In F. G. Castles (ed.), *The Impact of Parties: politics and policies in democratic capitalist states*. London: Sage, 21–96.

Castles, F. G. 1985:   *The Working Class and Welfare*. Wellington, New Zealand: Allen and Unwin.

Castles, F. G. 1994:   The wage earners' welfare state revisited: refurbishing the established model of Australian social protection, 1983–1993, *Australian Journal of Social Issues*, 29(2), 120–45.

Castles, F., Gerritsen, R. and Vowles, J. 1996:   *The Great Experiment*. Sydney: Allen and Unwin.

Castles, F. and Mitchell, D. 1992:   Identifying welfare state regimes. *Governance*, 5(1), 1–26.

Cawson, A. 1986:   *Corporatism and Political Theory*, Oxford: Blackwell.

Cerny, P. 1990:   *The Changing Architecture of Politics.* London: Sage.

Cerny, P. 1995:   Globalization and the changing logic of collective action. *International Organization*, 49(4), 595–625.

Cerny, P. 1997:   Paradoxes of the competition state: the dynamics of political globalization. *Government and Opposition*, 32(2), 251–74.

Childs, M. 1961:   *Sweden: The Middle Way*. New Haven: Yale University Press.

Clarke, T. and Clements, L. (eds) 1977:   *Trades Unions under Capitalism*. London: Fontana.

Collier, D. and Messick, R. E. 1975:   Prerequisites versus diffusion: testing alternative explanations of social security adoption. *American Political Science Review*, 69(4), 1299–315.

Commission on Social Justice 1994:   *Social Justice: strategies for national renewal*. London: Vintage Press.

Commonwealth Bureau of Census and Statistics (Australia) 1910– : *Official Year Book of the Commonwealth of Australia*. Canberra: Commonwealth Bureau of Census and Statistics.

Cook, J. and Watt, S. 1987:   Racism, women and poverty. In C. Glendinning and J. Millar, *Women and Poverty in Britain*, Brighton: Wheatsheaf pp. 53–70.

Cook, J. and Watt, S. 1992:   Racism, Women and Poverty. In Glendinning, C. and Millar, J. *Women and Poverty in Britain: the 1990s*. London: Harvester Wheatsheaf, 11–23.

Corti, L. and Dex, S. 1995:   Informal carers and employment. *Employment Gazette*, March. London Department of Employment/HMSO.

Coughlin, R. 1980:   *Ideology, Public Opinion, and Welfare Policy*. Berkeley: University of California Press.

Cox, R. 1993: Gramsci, hegemony and international relations: an essay in method. In S. Gill (ed.), *Gramsci, Historical Materialism and International Relations.* Cambridge: Cambridge University Press, 49–66.

Cram, L. 1997: *Policy-making in the EU: conceptual lenses and the integration process.* London: Routledge.

Crosland, A. 1964: *The Future of Socialism.* London: Cape.

Crozier, M., Huntington, S. P. and Watanuki, J. (eds) 1975: *The Crisis of Democracy.* New York: New York University Press.

Cutright, P. 1965: Political structure, economic development, and national social security programs. *American Journal of Sociology,* 70, 537–50.

Davies, G. and Piachaud, D. 1985: Public expenditure on the social services: the economic and political constraints. In R. Klein and M. O'Higgins (eds), *The Future of Welfare.* Oxford: Blackwell, 92–110.

De Swaan, A. 1988: *In Care of the State: Health Care, Education and Welfare in Europe and the USA in the Modern Era.* Cambridge: Polity.

Deacon, B. 1992: *The New Eastern Europe.* London: Sage.

Deacon, B. 1997: *Global Social Policy.* London: Sage.

Deakin, N. 1987: *In Search of the Postwar Consensus.* London: Suntory International Centre for Economics and Related Disciplines, LSE.

Delphy, C. 1984: *Close to Home.* London: Hutchinson.

Department of Health, 1989: *Working For Patients.* London: HMSO.

Department of Health and Social Security 1985: *The Reform of Social Security.* London: HMSO, Cmnd 9517, vol. 1.

Department of Social Security (DSS) 1995: *Family Resources Survey, 1993/4.* London: HMSO.

Dixon, J. and Scheurell, R. P. (eds) 1989: *Social Welfare in Developed Market Countries.* London: Routledge and Kegan Paul.

Dobson, A. 1995: *Green Political Thought,* 2nd edn. London: Routledge.

Donnison, D. 1979: Social policy since Titmuss. *Journal of Social Policy,* 8(2), 145–56.

Downs, A. 1957: *An Economic Theory of Democracy.* New York: Harper and Row.

Dryzek, J. and Goodin, R. E. 1986: Risk-sharing and social justice: the motivational foundations of the post-war welfare state. *British Journal of Political Science,* 16(1), 1–34.

Dunleavy, P. 1980: The political implications of sectoral cleavages and the growth of state employment. *Political Studies,* 28, 364–84 and 527–49.

Dunleavy, P. and Husbands, C. 1985: *British Democracy at the Crossroads: voting and party competition in the 1980s.* London: Allen and Unwin.

Dyer, C. 1978: *Population and Society in Twentieth Century France.* New York: Holmes and Meier.

Economist 1982a: Europe's socialists are losing their taste for power. 7 August.

Economist 1982b: The withering of Europe's welfare states. 16 October.

Economist 1997: Survey: The World Economy. 20 September.

Edelman, P. 1997: The worst thing Bill Clinton has done. *Atlantic Monthly,* March, 43–58.

Electoral Studies, 1989: *Electoral Studies,* 8(1), 102.

Emmanuel, A. 1979: The state in the transitional period. *New Left Review,* 113/4, 111–31.

Ensor, R. C. K. 1936:   *The Oxford History of England 1870–1914*. Oxford: Clarendon.

Equal Opportunities Commission (EOC) 1987:   *Women and Men in Britain: A Statistical Profile*. London: HMSO.

Ermisch, J. 1985:   Work, jobs and social policy. In R. Klein and M. O'Higgins, *The Future of Welfare*. Oxford: Blackwell, 59–71.

Esping-Andersen, G. 1985:   *Politics Against Markets*. Princeton: Princeton University Press.

Esping-Andersen, G. 1990:   *The Three Worlds of Welfare Capitalism*. Cambridge: Polity.

Esping-Andersen, G. 1997:   Hybrid or unique? The Japanese welfare state between Europe and America. *Journal of European Social Policy*, 7(3), 179–89.

Esping-Andersen, G. and Korpi, W. 1984:   Social policy and class politics in post-war capitalism: Scandinavia, Austria and Germany. In J. Goldthorpe (ed.), *Order and Conflict in Contemporary Capitalism*. Oxford: Oxford University Press, 179–208.

Esping-Andersen, G. and Korpi, W. 1987:   From poor relief to institutional welfare states: the development of Scandinavian social policy. In R. Erikson et al. (eds), *The Scandinavian Model: welfare states and welfare research*. Armonk, NY: Sharpe.

Eurobarometer 1993:   *Eurobarometer*, 40. Luxembourg European Commission.

Eurostat 1996a: Principal demographic trends in the EU in 1995, *Key Figures*, 11, 96.

Eurostat 1996b: *Social Portrait of Europe*, Luxembourg: EU.

Eurostat 1996c: *Basic Statistics of the European Union*, 33rd edn. Luxembourg: EU.

Evans, E. J. 1978:   *Social Policy 1830–1914: individualism, collectivism and the origins of the welfare state*. London: Routledge and Kegan Paul.

Ferrera, M. 1986:   Italy. In P. Flora (ed.), *Growth to Limits*, vol. 2. Berlin: De Gruyter, 385–482.

Ferrera, M. 1989:   Italy. In J. Dixon and R. P. Scheurell (eds), *Social Welfare in Developed Market Countries*. London: Routledge, 122–46.

Ferrera, M. 1996:   The 'southern model' of welfare in Social Europe. *Journal of European Social Policy*, 6(1), 17–37.

Finch, J. and Groves, D. 1983:   *A Labour Of Love: women, work and caring*. London: Routledge and Kegan Paul.

Firestone, S. 1979:   *The Dialectic of Sex*. London: The Women's Press.

Flora, P. (ed.) 1986:   *Growth to Limits*, vols 1 and 2. Berlin: De Gruyter.

Flora, P. (ed.) 1987a: *Growth to Limits*, vol. 4. Berlin: De Gruyter.

Flora, P. (ed.) 1987b: *State, Economy and Society*, 2 vols. London: Macmillan.

Flora, P. and Alber, J. 1981:   Modernization, democratization and the development of welfare states in Western Europe. In P. Flora and A. J. Heidenheimer (eds), *The Development of Welfare States in Europe and America*. London: Transaction Books, 37–80.

Flora, P. and Heidenheimer, A. J. (eds) 1981:   *The Development of Welfare States in Europe and America*. London: Transaction Books.

Foot, M. 1975:   *Aneurin Bevan*, vol. 2. London: Paladin.

Foucault, M. 1975: *Discipline and Punish*. Harmondsworth: Penguin.

Fowle, T. W. 1890: *The Poor Law*. London: Macmillan.

Fraser, D. 1973: *The Evolution of the Welfare State*. London: Macmillan.

Fraser, D. 1981: The English poor law and the origins of the British welfare state. In W. Mommsen (ed.), *The Emergence of the Welfare State in Britain and Germany 1850–1950*. London: Croom Helm, 9–31.

Fraser, N. 1989: Women, welfare and the politics of need interpretation. In P. Lassman (ed.), *Politics and Social Theory*. London: Routledge, 104–21.

Fraser, N. and Gordon, L. 1994: 'Dependency' demystified: inscriptions of power in a keyword of the welfare state. *Social Politics*, 1(1), 4–31.

Freeman, G. P. 1986: Migration and the political economy of the welfare state. *Annals of the American Academy of Political and Social Science*, 485, 51–63.

Friedman, M. 1962: *Capitalism and Freedom*. Chicago: University of Chicago Press.

Friedman, M. and Friedman, R. 1980: *Free to Choose*. London: Secker and Warburg.

Furniss, N. and Tilton, T. 1979: *The Case for the Welfare State*. London: University of Indiana Press.

Gale Research Company, 1985: *Encyclopaedia of Associations*. Detroit: Gale Research Co.

Gamble, A. 1981: *Britain in Decline*. London: Macmillan.

Gamble, A. 1988: *The Free Economy and the Strong State: the politics of Thatcherism*. London: Macmillan.

Garrett, G. and Mitchell, D. 1995: *Globalization and the Welfare State*. Canberra: Centre for Economic Policy Research, Australian National University.

Giddens, A. 1981: *The Class Structure of the Advanced Societies*. London: Hutchinson.

Giddens, A. 1985: *The Nation-State and Violence*. Cambridge: Polity.

Giddens, A. 1994: *Beyond Left and Right*. Cambridge: Polity Press.

Giddens, A. 1996: The Labour Party and British politics. In A. Giddens, *In Defence of Sociology*. Cambridge: Polity Press, 240–71.

Gilbert, B. B. 1966: *The Evolution of National Insurance in Great Britain*. London: Michael Joseph.

Gilbert, B. B. 1970: *British Social Policy 1914–1939*. London: Batsford.

Gilder, G. 1982: *Wealth and Poverty*. London: Buchan and Enright.

Ginsburg, N. 1979: *Class, Capital and Social Policy*. London: Macmillan.

Glass, D. 1940: *Population: Policies and Movements in Europe*. Oxford: Clarendon Press.

Glendinning, C. and Millar, J. 1987: Invisible women, invisible poverty. In C. Glendinning and J. Millar (eds), *Women and Poverty in Britain*. Brighton: Wheatsheaf, 3–27.

Glennerster, H., Power, A. and Travers, T. 1991: A new era for social policy. *Journal of Social Policy*, 20, 389–414.

Godfrey, M. 1986: *Global Unemployment: the new challenge of economic theory*. Brighton: Wheatsheaf.

Goldberg, G. S. and Kremen, E. (eds) 1990: *The Feminization of Poverty: only in America?* London: Praeger.

Golding, P. and Middleton, S. 1982: *Images of Welfare*. Oxford: Blackwell.

Goldthorpe, J. H. 1984:   *Order and Conflict in Contemporary Capitalism.* Oxford: Oxford University Press.

Goldthorpe, J. H., Lockwood, D., Bechofer, F. and Platt, J. 1968:   *The Affluent Worker.* Cambridge: Cambridge University Press.

Goodin, R. 1988:   *Reasons for Welfare.* Princeton: University of Princeton Press.

Goodin, R. E. and Le Grand, J. 1987:   *Not Only the Poor: the middle classes and the welfare state.* London: Allen and Unwin.

Goodman, R. and Peng, I. 1996:   The East Asian welfare state. In G. Esping-Andersen (ed.), *Welfare States in Transition.* London: Sage/UNRISD, 192–224.

Gordon, L. 1994:   *Pitied but Not Entitled: single mothers and the history of welfare.* Cambridge, Mass.: Harvard University Press.

Gorz, A. 1985:   *Paths to Paradise.* London: Pluto.

Gough, I. 1979:   *The Political Economy of the Welfare State.* London: Macmillan.

Gough, I. 1983:   Thatcherism and the welfare state. In S. Hall and M. Jacques (ed.), *The Politics of Thatcherism.* London: Lawrence and Wishart, 148–68.

Graham, H. 1987:   Women's poverty and caring. In C. Glendinning and J. Millar (eds.), *Women and Poverty in Britain.* Brighton: Wheatsheaf, 221–40.

Grammenos, S. 1982:   *Migrant Labour in Western Europe.* Maastricht: European Centre for Work and Society.

Gramsci, A. 1971:   *The Prison Notebooks.* London: Lawrence and Wishart.

Habermas, J. 1976:   *Legitimation Crisis.* London: Heinemann Educational.

Habermas, J. 1989:   The New Obscurity: the crisis of the welfare state and the exhaustion of utopian energies. In J. Habermas, *The New Conservatism.* Cambridge, Mass.: MIT Press, 48–70.

Hage, J., Hanneman, R. and Gargan, E. T. 1989:   *State Responsiveness and State Activism.* London: Unwin Hyman.

Hall, P. 1952:   *The Social Services of Modern England.* London: Routledge and Kegan Paul.

Hammar, T. 1990:   *Democracy and the Nation State: aliens, denizens and citizens in a world of international migration.* Aldershot: Avebury.

Hammar, T. and Lithman, Y. G. 1987:   The integration of migrants: experiences, concepts and policies. In Organization for Economic Co-operation and Development, *The Future of Migration.* Paris: OECD, 234–56.

Harris, J. 1977:   *William Beveridge: a biography.* Oxford: Clarendon Press.

Harris, R. and Seldon, A. 1979:   *Over-ruled on Welfare.* London: Institute of Economic Affairs.

Harris, R. and Seldon, A. 1987:   *Welfare Without the State: a quarter-century of suppressed public choice.* London: Institute of Economic Affairs.

Hartmann, H. 1981:   The family as the locus of gender, class, and political struggle: the example of housework. *Signs,* 6(3), 366–94.

Hay, J. 1975:   *Origins of the Liberal Welfare Reforms of 1908–14.* London: Macmillan.

Hay, J. 1978a: *The Development of the British Welfare State, 1880–1975.* London: Edward Arnold.

Hay, J. 1978b: Employers' attitudes to social policy and the concept of social control 1990–1920. In P. Thane (ed.), *The Origins of British Social Policy.* London: Croom Helm, 107–25.

Hay, R. 1977: Employers and social policy: the evolution of welfare legislation 1905–14. *Social History*, 4, 435–55.

Hayek, F. 1960: *The Constitution of Liberty*. London: Routledge and Kegan Paul.

Hayek, F. 1982: *Law, Legislation and Liberty*, 3 vols. London: Routledge and Kegan Paul.

Heath, A. and Evans, G. 1988: Working-class conservatives and middle-class socialists. In R. Jowell, S. Witherspoon and L. Brook (eds), *British Social Attitudes*, 5th edn. Aldershot: Gower, 53–69.

Heclo, H. 1974: *Modern Social Politics in Britain and Sweden: from relief to income maintenance*. London: Yale University Press.

Heclo, H. 1981: Towards a new welfare state? In P. Flora and A. Heidenheimer (eds), *The Development of the Welfare States in Europe and North America*. London: Transaction Books, 383–406.

Heikkinen, E. 1984: Implications of demographic change for the elderly population. In A. D. Lopez and R. L. Cliquet (eds), *Demographic Trends in the European Region*. Copenhagen: World Health Organization, 161–75.

Held, D. 1987: *Models of Democracy*. Cambridge: Polity.

Held, D. 1989: Citizenship and autonomy. In D. Held (ed.), *Political Theory and the Modern State*. Cambridge: Polity, 181–213.

Hennock, E. P. 1987: *British Social Reform and German Precedents: the case of social insurance 1880–1914*. Oxford: Clarendon Press.

Henriques, U. R. O. 1979: *Before the Welfare State*. London: Longman.

Hernes, H. 1987: *Welfare State and Woman Power: essays in state feminism*. Oslo: Norwegian University Press.

Hewitt, C. 1977: The effect of political democracy and social democracy on equality in industrial societies: a cross-national comparison. *American Sociological Review*, 42, 450–64.

Hicks, A. 1988: Social democratic corporatism and economic growth. *The Journal of Politics*, 50, 677–704.

Hicks, A. and Swank, D. 1984: On the political economy of welfare expansion: a comparative analysis of 18 advanced capitalist democracies, 1960–1971. *Comparative Political Studies*, 17(1), 81–119.

Hill, D. C. D. and Tigges, L. M. 1995: Gendering welfare state theory: a cross-national study of women's public pension quality. *Gender and Society*, 9(1), 99–119.

Hill, M. 1990: *Social Security Policy in Britain*. Aldershot: Edward Elgar.

Hills, J. 1994: *The Future of Welfare*. York: LSE/Rowntree.

Hills, J. 1997: *The Future of Welfare*, 2nd edn. York: LSE/Rowntree Trust.

Himmelstrand, U. et al. 1981: *Beyond Welfare Capitalism*. London: Heinemann.

Hindess, B. 1987: *Freedom, Equality, and the Market: arguments on social policy*. London: Tavistock.

Hirst, P. and Thompson, G. 1996: *Globalisation in Question: the international economy and the possibilities of governance*. Cambridge: Polity.

HM Treasury, U.K. 1979: *The Government's Expenditure Plans 1980–1*. London: HMSO, Cmnd. 7746.

Hutton, W. 1995: *The State We're In*. London: Cape.

Hyman, R. 1989a: Class struggle and the trades union movement. In R. Hyman (ed.), *The Political Economy of Industrial Relations*. London: Macmillan, 224–53.

Hyman, R. 1989b: *Strikes*. London: Macmillan.

Illich, I. 1973:   *Deschooling Society*. Harmondsworth: Penguin.

Illich, I. 1977:   *Disabling Professions*. London: Boyars.

Illich, I. 1978:   *The Right to Useful Employment*. London: Boyars.

Institute for Public Policy Research (IPPR) 1993:   *The Justice Gap*. London: IPPR.

Jackson, B. and Jackson, S. 1979:   *Childminder: a study in action research*. London: Routledge and Kegan Paul.

Jackson, M. P. 1987:   *Strikes*. Brighton: Wheatsheaf.

Jacobs, M. 1989:   What is sustainability? Paper presented to the Green Politics Seminar, Nottingham, May.

Jacobs, M. 1996:   *The Politics of the Real World*. London: Earthscan.

Jay, P. 1977:   Englanditis. In R. E. Tyrrell (ed.), *The Future That Doesn't Work*. New York: Doubleday, 167–85.

Jennings, E. T. 1979:   Competition, constituencies, and welfare policies in American states. *American Political Science Review*, 73(2), 414–29.

Jessop, B. 1988:   *Conservative Regimes and the Transition to Post-Fordism*. Colchester: University of Essex Papers.

Jessop, B. 1991:   Thatcherism and Flexibility. In Bob Jessop et al. (eds), *The Politics of Flexibility*. London: Edward Elgar.

Jessop, B. 1994:   The Schumpeterian workfare state. In R. Burrows and B. Loader (eds), *Towards a Post-Fordist Welfare State*. London: Routledge, 13–48.

Jessop, B., Bonnett, K., Bromley, S. and Ling, T. 1988:   *Thatcherism: A Tale of Two Nations*. Cambridge: Polity.

Johansen, L. N. 1986:   Denmark. In P. Flora (ed.), *Growth to Limits*, vol. 1. Berlin: De Gruyter, 293–381.

Johnson, R. J., Pattie, C. J. and Allsopp, J. G. 1988:   *A Nation Dividing? The electoral map of Great Britain 1979–1987*. London: Longman.

Jones, C. 1985:   *Patterns of Social Policy*. London: Tavistock.

Jones, C. 1993:   The Pacific challenge: Confucian welfare states. In C. Jones (ed.), *New Perspectives on the Welfare State in Europe*. London: Routledge, 198–217.

Jones, M. 1996:   Full steam ahead to a workfare state? *Policy and Politics*, 24(2), 137–57.

Jones, M. A. 1980:   *The Australian Welfare State*. London: Allen and Unwin.

Jones, M. A. 1996:   *The Australian Welfare State*, 4th edn. Sydney: Allen and Unwin.

Jones, T. 1993:   *Britain's Ethnic Minorities*. London: Policy Studies Institute.

Joshi, S. and Carter, B. 1984:   The role of Labour in the creation of a racist Britain. *Race and Class*, 25(3), 53–70.

Jowell, R. 1991:   *British Social Attitudes: 8th Report*. Aldershot: Dartmouth.

Junankar, P. N. and Kapuscinski, C. A. 1997:   Was Working Nation working? Canberra: Australian National University.

Kaim-Caudle, P. 1973:   *Comparative Social Policy and Social Security*. Oxford: Martin Robertson.

Katz, M. 1986:   *In the Shadow of the Poorhouse*. New York: Basic Books.

Kautsky, K. 1909: *The Road to Power*. Chicago: Bloch.

Kautsky, K. 1910: *The Class Struggle*. New York: Kerr.

Kautsky, K. 1983: *Selected Political Writings*. London: Macmillan.

Kavanagh, D. 1987: *Thatcherism and British Politics: the end of consensus?* Oxford: Oxford University Press.

Kavanagh, D. and Morris, P. 1989: *Consensus Politics from Attlee to Thatcher*. Oxford: Blackwell.

Kelsey, J. 1995: *The New Zealand Experiment: a world model or structural adjustment?* Auckland, NZ: Auckland University Press/Bridget Williams Books

Kemp, A. A. 1994: *Women's Work: degraded and devalued*. London: Prentice Hall.

Kennedy, F. 1975: *Public Social Expenditure in Ireland*. Dublin: The Economic and Social Research Institute.

Keohane, R. O. 1984: The world political economy and the crisis of embedded liberalism. In J. Goldthorpe (ed.), *Order and Conflict in Contemporary Capitalism*. Oxford: Oxford University Press, 15–38.

Keynes, M. 1973: *The General Theory of Employment, Interest and Money*. London: Macmillan.

King, D. S. 1987: *The New Right: politics, markets and citizenship*. London: Macmillan.

Klein, R. 1983: *The Politics of the NHS*. London: Longman.

Korpi, W. 1979: *The Working Class in Welfare Capitalism*. London: Routledge and Kegan Paul.

Korpi, W. 1983: *The Democratic Class Struggle*. London: Routledge and Kegan Paul.

Korpi, W. 1989: Power, politics, and state autonomy in the development of social citizenship: social rights during sickness in eighteen OECD countries since 1930. *American Sociological Review*, 54(3), 309–28.

Kristol, I. 1978: *Two Cheers for Capitalism*. New York: Basic Books.

Kudrle, R. T. and Marmor, T. R. 1981: The development of welfare states in North America. In P. Flora and A. J. Heidenheimer (eds), *The Development of Welfare States in Europe and America*. London: Transaction Books, 81–121.

Kuhnle, S. 1981: The growth of social insurance programs in Scandinavia: outside influences and internal forces. In P. Flora and A. J. Heidenheimer (eds), *The Development of Welfare States*. London: Transaction Books, 125–50.

Lane, J. E. 1995: The decline of the Swedish model, *Governance*, 8(4), 179–90.

Lane, J.-E. and Ersson, S. O. 1987: *Politics and Society in Western Europe*. London: Sage.

Lane, J.-E., McKay, D. and Newton, K. 1997: *Political Data Handbook*. Oxford: Oxford University Press.

Langan, M. and Lee, P. (eds) 1989: *Radical Social Work Today*. London: Unwin Hyman.

Lasch, C. 1978: *The Culture of Narcissism*. New York: Norton.

Lash, S. and Urry, J. 1987: *The End of Organized Capitalism*. Cambridge: Polity.

Le Grand, J. and Estrin, S. (eds) 1989: *Market Socialism*. Oxford: Clarendon Press.

Leibfried, S. 1993: Towards a European welfare state? In C. Jones, *New Perspectives on the Welfare State in Europe*. London: Routledge, 133–56.

Leibfried, S. and Pierson, P. (eds) 1995: *European Social Policy: Between Fragmentation and Integration.* Washington, DC: Brookings Institution.

Leman, C. 1977: Patterns of policy development: social security in the US and Canada. *Public Policy*, 25(2), 261–91.

Levine, D. 1983: Social democrats, socialism and social insurance in Germany and Denmark, 1918–1933. In R. F. Tomasson (ed)., *The Welfare State, 1883–1983: Comparative Social Research*, (6). London: Jai Press, 66–78.

Lewis, J. 1992: Gender and the development of welfare regimes. *Journal of European Social Policy*, 2(3), 159–73.

Lipset, S. M. 1969: *Political Man.* London: Heinemann.

Lister, R. 1993: Tracing the contours of women's citizenship. *Policy and Politics*, 21(1), 3–16.

McEvedy, C. and Jones, R. 1978: *Atlas of World Population History.* Harmondsworth: Penguin.

McIntosh, C. A. 1983: *Population Policy in Western Europe.* Armonk, New York: M. E. Sharpe.

McIntosh, M. 1978: The state and the oppression of women. In A. Kuhn and A. Wolpe (eds), *Feminism and Materialism: women and modes of production.* London: Routledge and Kegan Paul, 254–89.

McKay, A. 1998: Social security policy. In N. Ellison and C. Pierson (eds), *Developments in British Social Policy.* London: Macmillan, 112–29.

Mackie, T. T. and Rose, R. 1982: *The International Almanac of Electoral History*, 2nd edn. London: Macmillan.

Mackie, T. T. and Rose, R. 1991: *The International Almanac of Electoral History*, 3rd edn. London: Macmillan.

Maclean, M. and Groves, D. (eds) 1991: *Women's Issues in Social Policy.* London: Routledge.

Macpherson, C. B. 1987: *The Rise and Fall of Economic Justice.* Oxford: Oxford University Press.

Maddison, A. 1984: Origins and impact of the welfare state. *Banca Nazionale del Lavoro Quarterly Review*, 148, 55–87.

Madison, B. Q. 1980: *The Meaning of Social Policy.* London: Croom Helm.

Maguire, M. 1986: Ireland. In P. Flora (ed.), *Growth to Limits*, vol. 2. Berlin: De Gruyter, 241–384.

Maillat, D. 1987: Long-term aspects of international migration flows: the experience of European receiving countries. In Organization for Economic Co-operation and Development, *The Future of Migration.* Paris: OECD, 38–63.

Malthus, T. R. 1890: *An Essay on the Principle of Population.* London: Ward, Lock and Co.

Mann, M. 1970: The social cohesion of liberal democracy. *American Sociological Review*, 35(3), 423–39.

Marcuse, H. 1972: *One Dimensional Man.* London: Sphere.

Marshall, T. H. 1963: *Sociology at the Crossroads.* London: Heinemann.

Marshall, T. H. 1975: *Social Policy in the Twentieth Century.* London: Hutchinson Education.

Martin, A. 1997: *What Does Globalization Have to do with the Erosion of Welfare States? Sorting out the issues.* Bremen: Zentrum für Sozialpolitik.

Marwick, A. 1967: The Labour Party and the welfare state in Britain 1900–1948. *American Historical Review*, 73(2), 380–403.

Marx, K. 1973a: *Capital*. Harmondsworth: Penguin.

Marx, K. 1973b: *Surveys from Exile*. Harmondsworth: Penguin.

Middlemas, K. 1979: *Politics in Industrial Society: the Experience of the British System Since 1911*. London: André Deutsch.

Miliband, R. 1969: *The State in Capitalist Society*. London: Weidenfeld and Nicholson.

Millar, J. 1997: Gender. In A. and C. Walker (eds), *Britain Divided*. London: CPAG.

Minami, R., 1986: *The Economic Development of Japan: a quantitative study*. London: Macmillan.

Minford, P. 1987: The role of the social services: a view from the New Right. In M. Loney (ed.), *The State or the Market: politics and welfare in contemporary Britain*. London: Sage, 70–82.

Mishra, R. 1984: *The Welfare State in Crisis*. Brighton Wheatsheaf.

Mitchell, B. R. 1975: *European Historical Statistics 1750–1970*. New York: Columbia University Press.

Modood, T. and Berthoud, R. 1997: *Ethnic Minorities in Britain: diversity and disadvantage*. London: Policy Studies Institute.

Mommsen, W. J. (ed.) 1981: *The Emergence of the Welfare State in Britain and Germany*. London: Croom Helm.

Moran, M. 1988: Crises of the welfare state. *British Journal of Political Science*, 18, 397–414.

Moynihan, D. P. 1965: *The Negro Family: the case for national action*. Washington, DC: Office of Planning and Research, US Department of Labor.

Murray, C. 1984: *Losing Ground: American social policy 1950–1980*. New York: Basic Books.

Navarro, V. 1978: *The Rise and Fall of Economic Justice*. Oxford: Oxford University Press.

New Zealand Census and Statistics Office 1882–: *New Zealand Official Year-Book*: Wellington, New Zealand, Census and Statistics Office.

Niskanen, W. A. 1971: *Bureaucracy and Representative Government*. New York: Aldine-Atherton.

Niskanen, W. A. 1973: *Bureaucracy: servant or master?* London: Institute for Economic Affairs.

Nordlinger, E. A. 1981: *On the Autonomy of the Democratic State*. Cambridge, Mass.: Harvard University Press.

Nozick, R. 1974: *Anarchy, State and Utopia*. New York: Basic Books.

Oakley, A. 1974: *Housewife*. Harmondsworth: Allen Lane.

O'Connor, J. 1973: *The Fiscal Crisis of the State*. New York: St. Martin's Press.

O'Connor, J. 1987: *The Meaning of Crisis*. Oxford: Blackwell.

O'Connor, J. S. 1988: Convergence or Divergence? Change in welfare effort in OECD countries, 1960–1980. *European Journal of Political Research*, 16, 277–99.

O'Connor, J. S. 1996: Special issue: from women in the welfare state to gendering welfare state regimes. *Current Sociology*, 44(2), 124 pp.

O'Connor, J. S. and Brym, R. J. 1988: Public welfare expenditure in OECD countries: towards a reconciliation of inconsistent findings. *British Journal of Sociology*, 39(1), 47–68.

Offe, C. 1984:   *Contradictions of the Welfare State*. London: Hutchinson Education.

Offe, C. 1985:   *Disorganized Capitalism*. Cambridge: Polity.

Offe, C. 1987:   Democracy against the welfare state? *Political Theory*, 15(4), 501–37.

Offe, C. and Wiesenthal, H. 1985:   Two logics of collective action. In C. Offe, *Disorganized Capitalism*. Cambridge: Polity, 170–220.

Office of Population, Census and Surveys (OPCS), 1989:   *General Household Survey, 1987*. London: HMSO.

Official Year Book of the Commonwealth of Australia, 1923:   Melbourne: Australian Government.

Official Year Book of the Commonwealth of Australia, 1932:   Canberra: Australian Government.

Ohlin, B. 1938:   Economic progress in Sweden. *The Annals of the American Academy of Political and Social Science*, 197, 1–6.

Ohmae, K. 1990:   *The Borderless World*. London: Collins.

Olson, M. 1965:   *The Logic of Collective Action: public goods and the theory of groups*. Oxford: Oxford University Press.

Olson, M. 1982:   *The Rise and Decline of Nations: economic growth, stagflation, and social rigidities*. New Haven: Yale University Press.

Olsson, S. 1986:   Sweden. In P. Flora (ed.), *Growth to Limits*, vol. 1. Berlin: De Gruyter, 1–116.

Oppenheim, C. 1993:   *Poverty: the facts*, 2nd edn. London: CPAG.

Oppenheim, C. and Harker, L. 1996:   *Poverty: the facts*, 3rd edn. London: CPAG.

Orban, O. 1908:   *Le Droit Constitutionnel de la Belgique: II: Les Pouvoirs de l'Etat*. Liège: Dessain.

Organization for Economic Co-operation and Development 1966:   *Economic Growth, 1960–1970*. Paris: OECD.

Organization for Economic Co-operation and Development 1977:   *Towards Full Employment and Price Stability*. Paris: OECD.

Organization for Economic Co-operation and Development 1984:   *OECD Observer*, 126.

Organization for Economic Co-operation and Development 1985a: *Social Expenditure 1960–1990 problems of growth and control*. OECD: Paris.

Organization for Economic Co-operation and Development 1985b: *The Integration of Women into the Economy*. OECD: Paris.

Organization for Economic Co-operation and Development, 1986a: *OECD Observer*, 138.

Organization for Economic Co-operation and Development, 1986b: *Employment Outlook*. Paris: OECD.

Organization for Economic Co-operation and Development 1987a: *The Future of Migration*.

Organization for Economic Co-operation and Development 1987b: *Structural Adjustment and Economic Performance*. Paris: OECD.

Organization for Economic Co-operation and Development 1988:   *The Future of Social Protection*. Paris: OECD.

Organization for Economic Co-operation and Development 1989a: *Economies in Transition*. Paris: OECD.

Organization for Economic Co-operation and Development, 1994: *New Orientations for Social Policy*. Paris: OECD.

Orloff, A. S. 1988: The origins of America's belated welfare state. In M. Weir, A. S. Orloff, T. Skocpol (eds), *The Politics of Social Policy in the United States*. Princeton: Princeton University Press, 37–80.

Orloff, A. S. 1993: Gender and the social rights of citizenship: the comparative analysis of gender relations and welfare states. *American Sociological Review*, 38, 303–28.

Orloff, A. S. and Skocpol, T. 1984: Why not equal protection? Explaining the politics of public social spending in Britain, 1900–1911, and the United States, 1880s–1920. *American Sociological Review*, 49(6), 726–50.

Oshima, H.T. 1965: Meiji fiscal policy and agricultural progress. In W. W. Lockwood (ed.), *The State and Economic Enterprise in Japan*. Princeton: Princeton University Press, 353–89.

Owen, R. 1927: *A New View of Society and Other Writings*. London: Dent.

Paine, S. 1974: *Exporting Workers: the Turkish case*. Cambridge: Cambridge University Press.

Paine, T. 1958: *The Rights of Man*. London: Dent.

Pampel, F. C. and Williamson, J. B. 1988: Welfare spending in advanced industrial democracies, 1950–1980. *American Journal of Sociology*, 93(6), 1424–56.

Pampel, F. C. and Williamson, J. B. 1989: *Age, Class, Politics and the Welfare State*. Cambridge: Cambridge University Press.

Pampel, F. and Stryker, R. 1990: Age structure, the state, and social welfare spending: a reanalysis. *British Journal of Sociology*, 41(1), 16–24.

Panitch, L. 1986: *Working Class Politics in Crisis*, London: Verso.

Parry, R. 1986: United Kingdom. In P. Flora (ed.), *Growth to Limits*, vol. 2. Berlin: De Gruyter, 155–240.

Pateman, C. 1988: The patriarchal welfare state. In A. Gutmann (ed.), *Democracy and the Welfare State*. Princeton: Princeton University Press, 231–60.

Peacock, A. and Wiseman, J. 1961: *The Growth of Public Expenditure in the UK*. Oxford: Oxford University Press.

Pearce, D., Markandya, A. and Barbier, E. B. 1989: *Blueprint for a Green Economy: a report*. London: Earthscan.

Pedersen, S. 1993: *Family, Dependence and the Origins of the Welfare State*, Cambridge: Cambridge University Press.

Pelling, H. 1968: The working class and the origins of the welfare state. In H. Pelling (ed.), *Popular Politics and Society in Late Victorian Britain*. London: Macmillan, 1–18.

Pemberton, A. 1983: Marxism and social policy: a critique of the 'contradictions of welfare'. *Journal of Social Policy*, 12(3), 289–308.

Pen, J. 1987: Expanding budgets in a stagnating economy: the experience of the 1970s. In C. S. Maier, *Changing Boundaries of the Political*. Cambridge: Cambridge University Press, 323–61.

Perraton, J., Goldblatt, D., Held, D. and McGrew, A. 1997: The globalisation of economic activity. *New Political Economy*, 2(2).

Pfaller, A., Gough, I. and Therborn, G. (eds) 1991: *Can the Welfare State Compete?* London: Macmillan.

Piachaud, D. 1984: *Round About Fifty Hours a Week*. London: Child Poverty Action Group.

Pierson, C. 1986: *Marxist Theory and Democratic Politics*. Cambridge: Polity.

Pierson, C. 1991: Welfare states and social democracies: Sweden's 'Austro-Marxism' and the 'Social Democratic Road to Power'. *Research in Political Sociology*, vol. 5.

Pierson, C. 1998: 'Globalisation and the changing governance of welfare states: superannuation reform in Australia', *Global Society*, 12 (1), 31–47.

Pierson, P. 1994: *Dismantling the Welfare State? Reagan, Thatcher, and the politics of retrenchment*. Cambridge: Cambridge University Press.

Pigou, A. C. 1912: *Wealth and Welfare*. London: Macmillan.

Pigou, A. C. 1929: *The Economics of Welfare*. London: Macmillan.

Pimlott, B. 1988: The myth of consensus. In L. M. Smith (ed.), *The Making of Britain: echoes of greatness*. London: Macmillan, 129–41.

Piore, S. 1979: *Birds of Passage: migrant labour and industrial societies*. Cambridge: Cambridge University Press.

Piven, F. F. and Cloward, R. 1971: *Regulating the Poor: the functions of public welfare*. New York: Pantheon Books.

Piven, F. F. and Cloward, R. 1977: *Poor People's Movements: why they succeed, how they fail*. New York: Pantheon Books.

Piven, F. F. and Cloward, R. 1985: *The New Class War: Reagan's attack on the welfare state and its consequences*. New York: Pantheon.

Piven, F. F. and Cloward, R. A. 1986: The new class war in the US. In E. Oyen (ed.), *Comparing Welfare States and their Futures*. London: Gower, 47–63.

Ploug, N. 1995: The welfare state in liquidation? *International Social Security Review*, 2, 61–7.

Poguntke, T. 1987: New politics and party systems: the emergence of a new type of party? *West European Politics*, 10(1), 76–88.

Polanyi, K. 1944: *The Great Transformation*. New York: Rinehart.

Poulantzas, N. 1973: *Political Power and Social Classes*. London: Verso.

Poulantzas, N. 1978: *State, Power, Socialism*. London: Verso.

Przeworski, A. 1985: *Capitalism and Social Democracy*. Cambridge: Cambridge University Press.

Przeworski, A. and Sprague, J. 1986: *Paper Stones: a history of electoral socialism*. London: University of Chicago Press.

Quadagno, J. 1984: Welfare capitalism and the Social Security Act of 1935. *American Sociological Review*, 49, 632–47.

Quadagno, J. 1987: Women's welfare benefits and American exceptionalism. *Comparative Historical Sociology Newsletter*, 4(2), 1–2.

Quadagno, J. 1988a: *The Transformation of Old Age Security, Class and Politics in the American Welfare State*. Chicago: University of Chicago Press.

Quadagno, J. 1988b: From old-age assistance to Supplemental Security Income: the political economy of relief in the South, 1935–1972. In M. Weir, A. S. Orloff, T. Skocpol (eds), *The Politics of Social Policy in the United States*. Princeton: Princeton University Press, 253–63.

Quadagno, J. 1990: Race, class, and gender in the US welfare state: Nixon's failed family assistance plan. *American Sociological Review*, 55(1), 11–28.

Quadagno, J. 1994: *The Color of Welfare*. Oxford: Oxford University Press.

Rader, M. 1979: *Marx's Interpretation of History*. New York: Oxford University Press.

Rawlings, H. F. 1988: *Law and the Electoral Process*. London: Sweet and Maxwell.

Rawls, J. 1973: *A Theory of Justice*. Oxford: Oxford University Press.

Reede, A. H. 1947: *Adequacy of Workmen's Compensation*. Cambridge, Mass.: Harvard University Press.

Rein, M. 1985: Women, employment and social welfare. In R. Klein and M. O'Higgins (eds), *The Future of Welfare*. Oxford: Blackwell, 37–58.

Rein, M., Esping-Andersen, G. and Rainwater, M. 1987: *Stagnation and Renewal in Social Policy: the rise and fall of policy regimes*. New York: Sharpe.

Rhodes, M. 1996: Globalization and West European welfare states. *Journal of European Social Policy*, 4, 305–27.

Rimlinger, G. V. 1974: *Welfare Policy and Industrialization in Europe, America and Russia*. New York: John Wiley.

Ritter, G. A. 1985: *Social Welfare in Germany and Britain*. Leamington Spa: Berg.

Roberts, D. 1960: *Victorian Origins of the Welfare State*. New York: Yale University Press.

Rose, H. 1981: Rereading Titmuss: the sexual division of welfare. *Journal of Social Policy*, 10, 477–501.

Rose, R. and Peters, G. 1978: *Can Governments Go Bankrupt?* New York: Basic Books.

Rosenblum, G. 1973: *Immigrant Workers: their impact on American labor radicalism*. New York: Basic Books.

Sainsbury, D. (ed.), 1994: *Gendering Welfare States*. London: Sage.

Samuelsson, K. 1968: *From Great Power to Welfare State: three hundred years of Swedish social development*. London: Allen and Unwin.

Scase, R. 1977a: *Social Democracy in Capitalist Society: working class politics in Britain and Sweden*. London: Croom Helm.

Scase, R. 1977b: *Readings in the Swedish Class Structure*. Oxford: Pergamon.

Schmidt, M. G. 1983: The welfare state and the economy in periods of economic crisis: a comparative study of 23 OECD nations. *European Journal of Political Research*, 11, 1–26.

Schmidt, M. G. 1989: Social policy in rich and poor countries: socio-economic trends and political-institutional determinants. *European Journal of Political Research*, 17(6), 641–59.

Schneider, S. K. 1982: The sequential development of social programs in eighteen welfare states. *Comparative Social Research*, 5, 195–219.

Schottland, C. 1969: *The Welfare State*. New York: Harper and Row.

Schumpeter, J. 1976: *Capitalism, Socialism, Democracy*. London: Allen and Unwin.

Schwartz, H. 1998: Social democracy going down or down under: institutions, internationalized capital and indebted states. *Comparative Politics*.

Selbourne, D. 1985: *Against Socialist Illusion*. London: Macmillan.

Senior, N. A. 1865: *Historical and Political Essays*. London: publisher unknown.

Shalev, M. 1983: The social democratic model and beyond: 'two generations' of comparative research on the welfare state. In R. F. Tomasson (ed.), *The Welfare State, 1883–1983: Comparative Social Research*, 6. London: Jai Press, 315–51.

Shaver, S. 1988:   'Design for an Australian welfare state'. Paper presented to the BSA Annual Conference, Edinburgh, 28–31 March.

Shaver, S. 1989:   Gender, class and the welfare state: the case of income security in Australia. *Feminist Review*, 32, 91–108.

Sked, A. and Cook, C. 1984:   *Post-War Britain*. Harmondsworth: Penguin.

Skellington, R. 1996:   *'Race' in Britain Today*, 2nd edn. London: Sage.

Skidelsky, R. 1979:   The decline of Keynesian politics. In C. Crouch (ed.), *State and Economy in Contemporary Capitalism*. London: Croom Helm, 55–87.

Skocpol, T. 1980:   Political response to capitalist crisis: neo-Marxist theories of the state and the case of the New Deal. *Politics and Society*, 10, 155–201.

Skocpol, T. 1987:   America's incomplete welfare state. In M. Rein, G. Esping-Andersen and M. Rainwater, *Stagnation and Renewal*. New York: Sharpe.

Skocpol, T. 1992:   *Protecting Soldiers and Mothers: the political origins of social policy in the US*. Cambridge, Mass.: Harvard University Press.

Skocpol, T. and Amenta, E. 1986:   States and social policies. *Annual Review of Sociology*, 12, 131–57.

Skocpol, T. and Ikenberry, J. 1983:   The political formation of the American welfare state. An historical and comparative perspective. In R. F. Tomasson (ed.), *The Welfare State, 1887–1983: Comparative Social Research*, 6. London: Jai Press.

Sly, F. 1995:   Ethnic groups and the labour market. *Employment Gazette*, 103(6), 251–61.

Smith, A. 1895:   *The Wealth of Nations*. London: Routledge.

Smith, A. 1976:   *Theory of Moral Sentiments*. Oxford: Clarendon Press.

Smith, H. L. 1986:   *War and Social Change: British society in the Second World War*. Manchester: Manchester University Press.

Sombart, W. 1976:   *Why is There no Socialism in the United States?* New York: M. E. Sharpe.

Steering Group on Equal Opportunities for Women in the NHS 1988:   *Equal Opportunities for Women in the NHS*.

Stephens, J. 1979:   *The Transition from Capitalism to Socialism*. London: Macmillan.

Stockman, D. A. 1986:   *The Triumph of Politics*. London: The Bodley Head.

Swann, M. 1985:   *Education for All: the report of the committee of inquiry into the education of children from ethnic minority groups*. London: HMSO.

Tampke, J. 1981:   Bismarck's social legislation: a genuine breakthrough? In W. Mommsen (ed.), *The Emergence of the Welfare State in Britain and Germany 1850–1950*. London: Croom Helm, 71–83.

Tang, K.-L. 1997:   The case for the privatization of social welfare: three decades of public opinion evidence from Great Britain and the United States. *Scandinavian Journal of Social Welfare*, 6, 34–43.

Taylor, A. J. P. 1965:   *English History 1914–1945*. Oxford: Clarendon Press.

Taylor, C. L. and Hudson, M. C. 1983:   *World Handbook of Political and Social Indicators*. New York: Yale University Press.

Taylor-Gooby, P. 1985:   *Public Opinion, Ideology and State Welfare*. London: Routledge and Kegan Paul.

Taylor-Gooby, P. 1988: The future of the British welfare state: public attitudes, citizenship and social policy under the Conservative governments of the 1980s. *European Sociological Review*, 4(1), 1–19.

Taylor-Gooby, P. 1989: The role of the state. In R. Jowell, S. Witherspoon and L. Brook (eds), *British Social Attitudes: Special International Report*, 6th edn. Aldershot: Gower, 35–58.

Taylor-Gooby, P. and Dale, J. 1981: *Social Theory and Social Welfare*. London: Arnold.

Taylor-Gooby, P. and Papadakis, E. 1987: Consumer Attitudes and Participation in State Welfare. *Political Studies*, 35(3), 467–81.

Temple, W. 1941: The State. In *Citizen and Churchman*. London: Eyre and Spottiswoode. Reproduced in C. Schottland (ed.), *The Welfare State* (1967). London: Harper and Row, 20–4.

Temple, W. 1942: *Christianity and the Social Order*. London: Penguin.

Thane, P. 1982: *Foundations of the Welfare State*. London: Longman.

Thane, P. 1984: The working class and state 'welfare' in Britain, 1880–1914. *The Historical Journal*, 27(4), 877–900.

Thane, P. 1987: The coming burden of an ageing population? *Journal of Social Policy*, 7(4), 373–87.

Therborn, G. 1986: Karl Marx returning. *International Political Science Review*, 7(2), 131–64.

Therborn, G. 1987: Welfare state and capitalist markets. *Acta Sociologica*, 30(3/4), 237–54.

Tingsten, H. 1973: *The Swedish Social Democrats: their ideological development*. Totowa, NJ: Bedminster.

Titmuss, R. M. 1963: *Essays on the Welfare State*. London: Allen and Unwin.

Titmuss, R. M. 1974: *Social Policy*. London: Allen and Unwin.

Tomasson, R. F. 1969: The extraordinary success of the Swedish Social Democrats. *Journal of Politics*, 31(3), 772–98.

Tomasson, R. F. 1970: *Sweden: prototype of a modern society*. New York: Random House.

Tomasson, R. F., (ed.) 1983: *The welfare state, 1883–1983: Comparative Social Research*, 6. London: Jai Press.

Trattner, W. 1988: The federal government and needy citizens in nineteenth century America. *Political Science Quarterly*, 103(2), 347–56.

Tullock, G. 1976: *The Vote Motive: an essay in the economics of politics, with applications to the British economy*. Princeton: Princeton University Press.

Turner, B. S. 1986: *Citizenship and Capitalism: the debate over reformism*. London: Allen and Unwin.

Turner, B. S. 1990: Outline of a theory of citizenship. *Sociology*, 24(2), 189–217.

Ullman, H. P. 1981: German industry and Bismarck's social security system. In Mommsen, W. J. (ed.), *The Emergence of the Welfare State in Britain and Germany*. London: Croom Helm, 133–49.

United Nations 1948: *Universal Declaration of Human Rights*. New York: United Nations.

Urquhart, M. C. 1965: *Historical Statistics of Canada*. Cambridge: Cambridge University Press.

US Bureau of the Census 1996: *Poverty Statistics 1995* (online). Washington, DC: US Bureau of the Census.

US Bureau of Labor 1997: *Employment Statistics 1997* (online). Washington, DC: US Bureau of Labor.

US Bureau of Statistics 1975: *Historical Statistics of the United States: from colonial times to 1970*. Washington, DC: US Government Printing Office.

US Department of Commerce 1975: *Historical Statistics of the US*. Washington, DC: Department of Commerce.

Uusitalo, H. 1984: Comparative research on the determinants of the welfare state: the state of the art. *European Journal of Political Research*, 12, 403–22.

Van Parijs, P. (ed.) 1992: *Arguing for Basic Income*. London: Verso.

Van Parijs, P. 1995: *Real Freedom for All*. Oxford: Oxford University Press.

Waine, B. 1995: A disaster foretold? The case of the personal pension. *Social Policy and Administration*, 29(4), 317–44.

Walker, A. 1992: The poor relation: poverty among old women. In C. Glendinning and J. Millar (eds), *Women and Poverty in Britain: the 1990s*. London: Harvester-Wheatsheaf, 175–92.

Weale, A. 1983: *Political Theory and Social Policy*. London: Macmillan.

Webb, S. and Webb, B. 1910: *English Local Government: English poor law history*, vols 7–10. London: Longmans, Green.

Webb, S. and Webb, B. 1927: *English Local Government: English poor law history: Part 1: The Old Poor Law*. London Longmans, Green.

Weber, M. 1968: *Economy and Society*, 3 vols. New York: Bedminster.

Weir, A. 1974: The family, social work and the welfare state. In S. Allen, L. Sanders and J. Wallis, *Conditions of Illusion*. Leeds: Feminist Books, 217–28.

Weir, M., Orloff, A. S. and Skocpol, T. 1988a: *The Politics of Social Policy in the United States*. Princeton: Princeton University Press.

Weir, M., Orloff, A. S. and Skocpol, T. 1988b: Understanding American social politics. In M. Weir, A. S. Orloff and T. Skocpol (eds), *The Politics of Social Policy in the United States*. Princeton: Princeton University Press, 3–27.

Weir, M. and Skocpol, T. 1985: State structures and the possibilities for 'Keynesian' responses to the great depression in Sweden, Britain and the United States. In P. B. Evans, D. Rueschemeyer and T. Skocpol (eds), *Bringing the State Back In*. Cambridge: Cambridge University Press, 107–63.

White, S. 1997: Liberal equality, exploitation, and the case for an Unconditional Basic Income. *Political Studies*, 45, 312–26.

Whiteford, P. 1994: Income distribution and social policy under a reformist government: the Australian experience. *Policy and Politics*, 22(4), 239–55.

Wilensky, H. 1975: *The Welfare State and Equality: structural and ideological roots of public expenditure*. Berkeley: University of California Press.

Wilensky, H. 1976: *The 'New Corporatism', Centralization and the Welfare State*. London: Sage.

Wilensky, H. L. 1981: Leftism, Catholicism, and Democratic Corporatism: the role of political parties in recent welfare state development. In P. Flora and A. J. Heidenheimer (eds), *The Development of Welfare States in Europe and America*. London: Transaction, 345–82.

Williams, F. 1989: *Social Policy: A Critical Introduction: Issues of Race, Gender and Class*. Cambridge: Polity.

Williams, F. 1993: Gender, 'race' and class in British welfare policy. In A. Cochrane and J. Clarke (eds), *Comparing Welfare States*. Milton Keynes: Open University Press, 77–104.

Williamson, J. (ed.) 1994: *The Political Economy of Policy Reform*, Washington, DC: Institute for International Economics.

Wilson, E. 1977: *Women and the Welfare State*. London: Tavistock.

Wilson, W. J. 1987: *The Truly Disadvantaged: the inner city, the underclass, and public policy*. London: University of Chicago Press.

Winter, J. M. 1982: The decline of mortality in Britain 1870–1950. In T. Barker and M. Drake (eds), *Population and Society in Britain 1850–1950*. London: Batsford, 100–20.

Wolfe, A. 1979: *The Limits of Legitimacy*. London: Macmillan.

World Bank 1994: *Averting the Old Age Crisis*. New York: Oxford University Press.

World Bank 1997: *The State in a Changing World*. New York: Oxford University Press.

Zimmern, A. 1934: *Quo Vadimus*. Oxford: Oxford University Press.

Index